Avoiding Fraud and Abuse in the Medical Office

Brian Kalver, Esq

David B. Pursell, Esq

Megan C. Phillips, Esq

Michael F. Schaff, Esq

Paul W. Shaw, Esq

Robert A. Wade, Esq

AMERICAN
MEDICAL
ASSOCIATION

AMERICAN
HEALTH LAWYERS
ASSOCIATION

American Medical Association
Executive Vice President, Chief Executive Officer: Michael D. Maves, MD, MBA
Chief Operating Officer: Bernard L. Hengesbaugh
Senior Vice President, Publishing and Business Services: Robert A. Musacchio, PhD
Vice President and General Manager, Publishing: Frank J. Krause
Vice President, Business Operations: Vanessa Hayden
Publisher, AMA Publications and Clinical Solutions: Mary Lou White
Senior Acquisitions Editor: Elise Schumacher
Manager, Book and Product Development and Production: Nancy Baker
Director, Sales: J. D. Kinney
Senior Developmental Editor: Lisa Chin-Johnson
Production Specialist: Mary Ann Albanese
Marketing Manager: Lauren Jones

Internet address: www.ama-assn.org

The authors, editors, and publisher of this work have checked with sources believed to be reliable in their efforts to confirm the accuracy and completeness of the information presented herein and that the information is in accordance with the standard practices accepted at the time of publication. However, neither the authors nor the publisher nor any party involved in the creation and publication of this work warrant that the information is in every respect accurate and complete, and they are not responsible for any errors or omissions or for any consequences from application of the information in this book.

Additional copies of this book may be ordered by calling 800-621-8335 or from the secure AMA web site at www.amabookstore.com. Refer to product number OP 143309

ISBN 978-1-60359-105-8
BQ1709P034:12/09

Library of Congress Cataloging-in-Publication Data
Avoiding fraud and abuse in the medical office / Brain Kalver ... [et al.].
    p. cm.
  Includes bibliographical references.
  Summary: "This book provides physicians with information and examples of liability for physicians under both federal and state health care fraud and abuse legislation and how to be in compliance"—Provided by publisher.
  ISBN 978-1-60359-105-8
  1. Medical laws and legislation—United States. 2. Physicians—Malpractice—United States. 3. Medical care—United States—Corrupt practices. 4. Medicare fraud—Prevention. 5. Medicaid fraud—Prevention. I. Kalver, Brian. II. American Medical Association.
  [DNLM: 1. Practice Management, Medical—ethics—United States. 2. Fraud—prevention & control—United States. 3. Liability, Legal—United States. 4. Physicians—ethics—United States. W 80 A961 2010]
  KF3821.A98 2009
  344.7304'121—dc22

ACKNOWLEDGMENTS

Cynthia Conner, Vice President of Professional Resources and Will Harvey, Director of Business Development and Publishing for the American Health Lawyers Association (AHLA) would like to thank the authors on behalf of the Association for contributing their time and expertise to this project. We believe their dedication to the book ensures a useful guide for the intended audience.

The authors of Chapter 2 would like to thank Glenn Prives, who contributed to the research and writing of the chapter. Glenn graduated from Brooklyn Law School in the Class of 2009 and will join the firm of Wilentz, Goldman & Spitzer, PA in its Woodbridge, New Jersey office in Fall 2009.

ABOUT THE AUTHORS

Brian Kalver is an attorney with the firm of Wilentz, Goldman & Spitzer P.A. Kalver received his JD from the University of Pennsylvania Law School in 1989, and for the past 12 years his practice has focused primarily on health care matters. He has written numerous articles on health care law topics and given a number of presentations on health care law topics to professional legal and medical societies.

David B. Pursell is a partner in the health care department of Husch Blackwell Sanders LLP. He has practiced health care law for over 20 years, advising hospitals, physicians, professional corporations and other health care providers on issues facing the health care profession. These areas include hospital/physician contracting and joint venture issues; Medicare fraud and abuse and other health care compliance issues; Stark II and payment issues; tax-exempt entity compliance issues, business and tax planning for traditional and alternative physician practice structures; and GPO compliance issues. Pursell has been a frequent speaker at American Health Lawyers Association conferences, as well as other national and regional legal and accounting conferences on these issues. Pursell was graduated from Grinnell College in 1979 and received his JD from University of Missouri-Columbia in 1988, where he was a member of the Missouri Law Review and the Order of the Coif.

Megan C. Phillips is an attorney with the firm of Husch Blackwell Sanders LLP, where she practices exclusively in the firm's health care department. She advises clients on issues related to Medicare and

Medicaid reimbursement, Stark and anti-kickback analysis, state and federal licensure/certification of health care facilities, corporate health care transactions, HIPAA compliance, and various other regulatory matters. Phillips received her JD from the Washington University School of Law in St Louis, Missouri, in 2002, in which she was a member of the Journal of Law & Policy and the Order of the Coif.

Michael Schaff is the chair of the Corporate and Healthcare Departments and shareholder of Wilentz, Goldman & Spitzer PA. Schaff has been a member of the board of directors of the American Health Lawyers Association (AHLA) since 2006 and is a past chair of AHLA Physicians Organization Committee and editor of its newsletter.

Active in the New Jersey State Bar Association (NJSBA), he is a past chair and currently a director of the health and hospital law section. Schaff is an adjunct associate professor at the University of Medicine and Dentistry of New Jersey (UMDNJ) and at St. John's University. He is the vice chair of the editorial board for the New Jersey Lawyer Magazine, was the special editor of its issues on health law, patients' rights, internet law and nonprofit law. Schaff received his LLM (taxation) from Boston University; a joint JD/MBA from New York Law School and Bernard M. Baruch College, CUNY and his BA from Rutgers College. He has received many awards with respect to his representation of physicians and health care professionals, has published extensively, and is a frequent lecturer. Schaff has spoken on numerous national teleconferences and seminars and is quoted frequently in various publications. He has been selected for inclusion in Best Lawyers® list 2003–2009 and New Jersey Super Lawyers® list 2005–2009 (Top 100 attorneys).

Paul W. Shaw is a member of the litigation and health law departments of K&L Gates LLP in Boston, Massachusetts, where he concentrates in representing businesses and professionals in health care fraud and abuse investigations. Shaw has represented numerous health care clients involved in criminal fraud and abuse investigations and related civil proceedings by the federal government and state Medicaid Fraud Control

Units in Massachusetts and elsewhere in the United States. These clients include hospitals, physicians, medical practice groups, behavioral health providers, clinical laboratories, durable medical equipment suppliers, home health agencies and other health care providers. He has acted as counsel to a number of organizations, including the Massachusetts Medical Society and the New England Journal of Medicine.

Shaw has lectured and written extensively in the area of fraud and abuse before the American Health Lawyers Association, state medical societies and bar associations, with particular emphasis on statistical sampling and extrapolation procedures. He also assisted the Massachusetts Medical Society in developing a model physician compliance plan for use by small physician practices.

Shaw graduated from Georgetown University Law School in 1975. He is an adjunct professor at Suffolk Law School, where he teaches a course on health care fraud and abuse. Prior to joining Brown Rudnick, Shaw was a partner in the Boston law firm of Schwartz, Shaw and Griffith.

Robert A. Wade concentrates his practice in representing health care clients, including large health systems, hospitals, ambulatory surgical centers, physician groups, physicians and other medical providers. His expertise includes representing clients with respect to the Stark Act, Anti-Kickback Statute, False Claims Act, Emergency Medical Treatment, and Active Labor Act. Bob is nationally recognized in all aspects of health care compliance, including developing, monitoring and documentation of an effective compliance program. He has experience in representing health care clients with respect to issues being investigated by the Department of Justice and the Office of Inspector General as well as negotiating and implementing corporate integrity agreements. Bob is also the creator of Captain Integrity (www.captainintergrity.com), a unique compliance program branding and education resource, which has received national recognition and has been used by many hospitals, health systems and other providers.

TABLE OF CONTENTS

LIST OF FIGURES

PREFACE

Just weeks after the government publicized an expansion of a collaborative Medicare anti-fraud enforcement team, federal officials announced their first strike. It's likely to be the first of many to involve heightened scrutiny of physicians, according to legal experts.

As part of an ongoing effort, senior officials from the Depts. of Justice and Health and Human Services on June 24 announced criminal charges against 53 individuals—including doctors, beneficiaries, and health care company owners and employees—for allegedly scheming to submit a total of more than $50 million in false Medicare claims in the Detroit area.

THIS NEWS REPORT is far from unique. Headlines in a multitude of news sources chronicle specific instances of fraud and abuse enforcement involving physicians and targeting various areas of medical practice activity. Billing compliance, coding, clinical research, relationships with vendors, hospital transactions, and the quality of patient care are examples of the types of operations and activities that can generate liability for physicians under both federal and state healthcare fraud and abuse legislation.

Although the laws have been on the books for many years, the past decade has witnessed a tremendous increase in the government's efforts to enforce these laws, and this trend will continue in 2010 and beyond. As an example, the fiscal 2010 budget calls for infusing an additional $311 million—a 50% increase over 2009 funding—to strengthen Medicare and Medicaid fraud-fighting programs. In 2009 the Civil False Claims Act, the government's most potent enforcement tool, was amended to expand the government's reach under that law. Computerized investigation techniques and automated methods for analyzing billing patterns have further improved the efficacy and scope of fraud enforcement. With health care reform and its critical focus on reducing the cost of the national health care bill, we will see a continued expansion of anti-fraud activity, fueled by additional financial resources and stronger legislative weapons.

Now more than ever before, physicians need to understand how these laws affect the way they conduct business with other organizations, payers and patients, and how to structure transactions among themselves. In a ground-breaking partnership between the American Medical Association (AMA) and the American Health Lawyers Association (AHLA), this new guide *Avoiding Fraud and Abuse in the Medical Office* was specifically designed to address this need. Recognizing a desire to educate physicians on this topic with language and illustrations that are relevant to the medical profession, the AMA and AHLA recruited attorneys who are experts in educating and representing physicians on these matters. The result is a highly practical, easy-to-understand, and comprehensive resource on health care fraud tailored to provide physicians and practice managers with the answers to the questions that arise in their work environment.

The guide explains fraud and abuse laws in plain language using examples to illustrate the key principles. It starts with an overview chapter that introduces the governmental concerns, how governments discover fraud and abuse, and what physicians can do to avoid liability. This is followed by an extensive discussion of specific examples of fraud and abuse issues that arise in the physician office setting, and delineates best practices for compliance planning to eliminate potential liability. The analysis concludes by discussing what steps to take in the event that the practice runs afoul of governmental mandates. The guide also includes myriad sample documents which offer insight and assistance for compliance planning and examples of critical enforcement and defense documents.

We believe that physicians and their support staff will find this to be an invaluable guide in their efforts to avoid the devastating impact that a government investigation can have on their business.

References

1. *American Medical Association. AMNews.* July 6, 2009.

CHAPTER 1

Introduction to Fraud and Abuse for Physicians

David B. Pursell, Esquire, **and Megan C. Phillips,** Esquire

1.1 Introduction

In recent years, the US government has become increasingly concerned about the effect of fraud and abuse on federal health care programs such as Medicare and Medicaid. This concern has resulted in the implementation of federal laws, regulations, and guidance that are designed to prevent physicians and other health care providers from committing dishonest, wasteful, and other abusive acts that may have a negative effect on these programs. In addition to the federal laws, certain states have also passed fraud and abuse laws that prohibit conduct similar in scope to the federal laws, which in some circumstances may also apply to patients covered by commercial pay plans. While the subject matter of this book deals exclusively with the fraud and abuse laws related to federal health care programs, it is important to remember that a physician's particular state law should always be consulted to determine whether there are any unique fraud and abuse restrictions or other provisions that may affect a physician's practice.

The phrase "fraud and abuse" may conjure up images of physicians or other health care providers concocting schemes to defraud the government of millions of dollars. While the fraud and abuse laws have undoubtedly deterred individuals who may have sought intentionally to defraud the government, the real-life application of these laws encompasses much less nefarious acts. In fact, fraud and abuse can occur in situations where there is no clear intent or scheme to defraud the government at all. Because violations of these laws can result in significant fines, criminal penalties, and other severe consequences for physicians, it is in a physician's best interest to have a good understanding of the types of conduct that are prohibited by the fraud and abuse laws and the steps he or she can take to best avoid fraud and abuse liability.

While it may seem like a simple task to avoid engaging in fraudulent or abusive acts, the fraud and abuse laws have developed into a complex regulatory landscape that can be difficult to navigate. Even if a physician has the best of intentions to operate his or her practice in an ethical manner that complies with the fraud and abuse laws, the broad scope and complicated nature of such laws can make achieving and maintaining compliance difficult. One reason for this difficulty is that multiple fraud and abuse laws exist at both the federal and state level, and based on the facts and circumstances of a particular situation, different laws may apply. These laws prohibit different types of conduct, apply to different types of health care providers, and include their own technical definitions, restrictions, and exceptions that may have different effects on the operations of a physician practice and its dealings with other types of entities. While there is some overlap between the different fraud and abuse laws, each law ultimately stands on its own and may require a physician to implement separate safeguards to ensure compliance with each applicable law.

Because wading through the various requirements of the fraud and abuse laws can be a time-consuming and arduous process, particularly for a physician who is otherwise primarily engaged in the practice of medicine, the purpose of this book is to provide physicians with a user-friendly overview of the fundamental principles behind the fraud and abuse laws. In addition, it gives real-life examples of conduct that could trigger a government investigation and/or a fraud and abuse violation. These examples highlight areas where physicians should focus their compliance efforts and identify common pitfalls that they should avoid when operating their physician practices. This book will also provide suggestions to physicians on ways they can minimize their risk of fraud and abuse liability through implementing practices, policies, and procedures that are designed to maintain compliance with the fraud and abuse laws. Finally, this book will provide practical guidance to physicians on how best to proceed in the event that a fraud and abuse violation occurs.

1.2   What Is the Government Worried About?

While the government is concerned about fraud and abuse committed by federal health care program patients, contractors, and others, its regulatory and enforcement efforts generally target fraud and abuse committed at the provider level. A basic purpose of these laws is to prevent federal programs from making payments the government considers unnecessary or excessive. While some laws focus on proper coding, billing and documentation practices, others are geared toward deterring improper inducements, kickbacks, and self-referrals. For example, many of the fraud and abuse laws address situations where physicians or other health care providers have inappropriately billed Medicare, Medicaid, or other federal health care programs. Because providers typically bill federal health care programs directly for any services they provide to beneficiaries of federal health care programs, they have the opportunity to misrepresent or falsify the services provided on the claims they submit to obtain a greater reimbursement amount than the amount that they would otherwise receive. Therefore, the fraud and abuse laws were designed to control federal health care program costs by allowing the government to reclaim payments that should not have been made by federal health care programs, while also allowing fines and other penalties to be imposed on those who violate the fraud and abuse laws.

The government's ability to impose significant fines and other penalties on health care providers who violate the fraud and abuse laws encourages the health care industry to maintain its compliance with such laws. However, it is not always simple to categorize the types of activities that fall into the realm of fraud and abuse. While common sense dictates that certain acts would be considered fraudulent, fraud and abuse may also result from acts where the physician did not have any bad intent and did not even know that a law prohibited his or her conduct.

For example, it would clearly be inappropriate for a physician to bill Medicare for services that the physician knows he or she never provided to a patient, or intentionally code a service at a different reimbursement level than the service that was actually provided in order to obtain higher reimbursement. Other clearly fraudulent activities could involve deceiving the government into believing that services provided met federal health care program coverage requirements when in fact they did not. These activities would include falsifying supporting documentation, certificates of medical necessity, plans of care, or other records that may be necessary for a particular service to be covered under the Medicare or Medicaid program. As indicated above, activities of this type would likely demonstrate fraudulent intent to deceive the government to obtain reimbursement for services not provided, and would therefore likely be subject to the fraud and abuse laws.

On the other hand, fraud and abuse liability can sometimes result from run-of-the-mill billing errors or other actions that may not typically come to mind when describing fraud and abuse. For example, fraud and abuse can, in certain situations, include a physician engaging in sloppy billing practices, such as continually making coding or billing errors, submitting duplicate claims for reimbursement, or submitting claims to Medicare first when a nongovernmental payer was the primary payer. In addition, if a physician continually bills the government at a higher rate than it bills nongovernmental payers, or if the physician routinely waives coinsurance and deductible obligations for Medicare patients, the government could take the position that the bills submitted by the physician to Medicare misrepresent the physician's actual cost in providing such services. While these actions might not appear to be intentionally dishonest or wasteful, they may trigger fraud and abuse liability if the government can establish that these types of activities occur on a frequent basis such that the physician's pattern of conduct rises to the level of fraud and abuse.

In addition to the direct impact on the federal government due to false claims or other inappropriate billing practices engaged in by physicians, the federal government can also be negatively affected by inappropriate referral relationships between physicians and other health care providers. If a physician will receive some type of financial benefit as a result of making a referral to another health care provider, then the referral of the patient may be suspect under the fraud and abuse laws. Arrangements such as these concern the government, because the financial benefits received in exchange for referrals may encourage the physician or other health care provider to refer beneficiaries of federal health care programs for additional, unnecessary medical treatments. Because these referrals for additional treatments will also result in increased and unnecessary costs to federal health care programs, such activities may be subject to the fraud and abuse laws.

The government is also concerned about the negative effect that such referrals can have on the quality of care provided to beneficiaries of federal health care programs. When a physician or other health care provider refers a patient for unnecessary services, it is the patient who suffers the most direct consequences. For example, if a physician refers a patient for additional treatments in a manner that is not consistent with accepted sound medical practices, the patient could be subject to unwanted and medically unnecessary treatments that interfere with the patient's quality of life. The fraud and abuse laws therefore protect federal health care program beneficiaries from health care providers who may attempt to exploit beneficiaries' medical conditions and treatment options for their own financial gain.

Fraud and abuse also covers activities such as submitting a claim for a physician's service furnished by someone who is not licensed as a physician; employing or contracting with a person who has been "excluded" from the Medicare or Medicaid programs; and providing money (or anything else of value) to try and convince a Medicare or Medicaid patient to see a particular physician for services. Again, these types of activities potentially result in payment by federal health care programs for services that are not covered by the Medicare or Medicaid programs, that are not medically necessary, or that are not provided in accordance with professional standards of care. This type of conduct may unnecessarily increase federal health care program costs and therefore may be subject to the fraud and abuse laws.

All of the acts described above may have a negative effect on federal health care programs and could potentially qualify as fraud and abuse. The government's interest in reducing federal health care program costs has given it an incentive to deter, identify, and remedy instances of fraud and abuse quickly and efficiently. To address the issue of fraud and abuse and its effect on federal health care programs, the government has implemented various programs, issued guidance, created reporting mechanisms, and taken other steps to reduce instances of fraud and abuse. In addition to these methods of encouraging compliance, the various fraud and abuse laws are increasingly being used by the government to address the problem of fraud and abuse in the health care industry.

1.3   What Has the Government Done to Address Fraud and Abuse Problems?

For all of the reasons described above, the government has felt it necessary to draft laws, regulations, and various guidance not only to deter health care providers from engaging in fraudulent and abusive activities, but also to provide the government with an enforcement mechanism to identify and address such activities when they take place. The fraud and abuse laws clearly indicate that the government will not tolerate intentional deceptions or misrepresentations made by a physician to federal health care programs that result in unauthorized benefits to the physician. These laws also communicate to the health care industry that Medicare and Medicaid reimbursement rules and program guidance are to be taken seriously and that reimbursement under the federal health care programs cannot be treated as a blank check from the federal government. Furthermore, the fraud and abuse laws demonstrate that financial arrangements between physicians and other health care providers must have a legitimate purpose behind them and not be sham arrangements that merely exist to reward referrals from one provider to another. Fortunately, the government has also provided some resources that physicians can access that provide guidance on both appropriate conduct for physician practices and conduct to avoid, as well as guidance on the types of compliance issues the government is currently targeting.

The most notable of the fraud and abuse laws include the False Claims Act, the anti-kickback statute (AKS), and the federal physician self-referral law (also known as the *Stark Law*). The False Claims Act (FCA) generally prohibits a physician or other health care provider from *knowingly* submitting a false claim to a federal health care program. For purposes of the FCA, the requirement that a physician submit the claim "knowingly" can include situations where the physician either had actual knowledge that the claim was false or acted in reckless disregard or in deliberate ignorance of the truth or falsity of the claim. Therefore, it is not always necessary for a physician to have actual knowledge that a claim submitted to a federal health care program was false. For example, if a physician's staff submits incorrect claims to the government on the physician's behalf and the physician should have known that such claims were false because the government has published guidance that the physician's staff should have reviewed, the physician could still be held liable under the FCA. As a general rule, physicians and other health care providers should take appropriate precautions to ensure that they are not submitting false claims to federal health care programs. These precautions include remaining up to date on federal billing rules and requirements and implementing safeguards to ensure that claims are completed and submitted appropriately.

In addition to the type of conduct described above, the FCA was recently amended to prohibit a physician or other health care provider from knowingly concealing or knowingly and improperly avoiding or decreasing an *obligation* to pay or transmit money to the federal government. The term *obligation* is defined as an established duty arising from, among other things, the retention of overpayments made by the federal government. Therefore, physicians and other health care providers who knowingly and improperly retain overpayments received from a federal health care program may violate the FCA, even if the original claim submitted to the federal health care program was not fraudulent.

While the FCA targets the submission of false claims and the retention of overpayments, the AKS and Stark Law are geared more toward preventing inappropriate referrals of Medicare and Medicaid patients between health care providers. The AKS and the Stark Law are quite complicated, and each includes a whole host of definitions, restrictions, and exceptions that may vary depending on the type of conduct or relationship at issue, but the two statutes share a common goal. The government intends both statutes to help contain federal health care program costs by decreasing overutilization of program resources by physicians and other health care providers. Because a referral generally includes any request by a physician for an item or service, a physician may have many financial arrangements with entities that he or she refers to that could implicate the AKS and the Stark Law. For example, a physician may refer patients in a federal health care program to his or her employer; fellow group practice members and midlevel practitioners; other physicians, hospitals, and ancillary service providers; and other types of health care facilities. If a physician receives compensation or has an ownership or investment interest or other type of financial relationship with these entities or individuals, that relationship must be structured in a manner that does not violate the AKS or the Stark Law.

While the AKS and the Stark Law both are intended to prevent overutilization, the two statutes have important distinctions. The AKS is a criminal statute that makes it illegal for anyone to knowingly and willfully offer or solicit payment, or actually make or receive a payment of any form of financial benefit, whether in cash or in kind, in return for a referral of goods or services that are reimbursable under a federal health care program. The broad scope of this statute is not limited to a technical referral by a physician's written order; it applies to an attempt by anyone to influence or steer payment in return for goods or services that are reimbursable under a federal health care program. Therefore, many different types of arrangements between health care providers and other individuals can violate this statute. For example, if a manufacturer's representative offers to pay a physician to use a particular make of pacemaker in his or her patients, the manufacturer's representative has violated the statute, even though the representative has no actual ability to order the pacemaker for a particular patient or to implant it.

The AKS also has a *knowledge* requirement. This means that a person must knowingly and *willfully* violate the statute to be held liable. Generally, this means the government is required to prove that the individual knows that it is wrong to pay a kickback, but does not have to prove that he or she knows the actual language of the statute. Specific examples of how this statute applies in a physician's practice are discussed in the next chapter.

On the other hand, the Stark Law is narrower in scope than the AKS. The Stark Law prohibits a physician from making a referral of *designated health services* reimbursable under Medicare to an entity with which the physician has any type of financial relationship unless an exception specified in the statute or regulations applies to the financial relationship. Some of the distinctions are obvious from the wording of the law: it applies only to physicians; it applies only to the referral of designated health services; it applies only if those services are reimbursable under Medicare; and it applies only if the physician has a financial relationship with the entity to which he or she is making the referral.

The first distinction is that the Stark Law applies only to referrals made by physicians. For example, while it may be a crime under the AKS (if the parties have the necessary improper intent) for a supplier to offer to pay a physician to use a specific brand of supplies for which the physician would bill, those same actions would not be a violation of the Stark Law. However, if the physician had a financial relationship of any kind with a clinical laboratory (for example), the physician could not refer a Medicare patient to the laboratory, unless an exception applied to the physician's financial arrangement.

The Stark Law also only applies to referrals made by physicians to entities for designated health services that are reimbursable under the Medicare program. Designated health services include the following categories of services:

- Clinical laboratory services
- Physical therapy, occupational therapy, and speech-language pathology services
- Radiology and certain other imaging services
- Radiation therapy services and supplies
- Durable medical equipment and supplies
- Parenteral and enteral nutrients, equipment, and supplies
- Prosthetics, orthotics, and prosthetic devices and supplies
- Home health services
- Outpatient prescription drugs
- Inpatient and outpatient hospital services.

The Centers for Medicare and Medicaid Services (CMS) has developed detailed definitions for these designated health services (which CMS often refers to simply as *DHS*), some of which are based on the Current Procedural Terminology (CPT®) codes. These CPT code lists are updated periodically; the current list can be found on the CMS website at www.cms.hhs.gov/PhysicianSelfReferral/.

While the Stark Law is narrower in scope than the AKS, it is easier for the government to prove a violation of the Stark Law than the AKS. The Stark Law is a *strict liability* statute: In other words, the government does not have to prove that the physician making the referral or the entity to which the referral is made has improper intent or willful knowledge in order to result in a violation of the Stark Law. Therefore, if a physician makes a referral of designated health services reimbursable under Medicare to an entity with which the physician has a financial relationship (or with which the physician's immediate family member has a financial relationship), the Stark Law may apply regardless of whether the physician had any intent or knowledge to violate the Stark Law. A lack of knowledge or understanding of the Stark Law's rules would generally not serve as a defense of the physician's conduct. Because a violation of the Stark Law can result in serious financial and other consequences, physicians should closely examine any financial relationships they have with entities to which they refer designated health services.

It is also important to remember that the Stark Law applies to immediate family members of the physician, who are defined to include the physician's spouse; birth or adoptive parent, child, or sibling; stepparent, stepchild, stepbrother, or stepsister; father-in-law, mother-in-law, son-in-law, daughter-in-law, brother-in-law, or sister-in-law; grandparent or grandchild; and the spouse of a grandparent or grandchild. Therefore, if the physician's immediate family member has a financial relationship with an entity, an exception must apply to that financial relationship before the physician makes a referral to the entity. For example, if the granddaughter of a physician leases space for a coffee cart from a hospital at which the physician has privileges, the lease must be covered by an exception before the physician refers a Medicare patient to the hospital for inpatient or outpatient hospital services (or one of the other designated health services) or the hospital bills for those services. There is an exception that can be used in this example, but if the requirements of the exception are not met at the time the lease commences, the parties will violate the Stark Law if the referral is made. This example also illustrates another distinction of the Stark Law. It is not necessary for the financial relationship to have anything to do with the delivery of designated health services to create an issue under the Stark Law. The fact that the lease of space for a coffee cart by a physician's granddaughter is unrelated to the provision of inpatient and outpatient hospital services does not protect the physician or the hospital; an exception must be found and put in place or the parties have violated the Stark Law.

Because the general rule against referrals imposed by the AKS and the Stark Law could affect many arrangements that are necessary and serve a legitimate purpose, the government has implemented various exceptions to these laws that will protect common types of arrangements that are structured in a manner that the government believes do not create a risk of overutilization. Specific examples of exceptions available under the AKS and the Stark Law are described in more detail in later chapters. Generally, these exceptions protect many types of legitimate arrangements between physicians and other entities, provided that certain conditions are satisfied. For example, it is generally acceptable for an employed physician to refer patients to his or her employer even though the employed physician receives a financial benefit from his or her employer. In addition, physicians are generally permitted to refer to entities with which they have a service agreement or a space or equipment lease, if the arrangement is for legitimate items or services, the lease or service agreement is fair market value, and other requirements are met. Physicians can generally hold ownership interests in their group practices and refer to their fellow group practice members for both professional and ancillary services if specific conditions are satisfied. Physicians should consult the list of exceptions to the AKS and the Stark Law, and the specific requirements of each whenever he or she (or, his or her immediate family member) has a financial relationship with an entity to which referrals are made. Complying with such exceptions may mean the difference between a permissible and a prohibited arrangement under the fraud and abuse laws.

To take advantage of the protections afforded by the exceptions to the AKS and the Stark Law, physicians must generally structure the arrangement at issue to comply with the specific conditions required under the applicable exception. Once again, there is an important distinction between the AKS and the Stark Law. Under the AKS, the exceptions are referred to as *safe harbors*. That is, if the physician does not meet the requirements of the AKS safe harbor, he or she will not necessarily have violated the law, but the physician loses the benefit of knowing the arrangement is protected. In contrast, under the Stark Law, an exception that covers the financial arrangement must be met or the parties have violated the statute (eg, as described in the earlier example, the physician must find an exception to cover the lease of space for the coffee cart to avoid violating the Stark Law).

While a detailed analysis of each exception's requirements is beyond the scope of this chapter, there are several common elements to many of the AKS and Stark Law exceptions. For example, many of the exceptions require that the arrangements between the parties must be in writing, be signed by the parties, and specify all the items and services that are covered under the arrangement. Moreover, virtually every exception requires that the payments made under the arrangement are fair market value. Other conditions may include requiring that the agreement be for a term of at least 1 year and that the arrangement be commercially reasonable.

The most important aspect of the majority of the safe harbors and exceptions under the AKS and the Stark Law (and the most important element of complying with the AKS in the absence of a safe harbor) is that the compensation paid under an arrangement must be consistent with fair market value and not vary based on the volume or value of referrals made during the term of the agreement. While fair market value can generally be established by means of commercially reasonable methodologies such as appraisals or salary surveys, it will ultimately be determined on the basis of the facts and circumstances of a particular situation. The requirements of the AKS and Stark Law exceptions help ensure that the compensation paid under an arrangement is based on legitimate items and services provided under the arrangement, and not in exchange for referrals that may be made by a health care provider.

Generally, the more complicated the arrangement, the more complicated the requirements of an applicable exception will be. If a physician is interested in pursuing ownership, investment, joint ven-ture, or other more complicated relationships with an entity to which the physician refers patients in a federal health care program, such arrangements will require a detailed analysis under the AKS and the Stark Law to ensure that they are structured appropriately. Because of the complicated nature of the AKS and the Stark Law and their related exceptions, it is always beneficial to obtain legal counsel's opinion on any financial arrangements under which physicians will refer patients in federal health care programs to another entity.

1.4 How Does the Government Find Out About Fraud and Abuse?

The government can learn about fraud and abuse in various ways. For example, if a patient in a federal health care program suspects that a provider has fraudulently billed for services provided, he or she may contact the Medicare program directly to report the fraud and abuse. Patients in federal health care programs have access to the claims submitted by their providers, and may therefore, notice if an error has been made or if more questionable actions appear to be taking place. While patients in federal health care programs are encouraged to contact physicians directly if they believe a simple billing mistake has been made, they also have the option of directly contacting the Medicare contractor who paid the claim, or they may even contact the Office of Inspector General (OIG) to report fraud and abuse. In fact, the OIG maintains a hotline as a confidential means for patients in federal health care programs (or others) to report suspected cases of fraudulent activities.

In addition to reporting by patients in federal health care programs, the government can be notified of fraudulent activities through disclosure by a whistleblower. *Whistleblowers* are individuals who have knowledge of a potential fraudulent or abusive act and decide to disclose that information to the federal government. Whistleblowers could include a physician's previous or current partners, staff members, employees, agents, contractors, or anyone else who has knowledge of and decides to report an alleged fraud and abuse violation to the government.

Certain laws such as the FCA actually encourage whistleblowers to report violations of fraud and abuse laws to the government by allowing such individuals to share a portion of any damages awarded to the government based on the violation. In addition to providing a portion of the damage award, the FCA also protects employees, contractors, and agents who are discharged, demoted, suspended, threatened, harassed, or otherwise discriminated against in the terms and conditions of their employment as a result of disclosing such conduct to the government. Remedies for employees, contractors, and agents who are retaliated against under the FCA include reinstatement with the same seniority status the employee, contractor, or agent would have had but for the discrimination; 2 times the amount of back pay; interest on any back pay; compensation for special damages sustained as a result of the discrimination; litigation costs, and reasonable attorneys' fees.

The government can also learn about fraudulent activities directly from the health care provider who committed the violation. The OIG has set up a voluntary self-disclosure protocol that encourages health care providers to report certain fraudulent or abusive activities to the federal government. Currently, the self-disclosure protocol may only be utilized if the conduct includes a "colorable" (valid or genuine) antikickback statute violation, and therefore, may not be used if the disclosed conduct only violates the Stark Law. By disclosing AKS violations directly to the OIG, health care providers are able to work with the federal government to minimize potential fines or civil penalties, avoid criminal penalties, and reduce the amount of reimbursement that must be repaid to the government as a result of the violation. Use of the provider self-disclosure protocol generally requires that a provider admit that a violation of the AKS has occurred. If, however, there has been no clear violation of the AKS, but an overpayment has occurred, health care providers are able to work with their local Medicare contractors to address simple billing errors that do not rise to the level of fraud and abuse.

1.5   Why Should Physicians Care About Fraud and Abuse?

Engaging in fraudulent and abusive activities can have far-reaching consequences for physicians. If a physician has received reimbursement from a federal health care program in error, he or she is required (except in very limited circumstances) to return the overpaid amounts to such program. In addition to repaying overpaid or mistaken claims, the physician can also be subject to various penalties if the government becomes aware that it has made excess or unnecessary payments to a physician. Based on the facts and circumstances of a particular case and the fraud and abuse law that has been implicated, the potential penalties may vary. However, these penalties generally range from requiring the physician to return excess payments to the government, to significant civil or criminal penalties and assessments and exclusion from participation in federal health care programs in the future.

For example, a violation of the FCA can result in civil monetary penalties in the amount of $5500 to $11,000 per false claim, as well as an amount equal to 3 times the amount of damages sustained by the government as a result of the false claim, and/or exclusion from participation in Medicare, Medicaid, and other federal government health care programs. A violation of the AKS can result in criminal fines of up to $25,000 per violation, up to 5 years' imprisonment, or both. In addition, an AKS violation can result in civil monetary penalties of up to $50,000 per violation plus treble damages, or exclusion from participation in Medicare, Medicaid, and other federal government health care programs, or both. A violation of the Stark Law can result in a civil monetary penalty of up to $15,000 for each bill or claim that should not have been submitted, civil monetary penalties of up to $100,000 for engaging in a scheme to circumvent the Stark Law, fines for failing to report an entity's ownership, investment, and compensation arrangements when required, and/or exclusion from participation in Medicare, Medicaid, and other federal government health care programs.

These penalties can severely affect a physician and his or her practice. In addition to potential criminal penalties, the significant dollar amount of these fines can result in devastating financial consequences for a physician practice. These statutes impose criminal or civil penalties based on each claim submitted. As a result, the penalties can add up very quickly. For example, if a physician group performs and bills only 100 Medicare-reimbursable x-rays per year for 5 years, but fails to meet an applicable Stark Law exception for the compensation the group pays its own physicians, it potentially faces a penalty of $7,500,000 for those 500 x-rays. With any volume at all, the potential civil penalties become completely unmanageable (also greatly increasing the importance of the OIG's self-disclosure protocol discussed above). Furthermore, exclusion from the Medicare and Medicaid programs can also be a devastating penalty under the fraud and abuse laws. Exclusion from participating in these federal health care programs would limit the types of patients a physician could treat, who the physician could bill for services provided, and by whom a physician could be employed or with whom a physician could enter into contracts. Even without these severe consequences, merely being required to return the amount of the overpaid claims or being prohibited from billing federal health care programs for a period of time can have a debilitating effect on a physician practice.

1.6   What Can a Physician Do to Avoid Fraud and Abuse Liability?

A physician can take various steps to protect his or her practice from violating the fraud and abuse laws. An important initial step is establishing an effective compliance program. The OIG has provided guidance to various members of the health care industry, including physician practices, on how to set up and manage a compliance program. These are available at http://oig.hhs.gov/fraud/complianceguidance.asp. The guidance of the OIG should provide a helpful outline on practical ways a physician practice can prevent, reduce, and address instances of fraud and abuse. To stay current with fraud and abuse issues that are of particular interest to the government, it would also be useful for a physician practice to review the OIG's annual work plan on a regular basis. The work plan, which is also posted on the OIG web site, describes the areas of compliance in which the OIG plans to focus for the upcoming year. The work plan is divided into sections focusing on the different types of health care providers and includes a section on physician practices. Therefore, a physician can keep his or her compliance plan updated and consistent with the most recent positions taken by the OIG by reviewing the work plan each year as it is published.

In addition to setting up a compliance program, a physician practice should conduct internal audits at regularly scheduled intervals to make sure it complies with Medicare and Medicaid rules and regulations. If such audits are conducted on a frequent basis, they can identify issues and enable the physician practice to correct them before they rise to the level of fraud and abuse. Physicians can also implement procedures to ensure they are correctly coding and submitting claims to government payers. Educational programs on proper coding and documentation requirements may be particularly helpful to ensure that physicians and their staff members are acting in compliance with federal health care program coverage and other requirements.

These audits should include not only billing and coding of patient claims, but also a regular review of physician financial relationships to ensure that appropriate exceptions have been met. Any contractual or other financial arrangements the physician has with other providers should be reviewed to ensure that they comply with applicable exceptions to the fraud and abuse laws, particularly when referrals of patients in federal health care programs will flow between the parties. As referrals for federal health care program services may be subject to either the AKS or the Stark Law, or both, if there is a financial relationship between the parties, it would be wise to have any such arrangement reviewed by legal counsel to ensure that all requirements of applicable exceptions are satisfied.

Finally, physicians should keep abreast of the changing landscape of compliance and the practice of medicine. The government is continually updating both compliance statutes, as well as its interpretation of those statutes through regulations and other more informal announcements. The changes in these rules always seem to make compliance more complicated rather than simpler. Moreover, acts involving fraud and waste are easy targets when the government's fiscal responsibilities require an increase in revenue, which makes these acts prime targets for enforcement. Consequently, it is important that physicians keep themselves and their staff on top of these changing rules by taking advantage of educational opportunities on a regular basis.

CHAPTER 2

Examples of Physician Fraud and Abuse

Michael F. Schaff, Esquire, **and Brian Kalver,** Esquire

2.1 Introduction

At times, health care laws can seem intentionally vague. The lines between normal, lawful business and inappropriate conduct punishable by law can be difficult to define. Health care providers who are otherwise upstanding citizens step over that line fairly often, perhaps more often than we would like to admit. With the increase over the past several years in prosecutions of well-known institutions on charges of health care fraud, it is becoming more difficult to differentiate between the good guys and the bad guys.

This chapter will offer some examples of health care fraud and abuse in 10 different categories. This list and the accompanying examples focus on physicians, but many of the cases that will be described involve hospitals, drug companies, and other health care firms. All of the cases described involve allegations of fraud on federal health benefit programs, such as the Medicare or Medicaid programs. By one estimate, these 2 federally sponsored programs compose upward of 35% of the total national spending on health care.[1] While health care fraud is obviously not limited to Medicare and Medicaid, these programs make up the lion's share of the publicized cases and large awards and settlements.

The 10 common types of fraud and abuse described in this chapter are:

1. Billing for medically unnecessary services
2. Billing for services when none were provided
3. Failing to comply with billing requirements (eg, billing for the wrong service or wrong level of service and unbundling)
4. Failing to comply with coverage requirements (eg, services performed by nonphysician practitioners without the required physician supervision)
5. Failing to provide adequate or necessary services
6. Falsifying supporting documents
7. Kickbacks
8. Self-referral law violations
9. Inducements to beneficiaries
10. Employing excluded persons.

This list is not in order of frequency of prosecution or violation or of importance. In our experience, the greatest areas of concern for most physicians are kickbacks and self-referral laws.

The largest and most publicized health care fraud and abuse awards, settlements, and new prosecutions have fallen on large health care institutions, such as companies that manufacture and market pharmaceuticals and medical devices. Many of these cases involve allegations that payments, gifts, meals, travel expenses, discounts, etc that these companies gave to physicians were kickbacks. For example, in *US v. Forest Laboratories*, 03-10395, US District Court, District of Massachusetts, the US Attorney for the District of Massachusetts in Boston filed a complaint against Forest Laboratories "for alleged False Claims Act violations arising from the company's marketing the drugs Celexa and Lexapro for unapproved pediatric use and for paying kickbacks to induce physicians to prescribe the drugs."[2] The complaint alleged that the company's sales representatives, as well as physicians whom the company paid to make presentations to other physicians, promoted off-label use of the drugs for children and did not appropriately disclose research that had been done on the effectiveness and risk of pediatric use. The complaint also alleged that the company paid honoraria and fees to physicians for participation in local advisory boards, clinical trials, and "preceptorships," and that the company's sales representatives gave physicians restaurant gift certificates and provided lavish entertainment for physicians and their spouses and subsidies for office parties—and that all of the above were illegal kickbacks for prescribing Celexa and Lexapro.

The complaint outlined about $2 million in payments that the Medicaid program made for the off-label, pediatric use of these drugs and a little under $100,000 in payments the Medicaid program made for Celexa and Lexapro ordered by one particular physician over a 5-year period during which that physician received $5000 in payments from the company.[2] While the complaint was against the company (and not any of the physicians who were alleged to have received kickbacks), as discussed in section 2.6.7, prosecution of physicians for receiving kickbacks from pharmaceutical and medical device companies will probably become more common in the near future.

Some of the examples of fraud and abuse in this chapter will read as *obviously* criminal conduct. The perpetrators' stories as published by the press or by the government agencies that prosecuted them will present them as unsympathetic characters who, presumably, must have set out from the start to steal from the government's health care coffers. At best these were bad actors trying to take advantage of a vulnerable insurance system. They may have started out their careers with good intentions, but at some point they must have become desperate or lost their way and crossed a line that an upstanding citizen would never be expected to cross.

Other examples, however, will probably hit closer to home for many readers. Those include physicians or hospital administrators who seem to have been doing what came naturally in the furtherance of their practice or institution in a competitive and complicated environment. These perpetrators (and the word *perpetrator* hardly fits here) did not intentionally do anything wrong. They were careless and were caught looking the wrong way. Some readers will struggle to find a distinction between the example and things that they have personally done themselves, while others will make a natural assumption that there is more to the story that explains the bad outcome but that did not get published.

Most physician-clients who consult health care attorneys have thriving practices, come to the attorney for representation or advice in connection with an important business transaction, and are not in any sort of immediate legal jeopardy. In many instances, the transactions these attorneys work on require some degree of structuring or tailoring of the terms, either to avoid an outright violation of a fraud and abuse law or to establish parameters for a new relationship between the client and other health care providers to steer the parties away from a violation of fraud and abuse laws. At times, it is hard to pinpoint how much of a threat the fraud and abuse laws pose to these clients. However, these days, it is quite universally accepted that *all* health care providers must make it their business to understand fraud and abuse laws.

Over and above following their internal moral compass, all physicians and other health care providers should be taking affirmative steps to avoid violating health care laws. They should get expert advice whenever they are trying something new, and they should also periodically reevaluate the legal risk associated with their business as usual. It is hoped that readers of this chapter will come away with a better sense of what they should be watching out for, in terms of both novel possibilities and long-standing practices that could result in charges of health care fraud.

2.2   What Does "Fraud and Abuse" in Health Care Mean?

Fraud, by itself, is a word in common use in the law. Its general sense is using deception to get someone to give one something that one is not entitled to. In most jurisdictions, fraud is a crime defined by statute and a tort (ie, conduct for which a court may award damages to a plaintiff in a civil suit) is defined by common law (ie, legal precedents established by judicial decisions). While the legal definitions of fraud vary in a number of ways and contexts, the gist is generally consistent with the general sense of the word provided above. Abuse is a more nebulous concept. In the context of health care law, *abuse* is generally used to refer to overusing or misusing benefits provided by the government for personal advantage. Abuse can refer to a variety of statutory offenses that are intended to protect health care programs sponsored by the government. Abuse can also refer to conduct that is not necessarily proscribed by any law or regulation that insurance program administrators (such as the Centers for Medicare & Medicaid Services [CMS]) try to control by making changes to program policies and rules.

However, for purposes of this chapter, the phrase *fraud and abuse* means essentially the same thing as the term *health care fraud.* In 1977, President Jimmy Carter signed into law the Medicare-Medicaid Anti-Fraud and Abuse Amendments to the Social Security Act.[3] While historians may have better explanations of the roots linking the phrase *fraud and abuse* to practically all fraud against the federal health benefit programs, it appears that, at some point after 1977, the concepts became practically synonymous.

The types of fraud and abuse that are most often discussed involve payments by health care insurance programs to health care providers. Health care fraud can also involve health care that is paid for only by patients and not covered by any benefit program or other type of program, but these types of offenses generally are not as widespread, do not lead to massive penalties or settlements, and are not as common a topic.

2.3   Laws Used to Prosecute Fraud and Abuse; *Prominence of the Federal False Claims Act*

Fraud on any health benefit program (federally sponsored or otherwise) violates a federal statute enacted in 1996 (the federal Health Care Fraud Statute) that carries significant penalties: "Whoever knowingly and willfully executes, or attempts to execute, a scheme or artifice (1) to defraud any health care benefit program; or (2) to obtain, by means of false or fraudulent pretenses, representations, or promises, any of the money or property owned by, or under the custody or control of, any health care benefit program, in connection with the delivery of or payment for health care benefits, items, or services, shall be fined under this title or imprisoned not more than 10 years, or both."[4]

The federal Health Care Fraud Statute seems to address the field in a reasonably comprehensive matter: it sets out the prohibited conduct by using broad and familiar language ("defraud" and "obtain by means of false or fraudulent pretenses"); it provides for a very serious punishment of a large fine (up to $250,000 per violation) and the possibility of a very long prison term; and, since it is a federal law, it establishes the jurisdiction of federal prosecutors to bring cases. In fact, since its enactment, most of the criminal prosecutions for the sort of fraud and abuse discussed in the chapter have been brought under this statute.

Yet, fraud and abuse cases are brought under many other laws. There are certainly important differences between the federal Health Care Fraud Statute and some of these other laws, but they are largely redundant in that any of them could be used to prosecute the same acts: ie, the use of deception to get a health benefit plan (government sponsored or otherwise) to give a person something to which he or she is not entitled.

Some of the other laws used to prosecute health care fraud apply to fraud in a very general way, without regard to the type or context of the conduct or the identity of the victim. For example, charges have been brought under the federal mail fraud statute[5] and state general fraud or theft statutes. Health care fraud cases have also been brought under laws that proscribe any type of fraud in connection with insurance claims, but only when the victim is the federal government (eg, the federal criminal False Claims Act [FCA]),[6] or only when the victim is a federal health benefit program (eg, the Medicare-Medicaid Anti-Fraud and Abuse Amendments).[7]

Other cases have been brought under laws that prohibit more specific types of conduct that may not necessarily (but often would) constitute fraud under another law. (This discussion does not take into account the sort of other offenses that parties who are fearful of prosecution or facing a fraud investigation might commit [eg, by money laundering, obstruction of justice or perjury].) For example, the Social Security Act's Civil Monetary Penalties (CMP) Law[8] lists about a dozen different types of conduct that are prohibited in dealings with, or related to, the Medicare or Medicaid programs. Other important examples are the federal antikickback statute (AKS)[9] and the federal physician self-referral statute (the Stark Law),[10] which prohibit financial arrangements that may be perfectly appropriate (ie, not fraud) in other contexts.

In some instances, the choice of law used to prosecute health care fraud and abuse is dictated by the identity of the prosecutor or the means used to prosecute. The CMP Law authorizes the secretary of the US Department of Health and Human Services (HHS) to impose penalties through an administrative process in which many determinations are made by HHS that would be made by a judge if the case were brought in a judicial process. The federal civil False Claims Act (FCA),[11] with its private whistleblower or *qui tam* provisions is generally the only means for a private whistleblower to take up the prosecution of fraud on the Medicare program and benefit from the award or settlement. Class action suits against large health care companies by shareholders or by the users of their products or services are another form of private whistleblower suit, but the largest awards in these cases go to the class action attorneys who prosecute them.

(Federal laws include 2 different statutes sometimes referred to as the "False Claims Acts," one imposing civil penalties [ie, purely monetary penalties and administrative sanctions] and one that imposes criminal penalties [ie, both monetary fines and imprisonment, probation, or other limits on fundamental liberties]. In this chapter, we use FCA to refer to the *civil* False Claims Act.)

While the penalties that may be imposed under the CMP Law and the FCA are not as high as the fines that may be imposed under the criminal statutes, they still are very large. In cases involving a pattern of conduct that affected hundreds of claims, each claim might be a separate offense subject to its own penalty. As a result, prosecutions under the CMP Law and the FCA (without resort to the harsher criminal statutes) can be extremely intimidating and can elicit significant awards and settlements.

The FCA stands out as the most common basis for charges of fraud and abuse. Under the FCA, a person who "knowingly presents, or causes to be presented, [to the government] a false or fraudulent claim for payment or approval is liable . . . for a civil penalty."[12] Additionally, a person who knowingly makes a false statement to get a claim paid by the government; conceals property to defraud the government; delivers less property than the amount for which the government paid; makes a receipt of property to the government "without completely knowing that the information on the receipt is true"; knowingly buys public property from an officer of the government "who lawfully may not sell or pledge the property"; or "knowingly makes, uses, or causes to be made or used, a false record or statement to conceal, avoid, or decrease an obligation to pay or transmit money or property to the government" is liable for a civil penalty.[13]

Several aspects of a claim can be considered false. They include any data submitted in the claim ("codes, services performed, dates of service, eligibility of beneficiary, etc."), as well as details concerning the service provided, such as medical necessity, standard of care, and compliance with applicable laws and regulations.

The prominence of the FCA is probably due to several factors, including the right of private whistleblowers to bring suits in the FCA and to share in the proceeds of the suits they bring, judges' and prosecutors' familiarity with the legal standards necessary to prove a violation, and the generous monetary penalties available under the FCA. Even in cases where the charges include kickbacks or violation of self-referral laws (as opposed to claims for services that were not performed or overcharged), the FCA is typically the central charge. Courts addressing the issue have generally held that the FCA is violated by entities that receive Medicare program money from items and services ordered by physicians who received remuneration from the entity in violation of the AKS or who were prohibited from making referrals to the entity by the Stark Law.[14] Furthermore, use of the FCA in essentially all types of fraud and abuse cases allows the prosecutor to take advantage of the FCA's monetary penalty provisions, which are more generous than those available under the CMP Law, the AKS (which is a criminal statute), or the Stark Law.

A good example of the reach of the FCA is in the case of *United States ex rel Schmidt v Zimmer, Inc.*[14] In that case, a whistleblower charged Zimmer, a manufacturer, seller, and distributor of orthopedic implants, with violating the FCA by causing a hospital to submit claims for federally sponsored health benefits that were tainted by violations of the AKS and the Stark Law. Zimmer itself did not submit claims for benefits. However, the whistleblower alleged that Zimmer had contracted with Premier Purchasing Partners, a purchasing agent for a group of entities, including Mercy Health Systems, and those entities did submit claims for payment to the Medicare program. Under the contract, Zimmer would provide orthopedic implants to Premier participants for 5 years, and Premier participants were rewarded with several incentives, including reduced prices and bonuses, if they purchased a sufficient amount of Zimmer's products. Each Premier participant reported the costs associated with the purchase of the implants to the Medicare program but did not disclose the incentives they received under the contract. The Premier participants certified, as they were obligated to, that their claims were in compliance with all laws regarding the provision of health care services.[15]

The lower court in the case dismissed the charges against Zimmer, finding: "It is undisputed that Zimmer never submitted any cost reports: Zimmer could be liable under the FCA only if it caused Mercy to submit an allegedly false cost report. But the Amended Complaint does not allege Zimmer reviewed, approved, or received copies of Mercy's cost reports or participated in their preparation; nor does it allege Zimmer certified the truthfulness of Mercy's cost reports."[15] However, the federal appellate court overturned the lower court's decision, finding that, even though Zimmer did not submit claims or make any certifications concerning the hospital's claims, on the basis of the facts alleged, it was likely "that Zimmer knowingly assisted in causing the government to pay claims which were grounded in fraud."[16]

The FCA applies to claims against all manner of programs that are operated or funded by the US government that make payments or provide other types of benefits to the private sector or to governmental agencies.[16] The main intersection between physician practices and the US government programs covered by the FCA are the federally sponsored health benefit programs: Medicare, Medicaid, and TRICARE.

The penalties for violating the FCA are about as harsh as the toughest civil penalties under state insurance fraud laws, and the legal standards for proving a violation of the FCA are as well developed as most state insurance fraud laws. To prove a violation of the FCA or a state insurance fraud law, the prosecutor must show some level of intent by the accused. The legal standards for proving that the accused had the intent necessary to have committed fraud can range from proof that the defendant should have known that what he or she was doing was probably wrong, to proof that the defendant actually believed that what he or she was doing clearly violated the particular statute under which the defendant is being charged.[17] From the perspective of a prosecutor, it is relatively easy to convince a judge or jury of the former and relatively difficult to convince a judge or jury of the latter. Legal standards, such as intent requirement, are often moving targets, as the words of the applicable statute or case law precedent are interpreted and reinterpreted by judges and regulatory agencies.

The intent standard under the FCA is *knowingly*. The FCA provides that an individual makes a false claim knowingly if he or she:

1. has actual knowledge of the information;
2. acts in deliberate ignorance of the truth or falsity of the information; or
3. acts in reckless disregard of the truth of falsity of the information.[17]

However, no proof of specific intent to defraud is required.[17] This means that, as long as the provider intended to file the claim and knew that the claim was false, he or she does not have to intend to commit a fraud on the government to be prosecuted under the FCA.

While the bad intent requirements under some state insurance fraud laws may be even less rigid than the FCA, the federal agencies charged with protecting the federal benefit programs have more resources than any single state regulatory agency or prosecutor. Consequently, it should not be surprising that most of the examples of fraud and abuse in this chapter involve federal law and include an FCA claim or component.

The FCA was amended on May 20, 2009 by the Fraud Enforcement and Recovery Act of 2009 (FERA). It's important to note that the amended FCA makes the application of the FCA for failing to refund known-overpayments fairly explicit, by establishing FCA liability when a person "knowingly and improperly avoids . . . an obligation to pay or transmit money or property to the Government." FERA also expanded the ability of prosecutors and whistleblowers to get access to information to pursue FCA cases.

2.4   Enforcement

Title II of the Health Insurance Portability and Accountability Act of 1996 (HIPAA) established a national Health Care Fraud and Abuse Control Program (HCFAC) under the joint purview of the US attorney general and the Secretary of HHS.[18] The HHS Office of Inspector General (OIG) serves as the lead coordinator for federal, state, and local law enforcement efforts to identify and root out health care fraud and abuse. According to the HHS and Department of Justice (DOJ) *HCFAC Annual Report for FY 2007*, the goals of HCFAC are:

1. to coordinate federal, state, and local law enforcement efforts relating to health care fraud and abuse with respect to health plans;

2. to conduct investigations, audits, inspections, and evaluations relating to the delivery of and payment for health care in the United States;

3. to facilitate enforcement of all applicable remedies for such fraud;

4. to provide guidance to the health care industry regarding fraudulent practices; and

5. to establish a national data bank to receive and report final adverse actions against health care providers and suppliers.[19]

Pursuant to the Social Security Act, monetary recoveries from health care investigations, including fines, settlements, judgments, and penalties, must be deposited into the Medicare Trust Fund. In turn, a portion of the money from the Trust Fund is redirected into the HCFAC and utilized for additional enforcement prosecutorial efforts against health care fraud and abuse.[20] For example, in fiscal year 2007, HCFAC obtained $1.8 billion in health care fraud and abuse judgments and settlements. Of those recoveries, $249,459,000 was appropriated to the Fraud and Abuse Control Account for future enforcement investigations.[19]

Several federal agencies and departments, along with other groups, work separately and sometimes in collaboration to prosecute health care fraud and abuse as it impacts Medicare, Medicaid, and other federally sponsored programs.

Within HHS, CMS acts as the administrator of the Medicare and Medicaid programs. CMS itself cannot prosecute fraud and abuse violations but refers matters for investigation to the OIG and the DOJ. Besides fraud and abuse violations, CMS will also encourage the OIG and the DOJ to investigate overpayments of federal government funds to providers. CMS also establishes fraud and abuse policies for intermediary carriers to enforce against providers.[21]

The OIG was established by Congress to identify and eliminate fraud, abuse, and waste in HHS's programs and to promote efficiency in economy and departmental operations. Customarily, the OIG carries out its mission through nationwide fraud investigations and inspections. The OIG also issues fraud alerts and other guidance as a vehicle to identify perceived fraudulent and abusive practices in the health care industry. If the OIG uncovers a fraudulent claim, it can assess civil monetary penalties against the individual or entity and/or exclude that entity from participation in the federal health care programs. The OIG can also suspend and withhold a provider's payments under Medicare. The OIG has offices in all 50 states.[22]

The DOJ has a special counsel for health care to coordinate health care fraud enforcement among the DOJ, the US attorney's office, the Federal Bureau of Investigation, and the OIG. As a part of this initiative, each US attorney appoints a health care fraud coordinator and creates a health care fraud working group in each federal judicial district, including both criminal and civil attorneys, with the goal of coordinating the efforts of various program officials, investigative agencies, and private insurers. The DOJ may seek civil damages or penalties for fraud and abuse violations or it may prosecute violators under several criminal statutes.[23]

In addition to prosecution by government agencies, in some instances, private individuals (whistleblowers) can file a *qui tam* action to prosecute fraud and abuse. The FCA allows an individual who has knowledge of fraudulent practices engaged in by an entity to file a complaint.[24] The government then investigates the complaint and can choose to intervene in the action and prosecute the claim itself. If there is such intervention and the government wins the action, the individual receives 15% to 20% of the recovery plus costs and fees. If there is no intervention, the individual can still choose to bring the suit and, if victorious, will receive 25% to 30% of the recovery. Although the FCA is the only health fraud statute that provides for a *qui tam* action, as discussed above, other types of fraud and abuse, such as kickbacks and self-referral law violations, are subject to prosecution under the FCA and have been brought by private whistleblowers.

The Medicaid program, while funded in large part by the federal government, is operated at the state level, and federal law requires the establishment of Medicaid Fraud Control Units (MFCUs) for the states to enforce Medicaid fraud and abuse violations.[25] The states conduct the investigations and, if prosecution is deemed appropriate, the MFCUs pursue convictions in state courts by using state laws. Depending on the MFCU, the involvement of local prosecutors may be necessary to effect criminal proceedings. MFCUs also investigate Medicare fraud that is identified as a result of Medicaid investigations. States also use various other government agencies to combat fraud and abuse. These units include Medicaid inspectors general, Medicaid program integrity units, attorney general–consumer protection units, and state insurance fraud units.

Private entities that contract with CMS to administer and pay Medicare claims are required by law to have their own fraud and abuse investigative units and are important players in the fraud enforcement process. The Medicare Integrity Program requires private companies that process Medicare claims (Medicare intermediaries) to review the activities of providers for a variety of reasons, including fraud.[26] Medicare intermediaries are also obligated to audit provider costs reports and determine whether the carriers improperly paid or overpaid the providers, and the result of these audits are often referred to the fraud and abuse investigative units and become the starting point for a fraud investigation or prosecution.[27]

2.5   Penalties

Fraud and abuse may be punishable civilly, criminally, or both. In addition to the civil and criminal penalties, violators of fraud and abuse laws may be excluded from participating in federal health care programs. Given that these programs pay for such a large portion of total health care payments (especially in the many fields that cater heavily to older patients who are covered by Medicare), exclusion alone can result in financial ruin.

The maximum criminal penalties for violating the most common health care fraud charges are set forth below:

- Fraud on Medicare, Medicaid, or TRICARE programs
  - Imprisonment: 5 years
  - Fine: $25,000[28]
- Kickbacks involving Medicare, Medicaid, or TRICARE programs
  - Imprisonment: 5 years
  - Fine: $25,000[29]

- False claims: false, fictitious, or fraudulent claims
    - Imprisonment: 5 years
    - Fine: the greater of (a) $250,000 for an individual, $500,000 for an organization, or (b) twice the gross gain or loss from the offense[30]
- False statements relating to health care matters
    - Imprisonment: 5 years
    - Fine: the greater of (a) $250,000 for an individual, $500,000 for an organization, or (b) twice the gross gain or loss from the offense[31]
- Mail and wire fraud
    - Imprisonment: 20 years
    - Fine: the greater of (a) $250,000 for an individual, $500,000 for an organization or (b) twice the gross gain or loss from the offense[32]
- Health care fraud
    - Imprisonment: 10 years; if serious bodily injury results: 20 years; if death results: life
    - Fine: the greater of (a) $250,000 for an individual, $500,000 for an organization or (b) twice the gross gain or loss from the offense[33]
- Obstruction of criminal investigations of health care offenses
    - Imprisonment: 5 years
    - Fine: the greater of (a) $250,000 for an individual, $500,000 for an organization, or (b) twice the gross gain or loss from the offense.[34]

In a given case, the specific sentence within the ranges cited above is determined in accordance with the US Sentencing Guidelines.[35]

The Social Security Act establishes a number of CMPs for particular types of fraud and abuse. CMPs can be imposed by the Secretary of HHS through administrative proceedings and apply to the following acts:[36]

- Filing a claim for a service that was not provided
- Filing a false claim

- Filing a claim for a service provided by a nonphysician when the service was required to be provided by a physician
- Filing a claim for a service provided by a physician who misrepresented a material fact to become licensed
- Filing a claim for a service provided by a physician who misrepresented his or her certification by a medical specialty board
- Filing a claim for a service provided by a physician who was excluded from participation in the federal health care programs
- Filing a claim for a medically unnecessary service
- Filing a claim for a service improperly charged to the beneficiary
- Providing false information to the beneficiary
- Providing inducements to beneficiaries
- Contracting with a provider who is excluded from participation in the federal health care programs
- Providing or receiving a kickback.

The HHS Secretary can impose a CMP of up to $10,000 for engaging in most of these acts, and that penalty can be applied for each act, ie, for each item or service that was the subject of an improper claim.[36] For certain types of offenses, including certain violations of the AKS and Stark law, HHS has delegated to the OIG the authority to impose CMPs and also to exclude certain persons from participation in federal health benefit programs.[37] Each kickback paid or received can be the basis of a $50,000 CMP. Moreover, for any of the above offenses, the HHS Secretary can assess damages of up to 3 times the amount claimed for each item or service (or, in the case of a kickback, 3 times the amount paid or received) and can exclude the offender from participation in federal health care programs.[36] The HHS Secretary can also impose CMPs of up to $2000 per patient on hospitals that pay, and physicians who receive, a payment to induce the reduction of or limitation of services.

In addition to the CMPs described above, each violation of the FCA carries a maximum penalty of $10,000 and 3 times the amount of damages sustained by the government. If the trying court determines that the provider sued cooperated extensively with the government before being alerted that an action was filed against him or her, the maximum penalty is reduced to 2 times the amount of damages.[38]

Fraud and abuse can also result in a provider's or other person's exclusion from participation in federal health benefit programs.[39] Federal health care programs (other than the Federal Employees Health Benefits Plan) will not pay for items or services furnished, ordered, or prescribed by an excluded individual or entity, and this payment prohibition applies to the excluded person, anyone who employs or contracts with the excluded person, any hospital or other provider where the excluded person provides services, and anyone else, regardless of who submits the claims. If a person is convicted of felony health care fraud, or crimes related to program abuse, patient abuse, or controlled substances, the HHS Secretary is mandated to impose exclusion. Other offenses are grounds for exclusion at the discretion of the HHS Secretary. Under state law, a provider who is convicted of criminal fraud and abuse or found to have participated in a violation of a civil fraud and abuse statute may be subject to loss or suspension of a license to practice medicine or operate a health care facility. Short of exclusion by the OIG, fraud and abuse can constitute grounds for the CMS to revoke the Medicare billing privileges of a physician and the groups with which he or she is a member.[134]

Faced with the prospects of exclusion from participation in federal programs, criminal sentencing of executives, and even higher monetary fines or penalties, defendants can be put under tremendous pressure to settle with the various government agencies (or even whistleblowers) that are prosecuting them. In fact, the largest payments made as a result of federal prosecutions of health care fraud and abuse have been under the terms of settlement agreements and deferred prosecution agreements that spared the defendant from some or all of the penalties that could have resulted from the prosecution.

In addition to extracting payments from a settling provider, the government will typically require a provider who settles a fraud claim to sign a corporate integrity agreement (CIA). Under a CIA, the entity agrees to submit to fraud and abuse auditing, reporting, and other obligations for a predetermined period of time. As fraud settlements are on the rise, so are CIAs. The following are customary requirements of a CIA:

- Three- to 8-year term
- Establishment of a corporate compliance program
- External monitoring of billing and quality of care conduct
- Required disclosure program
- Removal of excluded individuals
- Reporting of overpayments
- Annual compliance reports
- Enhanced OIG inspection and audit authority
- Enhanced document retention
- Specified penalties
- Exclusion for breach.

Examples of provisions typically included in a CIA for an individual and/or small physician practices include:

- Designation of a compliance contact
- Posting of notice of commitment to comply with all federal health care program requirements including a means by which patients can address billing concerns
- Distribution of written policies and procedures to all employees and contractors
- Training and certification of all employees and contractors
- Development of procedures to comply with the AKS and Stark law for future arrangements
- Obtaining independent review of the practice's compliance with the CIA
- Screening of all employees, contractors, and agents to ensure that none is excluded from participation in the federal health care programs
- Notification of OIG of any government investigation or legal proceedings

- Reporting of all overpayments
- Notification of OIG of new business units or locations
- Submission of an implementation report to OIG
- Submission of annual reports on compliance to OIG
- The right of OIG to inspect, audit, or review the practice's books, records, and other documents
- Retention of all documents and records regarding reimbursement from the federal health care programs for 6 years
- Penalties for failure to comply (varies on the basis of the exact act).[40]

Complying with a CIA can be expensive and can require extensive changes in the way a provider conducts business.

2.6   Examples of Fraud and Abuse

This section of the chapter describes a number of different fraud and abuse cases that have resulted in penalties or settlements paid to the government and, in many cases, shared with whistleblowers. It also lays out a top 10 list of fraud and abuse examples with a focus on the conduct of physicians.

For some types of fraud and abuse, a hypothetical example involving "Dr X" has been provided. These Dr X cases are scenarios involving a well-meaning physician (like those reading this book). The Dr X scenarios could be cases of fraud and abuse in an incipient stage.

In recent years, the largest fraud recoveries have been from large institutions, such as hospital chains and companies that manufacture and market pharmaceuticals and medical devices. For example, in January 2009, drug makers Eli Lilly and Pfizer both said that they would pay fines to settle federal criminal charges that they had illegally marketed certain drugs.[41] Eli Lilly agreed to pay $1.4 billion stemming from its marketing of the antipsychotic drug Zyprexa, and Pfizer planned to pay $2.3 billion related to its marketing of the anti-inflammatory drug Bextra.[41] In 2007, the Purdue Frederick Company, producer of the painkiller Oxycontin, paid $634.5 million in criminal and civil penalties related to marketing of that drug.[41] In 2000 and 2003, hospital chain HCA (formerly Columbia/ HCA) entered into settlements under which it agreed to pay the federal government over $1.4 billion, and in 2006, hospital chain Tenet entered into a settlement agreeing to pay the federal government over $900 million for various fraud and abuse offenses related to the way they billed federal health care programs and relationships with referring physicians.[42]

Physicians may take some comfort from the fact that government agencies and whistleblowers appear to have focused most of their attention on companies whose schemes are carried out on a grand scale. A pharmaceutical or device manufacturer's act of misconduct can easily have an identical effect on hundreds or thousands of claims to federal programs for millions or even billions of dollars. The monetary penalties that could be generated by prosecuting any one scheme are also in the millions or even billions of dollars. Looked at purely as a business proposition, weighing the risks and rewards (which is the way a potential whistleblower with no particular ax to grind would look at it), the decision as to whether to marshal the resources necessary to investigate and then prosecute a large company will often be an easy one, especially if the recovery is going back into the program's funds.

The decision to prosecute any particular physician who is suspected of committing a fraud and abuse offense is more complicated. The more complicated cases will not be as appealing to prosecutors, and a policy of strict enforcement is not going to be feasible. As a result, the focus on large institutions is probably fairly heavily influenced by the economics of prosecution and not entirely by the government's policy priorities or by some sympathy that the public holds for physician defendants.

While prosecutors have focused primarily on the bigger fish, there have been instances where physicians who played a supporting role in an institution's misconduct have been prosecuted. For example, in 2007 a physician who wrote fraudulent prescriptions for medically unnecessary durable medical equipment (DME) and was compensated for these prescriptions was convicted. The DME owner was sentenced to 63 months' imprisonment, but the physician also received 36 months in jail. Together, the parties had to pay $1.3 million in restitution.[42]

Federal health officials and prosecutors have signaled recently that they will devote more resources to investigate and prosecute physicians who accept money or other incentives from drug and DME companies for using their products. In an article published in the *New York Times* on March 3, 2009, entitled "Crackdowns on Doctors Who Take Kickbacks," Lewis Morris, chief counsel to the OIG, expressed the desire to "make examples of a couple of doctors so that their colleagues see that [taking kickbacks from drug and device companies] isn't worth it." The *New York Times* reported that "within a few months, officials plan to file civil and criminal charges against a number of surgeons who they say demanded profitable consulting agreements from device makers in exchange for using their products."[41]

More examples of fraud and abuse prosecutions against all types of health care business can be found in the OIG Annual Reports, available on the OIG's website at www.oig.hhs.gov/publications/hcfac.asp.

2.6.1   Billing for Medically Unnecessary Services

Health benefit plans typically only cover services that are medically necessary, with certain exceptions, such as the Medicare program's limited types and amounts of certain preventive care and medical screening services, hospice care, and certain experimental treatments. The statutes governing the Medicare program, for instance, mandate that most covered services be "reasonable and necessary for the diagnosis or treatment of illness or injury or to improve the functioning of a malformed body member."[43] The CMP Law provides for penalties for any person who knowingly presents claims to a federal health care program for a pattern of items or services that the person knows or should know are not medically necessary,[44] and providing services substantially in excess of those needed by the patient is grounds for exclusion from participation in federal health care programs.

Whether a particular diagnostic test, treatment, or other service was medically necessary can be a difficult and even subjective question, although there is a regulatory framework for establishing parameters for the necessity of particular services.[45] Submitting a larger than expected number of claims for expensive procedures is a frequent starting point for audits that lead to charges of fraud and abuse based on submission of claims for medically unnecessary services.

Some of the examples in this section appear, on the face of things, indefensible. However, most providers can probably imagine how at least some of the defendants ended up billing for services that were medically unnecessary. Providers, over time, develop methods of treating patients that they believe are in the patients' best interests. The mere notion of second-guessing one's clinical decisions to conform to an insurer's policies can sometimes present a moral dilemma for a provider, and also rouse fears of being accused of malpractice for providing substandard care or not performing a test that would have provided the right diagnosis. Readers will have to read between the lines in the examples below to decide where the defendants fall on the spectrum that runs from unscrupulous to reckless to careless to stubborn to purely unlucky.

In the case of *United States ex rel Thomas Gayeski v Linda Bland*, a neurosurgeon was accused of performing multiple unnecessary neurosurgical procedures at a hospital on the same patients on successive days.[46] The accusation was brought under the FCA by a whistleblower who was an anesthesiologist at the same hospital, and the federal government joined the case. In addition to performing unnecessary surgeries, the complaint alleged that the neurosurgeon worked only 2 days per week and unnecessarily performed many procedures at night, which resulted in further increases to the payments received from the federal health care programs.[46] The patients remained in the hospital for longer stays and had extra follow-up office visits, generating higher payments not only to the neurosurgeon, but also to the hospital. The case was settled in 2007 with the hospital and the neurosurgeon agreeing to pay $1.275 million.[47]

In 2009, the DOJ announced that 3 physicians who were part owners of 2 medical clinics pled guilty to defrauding the Medicare program of $5.3 million by billing for treatments and drugs that were not medically necessary.[48] The clinics specialized in the treatment of patients infected with Human Immunodeficiency Virus (HIV). According the DOJ's press release, the clinic owners had entered into kickback arrangements with their patients, who were Medicare beneficiaries, under which the

beneficiaries were paid every week for their Medicare billing information, which the clinics used to submit the fraudulent bills. The patients'
blood samples were altered by the owners to give the appearance that
the patients required the treatments and drugs.[48]

In 2006, the DOJ accepted payment of more than $25 million to settle
with a network of affiliated physician groups accused of billing Medicaid
for critical neonatal services when the infants in question were not
critically ill. According the DOJ,

> [The network] admitted infants to hospital neonatal intensive care
> units using a CPT code for admission of critically ill infants, when as
> many as one-third or more of those infants were not in fact critically
> ill. [The network] used critical/unstable and critical/stable CPT codes
> for subsequent days of treatment, when as many as 50% or more of
> those infants were not in fact critically ill. [The network] also used
> critical/unstable and critical/stable CPT codes on discharge days, when
> as many as 85% or more of those infants were not in fact critically ill.[48]

In 2007, a husband and wife, both licensed occupational therapists,
were charged with defrauding the Florida Medicaid program out of more
than $200,000.[49] The couple billed Medicaid for providing 2 or 3 differ-
ent types of services during the same 15 minutes of face-to-face therapy,
although Medicaid could only reimburse for 1 treatment per 15-minute
interval. The husband and wife were charged with grand theft and
organized scheme to defraud, both first-degree felonies, and funds from
several of their bank accounts were seized.[49]

In the HCA settlement cited above, an important charge was that the
company's hospital laboratories engaged in many instances of adding
unnecessary tests onto orders for simple blood tests and then billing the
government for both the necessary and unnecessary tests.[42]

> Dr X is an ear, nose, and throat physician. An unusually high
> percentage of his patients complain of chronic conditions that have
> persisted for many years. The reason for this is not clear but could
> have something to do with local air quality, or the fact that many of
> them worked for one of several large industrial employers, or perhaps
> that word of Dr X's success in providing many patients with relief

has spread in the community. Many years ago, Dr X started using relatively advanced tests to assist him in diagnosing patients and in making ongoing adjustments to their medications and determining when a surgical procedure is necessary. Dr X, more than other ear, nose, and throat physicians in the area, is skeptical about the benefits of surgery for these types of patients and does relatively few surgeries. In the past 10 years, Dr X has purchased various types of testing equipment and performed some tests in his office that are usually performed at a hospital or other special testing facility. He uses these tests whenever he believes the information will be useful, which is quite often, and sometimes several times in a short period when the patient's condition has flared up or when he is modifying the patient's care plan. Over the years, the local Medicare carrier and one private insurer have audited small numbers of his claims and demanded repayment of several thousand dollars, asserting that many of the tests on the claims were not medically necessary. It is not unthinkable that Dr X's proclivity for testing could lead to a referral to a fraud unit and, eventually, an OIG report reading "Dr X agreed to pay to the government twice the amount that he had been paid for unnecessary diagnostic tests to settle allegations that he submitted false claims to federal health benefit programs."

2.6.2   Billing for Services Not Provided

There is no need to lay out the laws that prohibit billing for services that were never provided or why intentionally obtaining payment for services that were never provided is fraudulent, but the CMP Law does specifically provide that knowingly submitting claims for a service that a person knows or should know was not provided is grounds for a CMP.[50] The examples in this section do not seem particularly sympathetic. Aside from an unnoticed billing error, it is hard to find an excuse or gray area to explain or justify billing for a service when *no* service was provided. However, as the hypothetical scenario at the end of this section shows, the legal distinction between miscoding and billing for a service that was not provided may not always be as clear as it seems to be in the examples that follow.

In the case of *United States v Awad*, a physician contracted with a nonphysician who owned a billing company and a respiratory therapy company to evaluate patients and supervise therapists.[51] The physician began seeing Medicare patients at board-and-care facilities where he performed initial assessments on patients to determine whether they required respiratory treatment. Both the California Department of Health Services and Medicare conducted audits of the physician's files as a result of patient complaints that the physician billed for services that were not actually provided. The audits uncovered a number of suspicious billing practices, including seeing up to 114 patients per date of service and numerous occasions on which 90 or more patients were seen on one day, billing for visits with patients at board-and-care facilities when the patients were hospitalized elsewhere on the dates claimed, and consistent use of the place-of-service code reserved for office visits when visits took place at board-and-care facilities. The physician's billings for a certain respiratory treatment were 14 times the number, and 18,000 times the amount, than those of the next highest biller in the region for that type of treatment. A follow-up investigation revealed that the physician billed Medicare for more than $460,000 for treatments performed by his therapists while he was out of the country.[52] The physician in this case was sentenced to 180 months' imprisonment, 3 years' supervised release, restitution in the amount of $2,625,722, and a $2800 special assessment, and the federal appeals court affirmed his conviction on appeal.[53]

In 2009, DOJ charged a cardiologist with accepting fraudulent reimbursements. The cardiologist allegedly obtained information about patients at a hospital at which he had privileges and then used this information to his personal advantage without their consent. He then arranged for others to bill Medicare for services never actually rendered to these patients. According to the DOJ's charges, in most cases the cardiologist waited nearly a year after the falsified date of treatment before filing the claims. Moreover, he filed multiple claims for the highest level of cardiac care for each of these patients.[54]

In contrast to the fairly stark allegations of billing for services not provided, described above, the next hypothetical scenario is a case where a casual approach to documenting and coding results in the same type of charges.

Dr X is a podiatrist. He is well known in the community and occasionally (a few times in an average week) receives requests for consultations from other specialists in the area, such as orthopedists, neurologists, and pain management specialists. His office is low tech, and during his 20 years in practice, his billing has always been done by a staff of one with limited training. Sometimes Dr X gets a written order for the consultation from the patient; other times the specialist contacts Dr X's office and requests the consultation on the phone, and other times the patient tells Dr X when making the appointment that the specialist requested the consultation. After examining the patient, Dr X sends a copy of his chart notes to the specialist, which are very detailed and legible, and bills for a consultation. Over the years, Dr X billed for hundreds of these consultations. Recently, one of his billers mentioned that it seemed odd that the consultation order was not always in the chart, but no payer ever questioned any of his claims for payment for consultations. The specialists would sometimes call him with a question about his chart notes but never asked for anything else in writing.

On the basis of the hypothetical facts laid out above, most readers would probably agree that Dr X may have been overpaid on some or many of the claims he submitted for consultations, but that the facts present do not suggest fraud. However, the facts could either be construed as a case of miscoding (office visits as consultations) or improper documentation, or be cast as a more menacing charge of billing for services (consultations) that were never performed. The difference in approach, and the decision as to how the case is prosecuted, could have a very significant effect on Dr X's willingness or ability to withstand a settlement offer.

2.6.3   Failing to Comply With Billing Requirements

A physician who *intentionally* fails to comply with billing requirements that the physician *knows* are applicable and has the *intent* of obtaining a payment from a health benefit plan that the physician *knows* he or she would not otherwise have received if he or she had complied with the billing requirements, which results in the physician receiving reimbursement that is higher than he or she is entitled to, commits fraud. With all of the italicized terms demonstrating intent and knowledge in the preceding sentence, there should be enough to establish the requisite findings for a conviction of fraud under the federal Health Care Fraud Statute and liability under any of the other criminal or civil fraud and abuse statutes discussed in this chapter (with the proviso that the other federal statutes apply only when federal programs are affected, and that there may be constitutional limits on the application of any federal statute).

However, as every physician knows, many of the rules of medical billing are very hard to understand and/or are subjective. Guidance from numerous sources is constantly flooding into physician offices, via mail, fax, and e-mail. Wading through the voluminous correspondence to pick out relevant material takes more time than the typical physician is likely to have to devote to this task. Essentially similar questions about the proper way to bill for a certain service under a certain set of circumstances might be answered in different ways, by different people, or by the same people on different days. Left unchallenged, some payment determinations will be completely irrational and inexplicable.

Yet, both sides need to keep moving forward with a business that requires settling a continuous and very large volume of claims. Physicians need to be paid and cannot necessarily afford to have faith that the payer's appeal process will result in a fair settlement, and payers need to minimize the amount of time they devote to resolving questions on any particular claim or from any particular physician. The result: physicians and payers both cut corners when trying to get to the bottom of a thorny billing question.

Unlike the unsympathetic examples in the preceding section of fraudulent billings for services that were never provided, readers are likely to be able to see a more familiar scenario in the cases described in the following subsections. The question raised by many of these cases is at what point a provider's careless or aggressive use of codes and other billing protocols become fraud.

2.6.3.1   *Miscoding*

Procedure coding and other medical billing rules generally dictate what payers will and will not pay for. However, good patient care does not end with the Current Procedural Terminology (CPT®) code, and physicians sometimes interpret the CPT codebook broadly so that they can submit claims for services that their patients need and expect. This sort of practical approach to the technical rules of medical billing can have disastrous results.

In *United States v Rousseau*, a podiatrist was prosecuted for failing to comply with billing requirements regarding treatment that he provided to 20 Medicare patients.[55] The podiatrist claimed that he treated these patients for "fungus infections of the toenails and ingrown toenails" and filed a claim with Medicare stating as such. In fact, the only services provided were a trimming of the toenails and other minor procedures. The services actually rendered were not reimbursable under Medicare. The podiatrist's conviction was upheld on appeal.[56]

2.6.3.2   *Upcoding*

Another common type of billing error occurs when a provider performs a service that is covered, but *upcodes* by billing for a higher level or otherwise more expensive service than the one that was performed.

In *United States v Augustine Medical, Inc*, a physician founded a manufacturing company and invented a product called "Warm-Up Active Wound Therapy."[57] Pursuant to the Medicare coding system, Warm-Up was to be billed as a medical supply under a specific code, which reimbursed the manufacturer at a lower payment level than the owners of the company wished. Instead, the company directed providers who used Warm-Up to use a different code for billing purposes to reap a higher reimbursement fee. The owners of the company were convicted of several counts of fraud.[58]

Another, more troubling example of upcoding cited by the OIG was the case of a dermatologist who falsely informed patients that they had cancer when laboratory results indicated that their tissue specimens were benign.[59] He then performed surgeries on the basis of these false diagnoses.

A jury found him guilty of upcoding surgical procedures, billing for unnecessary procedures, and improperly billing for follow-up office visits. The dermatologist was sentenced to over 10 years in prison and required to pay $1.3 million in restitution and a $175,000 fine.[59]

In 2004, an administrative law judge issued a decision imposing CMPs of $126,000 and a 7-year exclusion against a physician whom the judge found to have submitted 126 false claims to the Medicare program seeking reimbursement for an expensive nuclear medicine test when, in fact, he had provided only a simple, inexpensive spirometry test.[59]

2.6.3.3   Unbundling

Unbundling is, from a payer's perspective, obtaining higher payment than a provider is entitled to by submitting separate claims, or separate charges on a single claim, for various tests or procedures that are required to be bundled together and paid for by a single, lower payment. A simple example would be the charge for a complete blood count (CBC). CBCs involve up to a dozen or more tests, but a standard automated test performs the panel of tests at once, so that each test does not have to be run separately. The CPT coding system used by Medicare and other payers includes individual codes for CBCs that result in a single payment for the entire panel. Bundling is also used in other contexts, such as the bundling of a procedure with certain preadmission or follow-up services in connection with that procedure, and the bundling of a wide array of services provided to patients admitted to a hospital as an inpatient or an outpatient in connection with the admission.

In 2005, an anesthesiologist and an anesthesiology practice group agreed to pay a $50,000 and $130,000, respectively, and enter into a CIA to resolve their civil liability for, among other things, the practice group separately billing for preoperative patient evaluations for pain management procedures that were bundled into the payment for the procedure. The group billed for pain management services for patients even though it also billed for preoperative anesthesia services for separate patients awaiting surgery.[60]

Bundling rules can become particularly complicated when the services that are often provided by one provider are bundled with services provided by another provider. Over time, payers have developed *edits* to call attention to claims for unbundled services, and, in some instances, automatically rebundle the claims. Providers frequently complain that these automatic edits result in payment errors when they fail to take into account the circumstances that justify separate billing in certain cases.

Unbundling can also be used to refer to schemes to get physicians to order unnecessary tests by having them order panels of tests that included tests that are not part of a standard panel and then separately bill for these nonstandard tests. This was a component of the infamous lab scam cases, including the case against National Health Laboratories that resulted in a settlement of $111 million in 1992 as well as a prison term for the company's chief executive officer.[60]

2.6.3.4   *Improper Cost Reports*

Hospitals and certain other health care providers file annual cost reports with Medicare and Medicaid to obtain payment.[61,62] When reimbursement of the provider's actual costs is a component of payment, the provider is generally only entitled to reimbursement for costs related to care provided to patients in the particular program. Providers are required to allocate their costs into cost centers to enable the federal programs to identify the costs that are eligible for reimbursement. Providers also must designate on their cost reports how much of their costs are properly allocated to the Medicare and Medicaid programs and how much to other patients.[63] The following are types of fraud that can be committed by providers when reporting their costs:

- Including expenses that are not related to patient care
- Inflating expenses that are related to patient care
- Shifting costs to reimbursable cost centers or to cover patients
- Failing to disclose the related status of business entities with whom the provider is dealing.

Cost reports involve technical accounting rules, and FCA cases involving improper cost reports are among the most complicated fraud and abuse cases.

United States v Bourseau[64] involved a hospital that had filed for Chapter 11 bankruptcy and was operated under a reorganization plan approved by the bankruptcy court. The federal government charged the hospital and its owners with filing false claims by including in its cost report legal fees incurred in connection with the bankruptcy proceeding, interest and lease payments that were not made within the time limits established under the cost reporting regulations and/or were made to related entities, also in contravention of the cost reporting rules, and misreporting certain other costs. In finding an FCA violation, the court found that the hospital knew or should have known of these mistakes when it filed the reports, and the hospital was not spared from penalties under the FCA (including treble damages) by the fact that the Medicare intermediary did not adjust or audit the hospital's cost reports.[65]

In 2005, a co-owner and chief financial officer (CFO) of 2 home health agencies allegedly filed claims for his salary as CFO in cost reports from 1994 through 1998.[66] According to the OIG, at the times in question, he was employed as a full-time electrician or a full-time real estate agent. He agreed to pay $20,000 and received a permanent exclusion from participation in the federal health care programs to resolve his civil liability.[66]

In *United States v Collins*, the owner of several nursing homes submitted falsely inflated expenses for Medicaid reimbursement.[67] Cost reports were to include actual expenses for items such as salaries, food, maintenance, and depreciation. The government compared the owner's cost reports to the nursing homes' tax returns and financial books and uncovered discrepancies between the numbers reported and those stated in the books.[67] For instance, the cost report indicated salary expenses at $82,070, but the tax returns and books showed $72,070 for the same items. The owner was convicted, sentenced to prison, and fined.[68]

Shifting costs takes place when a provider takes the costs for one type of expenses and reports that as another type, resulting in a higher reimbursement. In *United States ex rel Geisler v IMED Corp*, the defendant corporation sold equipment used by Medicare beneficiaries including intravenous pumps.[69] According to the district court,

> the gist of the alleged scheme was to shift the costs of the goods to the pumps, which as 'capital' goods were reimbursed by Medicare at their full cost, and away from the disposables, which were reimbursed at a lower rate under a Medicare program known as PPS that groups disposables with other predetermined operating costs.[69]

In *United States v Alemany Rivera*,[70] a hospital medical director led the hospital into business dealings with a medical equipment supplier whose parent company he controlled. The hospital obtained a mortgage loan for remodeling and expansion. To profit from this loan, the equipment supplier, which was essentially controlled by the medical director, sold equipment and furnishings to the hospital at inflated prices and did not even deliver a large amount of the contracted equipment.[71] The medical director was subsequently convicted, imprisoned, and fined.[70]

2.6.3.5 *Inflating Claims*

Inflating claims, also known as *padding claims*, typically occurs when a provider adds additional hours and/or dates of treatment to the bills even though such treatment was never provided. The CPT code itself does not change, but the amount of time designated per code is artificially enlarged.

In *United States v Cabrera-Diaz*, an anesthesiologist who provided services to Medicare patients billed a Medicare intermediary for his claims.[72] The Medicare intermediary audited the anesthesiologist's claims and compared the claims filed to the medical records of certain of the anesthesiologist's patients. The audit revealed that for several years, the anesthesiologist "overstated, falsely reported, unsupported, or undocumented the anesthesia time" for most patients. In 1994, the physician billed for 99,720 minutes of anesthesia time, but the records supported only 21,371 minutes. As a result, the Medicare intermediary determined that the anesthesiologist had falsely claimed $237,600.39 in reimbursement in 1994.[73]

Under Medicare's hospital payment system, hospitals are paid predetermined amounts for each patient depending on the diagnosis-related group to which the patient is assigned, as well as certain features of the hospital. Additional outlier payments are made for atypical cases that generate relatively higher costs for the hospital. On December 7, 2001, the OIG released the findings of an audit that it conducted of Brigham and Women's Hospital for fiscal year 1999.[74] The review concluded that Brigham and Women's billed $237,089 in charges involving services that were not ordered by a physician, represented an inappropriate admission, were not provided or were not ordered by a physician, or were duplicate billings. Further, the OIG also identified $525,143 in erroneous pharmacy charges or incorrectly billed lung acquisition charges. The OIG determined that this resulted in an outlier overpayment of $295,671.[74]

Over the past few years, excessive outlier payments have been the subject of a large number of FCA abuse prosecutions, resulting in some very large settlements. In the Tenet case cited earlier, accusations were made that Tenet inflated its claims to obtain outlier payments despite the absence of a proportional rise in patient care and medical supply costs.[75] In 2006, a nonprofit health care system that operated 9 hospitals was forced to pay $265 million to the federal government as part of a settlement for allegations that it inflated charges for treating seriously ill patients by more than $500 million.[76] In addition to the financial penalty, the hospital system agreed to be audited by an outside monitor for 6 years.[76]

2.6.3.6 *Retaining Overpayments*

The Social Security Act makes it a crime to conceal or fail to disclose an overpayment with the intent of securing a benefit that is not due.[77] The FCA includes a prohibition against using a false record or statement to conceal, avoid, or decrease an obligation to pay or transmit money or property to the federal government—the Reverse False Claims Act.[78]

The OIG's published guidance to various types of health care providers, including individual physicians and small physician group practices, stresses that providers should refund any federal program overpayments they identify to the program intermediary that paid it:

> One of the most important components of a successful compliance audit protocol is an appropriate response when the physician practice identifies a problem. This action should be taken as soon as possible after the date the problem is identified. The specific action a physician practice takes should depend on the circumstances of the situation. In some cases, the response can be as straightforward as generating a repayment with appropriate explanation to Medicare or the appropriate payor from which the overpayment was received. In others, the physician practice may want to consult with a coding/ billing expert to determine the next best course of action. There is no boilerplate solution to how to handle problems that are identified.

It is a good business practice to create a system to address how
physician practices will respond to and report potential problems.
In addition, preserving information relating to identification of the
problem is as important as preserving information that tracks the
physician practice's reaction to, and solution for, the issue.[79]

While overpayments occur as a result of a variety of errors, either by
the provider or by the payer, failure to call them to the attention of the
payer can result in further errors in claims processing, and could also
lead to investigations for submitting further claims knowing that they
will result in further overpayments. The OIG encourages providers who
have a legal compliance program to bring significant overpayments to
the attention of their compliance officer.

In 2006, a Nebraska hospital paid $4 million to the federal government
and the state of Nebraska to settle allegations that it knowingly failed
to disclose and failed to return overpayments made by the federal Medicare
and the Nebraska Medicaid programs.[80] This settlement was part of a
series of settlements of FCA claims against hospitals brought by a whistleblower who had worked for Healthcare Financial Advisers, a consulting firm that had advised the hospitals with regard to their cost reports,
including a $24.5 million settlement paid by a subsidiary of Cigna Corp.

The FCA was amended on May 20, 2009 by FERA. It's important to
note that the amended FCA makes the application of the FCA for
failing to refund known-overpayments fairly explicit, by establishing
FCA liability when a person "knowingly and improperly avoids . . . an
obligation to pay or transmit money or property to the Government."
FERA also expanded the ability of prosecutors and whistleblowers to get
access to information to pursue FCA cases.

2.6.3.7 Miscellaneous

In March 2009, the OIG reported that it had entered into a $2 million
settlement with a radiology group that was one of the largest CMP
settlements it has ever negotiated.[81] The OIG alleged that the defendants improperly provided diagnostic tests without the required treating physicians' orders, billed for certain tests under CPT codes not

supported by the medical records, and failed to satisfy certain other Medicare billing and coverage requirements.

The OIG has established a standing offer to limit the civil penalties that it will apply to violations of federal civil, criminal, and administrative laws if the provider follows the OIG's Provider Self-Disclosure Protocol. Until recently, the Provider Self-Disclosure Protocol required the provider to submit the following information:

- The name, address, provider identification number, and tax identification number of the provider
- Whether the provider has knowledge that the matter is under current inquiry by a government agency or contractor
- Whether the provider is under investigation or other inquiry for any other matters relating to a federal health care program
- A full description of the nature of the matter being disclosed, including the type of claim, transaction or other conduct giving rise to the matter, the names of entities and individuals believed to be implicated and an explanation of their roles in the matter, and the relevant periods involved
- The type of health care provider implicated and any provider billing numbers associated with the matter disclosed
- The federal health care programs affected, including government contractors
- The reasons why the disclosing provider believes that a violation of federal, criminal, civil, or administrative law may have occurred
- A certification by the provider that the submission contains truthful information and is based on a good faith effort to bring the matter to the government's attention for the purpose of resolving any potential liabilities to the government.[82]

On April 15, 2008, in an open letter to health care providers, the OIG modified the protocol. In addition to the information required above, the OIG now also requires submission of the following information:

- A complete description of the conduct being disclosed
- A description of the provider's internal investigation or a commitment regarding when it will be completed

■ An estimate of the damages to the federal health care programs and the methodology used to calculate that figure or a commitment regarding when the provider will complete such estimate

■ A statement of the laws potentially violated by the conduct.[83]

2.6.4   Failing to Comply With Coverage Requirements

Like medical billing rules, health benefit coverage rules can be highly technical and unintuitive. As with the other types of complex fraud and abuse cases, cases of this type are usually brought under the FCA.

2.6.4.1   Billing for Services Not Personally Rendered

Certain types of services must be provided by an individual with specified credentials, such as a license to practice medicine or physical therapy in the state where the service is provided. For example, in 2005, a psychologist was charged with submitting claims to the Medicare program for psychiatric services. The psychologist submitted claims under the name and provider number of a licensed psychiatrist with whom he was working in order to obtain Medicare reimbursement. The psychologist paid a $25,000 penalty and was excluded from federal health care programs for 3 years.[84]

In *United States v Singh,* a physician was convicted of violating the federal Health Care Fraud Statute, as well as other crimes related to the distribution of controlled substances from his pain management practice.[85] The pain practice's nurses were expected to treat patients without supervision when the physician was not present, and the practice routinely and inappropriately billed level 4 and 5 office visits when only a nurse had seen the patient. Even though medical billing is complex and physicians may misinterpret the CPT code book, a physician should clearly understand that billing for an unsupervised nurse visit as a physician-supervised visit will result in significant overpayments to the practice. In its thorough review of the physician's conviction, the court noted that the American Medical Association (AMA) coding manual highlighted and clearly set out the rule that physician presence is required to bill for office visits above a level 1, and this concept was even printed on the superbill form used by the practice.[86]

A number of fraud and abuse prosecutions have involved fairly common practices in which physicians working in hospitals or other facilities delegated tasks to assistants who were trained to perform those tasks under supervision by an individual with higher credentials, but coverage rules required that the services, or particular aspects of the services, be personally performed by the higher-licensed individuals. In most of these cases, the physicians and hospitals were probably highly sensitive to the need to ensure that care was provided in a clinically appropriate manner, if for no other reason than to avoid liability for malpractice. Systems were probably in place to ensure that practitioners were adequately trained in the tasks they performed, and that patient safety was not compromised. Nevertheless, the service was not eligible for coverage unless the physician personally performed the particular task, and the claims submitted to the government payers for these ineligible services were grounds for liability under the FCA.

In *Minnesota Association of Nurse Anesthetists, United States, ex rel v Allina Health System Corp*, a group of anesthesiologists and a hospital system were accused of billing for services that were not eligible for coverage under the Medicare Part B benefit for anesthesiologists' services that required the anesthesiologists' presence in the operating room at certain times.[87] This was an FCA action and was brought by a competitor (the whistleblower was an association of competing health care practitioners). The case continued after the government declined its option to intervene and was ultimately settled partly on the basis of different but related claims by the government. The case survived the hospital's motion to dismiss (which was first granted and then overturned on appeal) when the appellate court considered complicated questions concerning the proper interpretation of the Medicare regulations, guidance published by CMS, and communications between the Medicare intermediary and the hospital, and advice given by the hospital's in-house counsel, in determining that the whistleblower may be able to prove in a trial that the defendants had the requisite state of mind to violate the FCA. The hospital system eventually settled the whistleblower claims (along with a separate charge brought by the government that the hospital system had retained overpayments related to the anesthesia billing) by refunding $13 million in overpayments and paying $3 million in interest and expenses. The whistleblower received $1.12 million of the overpayments, and the hospital agreed to a 5-year CIA.[88]

In 2005, the University of Washington (UW) Medical School paid a $35 million penalty to the government for improper billing to Medicare and Medicaid.[89] Specifically, UW Medical School physicians repeatedly billed the government programs for procedures and treatments performed by medical residents, who are not permitted to bill the federal health care programs.[89]

The UW Medical School is a late entry in a series of substantial settlements by teaching hospitals for improper coding given the level of supervision that attending physicians routinely provided for residents treating patients. In what became known as the *physicians at teaching hospitals* or PATH audits, the DOJ and HHS, through the OIG, audited teaching hospitals across the country in the late 1990s to determine whether teaching physicians who billed Medicare for services rendered by residents provided (and documented) sufficient personal supervision for the delivery of the service to payment under Part B for services performed by a resident under the personal supervision of the teaching physician.[89] A 1995 settlement under which the University of Pennsylvania agreed to pay approximately $30 million in disputed billings and damages kicked off a series of similar PATH settlements, including ones with the following institutions:

- University of Pennsylvania: $30 million
- Thomas Jefferson University: $12 million
- University of Virginia: $8.6 million
- University of Pittsburgh: $17 million.[89]

2.6.4.2 *Inadequate Supervision of Unlicensed Employees*

Another violation of billing requirements occurs when a physician fails to provide adequate supervision of employees. In most states, certain employees must be supervised by a physician at all times or when performing certain procedures.

For example, a physician who owned a physical therapy clinic billed federal programs $16 million and collected $7 million for therapy provided by unqualified, inadequately trained, unlicensed technicians working without physician supervision.[59] The physician was convicted on 16 counts of fraud.[59]

2.6.5   Failure to Provide Adequate or Necessary Services

The federal government has recently employed the health care fraud laws to attack substandard or inadequate care, particularly with regard to nursing homes and other facilities that are charged with caring for residents who are unable to speak up for themselves.

In December 2005, a nursing home settled allegations for $2.5 million that it billed for services when the quality of care was so poor that it was not provided as charged or was worthless to the patients.[90] The complaint was filed by 5 whistleblowers in 2002 who alleged a systemic failure by the nursing home to provide appropriate care to its residents, resulting in the premature death of several patients. The failure of care was alleged to be due to severe understaffing (with 1 or 2 RNs staffing the subacute unit per shift, caring for up to 55 medically needy patients), inadequate staff training, high staff turnover, an ineffective medical director (who lived 40 minutes from the home, was allegedly often unreachable by phone, and sent an assistant to attend his patients at the home), poor nursing documentation, and insufficient budgetary allowances.[90]

In *United States ex rel Aranda v Community Psychiatric Centers of Oklahoma, Inc*, a psychiatric hospital was accused of providing an unsafe environment for its patients.[91] The hospital understaffed shifts, failed to monitor equipment, and made inappropriate housing assignments based on the needs of its patients. As a result, some patients suffered from physical injuries and sexual abuse.[92] However, this did not stop the hospital from filing claims for services rendered with Medicaid and certifying that it met all applicable statutes.[93] The court let the case go forward because it reasoned that participation in Medicaid is conditioned on meeting certain quality of care standards, which may have been violated by this hospital.[92] Eventually, the facility was closed and the case settled for a payment of $750,000.[94]

2.6.6   Falsifying Supporting Documents

Falsifying supporting documents is often a companion charge to the filing of false claims, prosecuted under the False Statements Act, which is a companion statute to the FCA. To be guilty of making a false statement, the following elements must be proved: (1) the individual submitted a statement to the government; (2) this statement was false; (3) this statement was material; (4) this statement was made knowingly and willfully; and (5) this statement pertained to some activity within the jurisdiction of the federal government.[95] A false statement made to a private insurance company with which the government has contracted to administer federal health programs' claims is considered to be in violation of the False Statements Act. To be material, the statement merely has to be intended to influence government action, even if it fails to actually do so. The statement must be made knowingly and willfully, but this does not mean that the individual must know that making the statement is illegal.

Referring again to the UW Medical School fraud first mentioned in section 2.6.4.1, an additional charge levied against the school was that "the doctors systematically created false documentation to support the false Medicare claims, including falsifying documents to claim they were present while services such as dialysis were performed."[89]

A false entry in a supporting document, such as a patient chart, can constitute a false statement even if that document is not submitted with the claim. In *United States v Rutgard*, a physician ordered a number of procedures that were deemed to be not medically necessary.[96] Consequently, he was charged with a battery of health care fraud counts.[96] Among these charges was one for making false statements because he recorded all of the notes regarding the unnecessary entries in patient charts. It did not matter that the charts themselves were not sent with the claims for reimbursement.[97]

2.6.7   Kickbacks

There is no remembrance of them of former times; neither shall there be any remembrance of them of latter times that are to come, among those that shall come after.[98]

Kickbacks hold a special place in the annals of fraud and abuse. The forces of entrepreneurial creativity and optimism in the health care industry continue to grind away in an epic battle with the anti-kickback statute (AKS). A criminal prosecution under the AKS can result in a maximum fine of $25,000, imprisonment up to 5 years, or both, and is grounds for automatic exclusion from federal health care programs. The OIG has the authority to bring civil prosecutions under the AKS on behalf of HHS and may initiate administrative proceedings to impose CMPs and to exclude such party from the federal health care programs. Government prosecutors and private whistleblowers can also bring civil prosecutions under the FCA alleging that AKS violations resulted in the submission of false claims (see discussion of FCA in section 2.3).

As many health care law attorneys can recite in their sleep, "the anti-kickback statute makes it a criminal offense to knowingly and willfully offer, pay, solicit, or receive any remuneration to induce or reward referrals of items or services reimbursable by a federal health care program."[99] The AKS has been applied to every sort of transaction between or among health care providers, manufacturers of health care products, and other people and firms with business that involves health care.

The OIG has published a number of special fraud alerts, special advisory bulletins, advisory opinions, and other statements expressing their concern that many types of transactions are suspect and could be prosecuted under the AKS. Some of the transactions that the OIG warns of have been going on for many years, and others are novel (or were novel at the time of the OIG's warning). Some are very simple (eg, gifts from drug manufacturers to physicians) and some are complicated (eg, contractual joint ventures involving multiple legal entities). Many are commonplace. Furthermore, prosecutions have been brought against many of the types of arrangements, including the arrangements described in the OIG's statements.

A party's *intent* is central in determining whether it is violating the AKS. A payment that is made, or an investment offered, with a heart that is pure and a mind that is free from any intent to induce referrals does not violate the statute. Even an envelope stuffed with cash received directly from the Medicare program and passed under a table from a hospital executive to a surgeon does not violate the AKS if it was not given with the intent of inducing or rewarding referrals— although such a transaction screams out for an answer to the question of *why* the envelope was passed. As the OIG reiterates in each advisory opinion that it issues: "The [AKS] has been interpreted to cover any arrangement where <u>one</u> purpose of the remuneration was to obtain money for the referral of services or to induce further referrals."[99] Faced with the threat of the staggering potential penalties for a violation of the AKS, paying a large financial settlement may seem a safer course of action than arguing over intent in a court or in an HHS administrative proceeding. About one-third of the civil fraud and abuse settlements that the OIG reported on its website for 2008 involved allegations of AKS violations.

Statutory and regulatory safe harbors offer protection from prosecution for certain arrangements that meet all of the safe harbor requirements, but the scope of this protection is very limited. For many of the transactions that physicians propose, no safe harbor is available or compliance with a safe harbor would require modifications to the proposal that wipe out or dramatically reduce the benefits to the parties. A good example of this is when hospitals and physicians in the same community identify a need or an opportunity to compete to provide certain health care services to their own patients, and propose to jointly invest in a business that provides those services. The only safe harbor for this type of arrangement applies when the investment is in a publicly traded company or in a medically underserved area, or when business is not largely driven by referrals from its investors.[100] The safe harbor could not be used unless the investors knew that the business would attract a lot of patients from outside sources, and it would require finding investors who are not sources of referrals or services for the business to provide most of the capital and own most of the business.

Some of the most frequently considered safe harbors are the ones that apply to payments made to a party who is a source of referrals as rent for space or equipment or as compensation for services if the payment is "consistent with fair market value in arms-length transactions and . . . not determined in a manner that takes into account the volume or value of any referrals or business otherwise generated between the parties" and is set forth in a written agreement with a term of at least 1 year.[101] The safe harbor can often be used to establish the terms for simple transactions where the fair market value is easy to ascertain (such as rent for unfinished office space in a large commercial office building). In many situations where a physician is being compensated for his or her personal labor, the personal service safe harbor may be relied on (provided that a good basis can be found for establishing the fair market value of the particular services that the physician provides). However, there are only so many hours in a day. For a physician whose calendar is already full, the safe harbor is of limited use. Entrepreneurial proposals that would allow physicians to generate revenue or profit from the ties they have developed with the recipients of their referrals are not likely to fit in any safe harbor.

For some seemingly simple transactions, the door is left ajar for AKS prosecution in which the precise fair market value is not 100% clear. Even where the parties are confident that they have complied with a safe harbor's fair market value requirement, any complex business arrangement that generates health care business either as its central purpose or as an ancillary feature is likely to be at risk for prosecution under the AKS.

The OIG issues advisory opinions to parties seeking to protect an existing or proposed arrangement from prosecution under the AKS. When issuing these opinions, the OIG generally accepts the requestor's description of the arrangement and representations concerning relevant circumstances and how the arrangement will be carried out. The OIG issues opinions that grant this protection when the arrangement described either clearly does not implicate the AKS, clearly fits in a safe harbor, or presents very little risk of federal program abuse when weighed against the benefits the program is likely to produce for program beneficiaries and for the public. With these narrow criteria, many complex arrangements will not be eligible for a positive advisory opinion that will protect it from prosecution under the AKS.

Since 1997, the OIG has issued more than 200 advisory opinions. While the guidance provided by the advisory opinion is very important, it covers somewhat limited ground. In terms of providing groundwork for structuring complex arrangements among health care providers, the guidance offered by the advisory opinions does not expand much on the safe harbors. Of the 200 opinions, many address arrangements that appear on their face to have a purely charitable intent and pose only a limited risk of inducing any referrals. Many are redundant in that they address similar or identical situations. Many are negative, ie, the opinion states that the OIG was not willing to provide protection from prosecution because it determined that the arrangement posed more risk to the program than the OIG would abide. Like the OIG's other cautionary publications concerning the AKS, these negative advisory opinions serve as warnings that arrangements that may have become commonplace may be fertile grounds for AKS scrutiny.

The fraud and abuse cases that generate the largest fines and settlements and grab the most headlines have involved fines and settlements imposed on large institutions, such as hospitals and pharmaceutical and device manufacturers, and many of these cases included allegations that the AKS was violated when the institution gave physicians remuneration for referrals. While the publicized prosecutions of the physicians who received this remuneration are fewer and less eye-catching, they do occur, and, as discussed in the introduction to this chapter, prosecution of physicians for AKS violations may be about to become more common.

For example, in October 2008, the US attorney for the Western District of Missouri reported that a physician clinic with more than 100 physicians agreed to pay $1 million to settle claims that it had participated in prohibited financial relationships with a hospital dating back to 1996. In February of 2008, the hospital agreed to pay $60 million for its role in the arrangement.

Prosecutions were brought against a number of urologists in the wake of a massive $875 million settlement with TAP, the manufacturer of the prostate cancer drug Lupron.

At the heart of the scheme was TAP's overt or tacit encouragement of doctors to bill Medicare for Lupron at an imaginary average wholesale price provided by TAP to the *Red Book*, an industry publication used by Medicare and other payers to establish payment schedules for reimbursable prescription drugs, and marketing the profit opportunity that this created to urologists to induce them to purchase and order it for their patients.[102]

However, this pharmaceutical pricing scheme was reinforced by providing urologists with additional inducements, including volume discounts, rebates, education grants, junkets, off-invoice pricing, free goods, credit memos, supposed consulting fees, and debt forgiveness. Several urologists pled guilty to charges of conspiring with TAP and incurred sentences of probation and fines and sanctions against their medical licenses. Others appear to have settled without criminal involvement, typically in the tens of thousands of dollars. About a year after the TAP settlement, Astrazeneca, the maker of the competing drug Zoladex, agreed to a $355,000 settlement for the methods they used to market their product, and that affair also resulted in prosecutions of physicians.[103]

The following sections provide descriptions of some recent prosecutions of pharmaceutical companies, hospitals, or other health care companies for paying kickbacks to physicians, or of physicians for receiving kickbacks. Also included are descriptions from OIG advisory opinions and other OIG publications that demonstrate how the OIG analyzes complicated arrangements. The examples are grouped into categories based on the type of payments or other remuneration involved, but, in many cases, there were allegations that more than one type of illegal remuneration was given.

2.6.7.1 *Items and Services Provided Without Charge (eg, Gifts)*

The examples in this section run the gamut from straightforward transactions that benefited referring physicians (such as gifts) to transactions where the benefit to the physician is not so clear (eg, patient transportation or the services of an athletic trainer provided to a school).

In 2006, 2 south Florida pulmonologists agreed to pay $65,066 and $57,030, respectively, and entered into a 3-year CIA to resolve their civil liability for alleged violations of the AKS and the Stark Law. According to the OIG, the pulmonologists accepted gifts, including Miami Dolphins tickets and meals, from a DME supplier in exchange for patient referrals.[104] While the number and value of these gifts was not reported, they could have been similar to the gifts, entertainment, and meals that many physicians receive (or at least until recently received) from drug company representatives. South Florida, with its high concentration of Medicare recipients, has been a regular focus of the OIG's fraud prevention and enforcement activities.

In 2007 a home health service provider agreed to pay $86,327 to resolve its civil liability for allegedly paying kickbacks, after it disclosed its conduct to the OIG. According to the OIG, the firm had entered into 2 arrangements that provided free nursing services to beneficiaries and physicians with the intent to induce federal health care program referrals from them.[104]

In 2007, after it disclosed its conduct to the OIG, an Illinois hospital agreed to pay $20,000 to resolve its civil liability for alleged violations of the AKS and the CMP Law prohibitions against beneficiary inducements. The OIG alleged that the hospital provided free transportation to 384 outpatient orthopedic surgery patients of a physician on the hospital's medical staff.[104] The transportation services in this case were provided to patients, not the physicians, and presumably benefited the physicians only indirectly by making their patients more likely to use their services. The OIG has published its concerns about free transportation provided to patients in the past.[105]

HealthSouth agreed to pay $100,000 to resolve its liability under the CMP Law for entering into sponsorship arrangements with a high school when the school's team physician was a significant referral source for HealthSouth. Under the terms of the sponsorship arrangements, HealthSouth agreed to provide an athletic trainer to the school whose salary the school supplemented by payments to HealthSouth. According to the OIG, the agreed-upon payment amount was less than the cost of the salary and benefits of the trainer provided, and HealthSouth had agreed to these arrangements, in large part, to induce the high school's team physician to continue making referrals to HealthSouth.[104]

In 2006, after it disclosed its conduct to the OIG, a public hospital agreed to pay $175,000 and enter into a 3-year CIA to resolve civil liability for, among other things, failing to bill a certain physician independent practice association for the employment benefits provided to a hospital employee assigned to the independent practice association.[104]

On the bright side, in advisory opinion 08-05, the OIG advised a drug company that it would not be prosecuted under the AKS for putting computer installations in physicians' offices free of charge. The OIG considered the installations to be "limited purpose kiosks—which amount to little more than high-tech interactive brochures [and] have no independent value to the Participating Physicians."[106] The kiosks, presumably, promoted the company, albeit without naming any particular drugs, and patients could use them to complete questionnaires that would help determine whether they should discuss symptoms of 1 of 4 conditions with their physician. Physicians would not receive any rent for hosting the kiosks or, the OIG wrote, be reimbursed for the cost of the electricity needed to run them. In analyzing the proposal, the OIG noted:

> It seems unlikely that the kiosk-generated questionnaires would save any appreciable amount of physician or staff time. We believe the kiosks, as described above, would not enhance the attractiveness of the Participating Physicians' office practices to prospective patients such that they would be likely to select a Participating Physician because he or she offered a kiosk in the waiting room.

Advisory opinion 08-05 demonstrates how careful the OIG is in considering the subtlest of benefits before issuing an approving opinion.

2.6.7.2   *Waiving Co-Pays and Deductibles*

The practice of waiving co-pays and deductibles provided under federal health benefit programs implicates various fraud and abuse laws. A co-payment is a fixed dollar amount paid by a beneficiary when receiving medical services. A deductible is an amount that is required to be paid before the insurer or third-party payer is obligated to pay for the medical services. Deductibles are typically based upon a percentage of the fee charged for the service. In May, 1991, the OIG issued a special Fraud Alert titled *"Routine Waiver of Co-Payments or Deductibles under Medicare Part B."* Pursuant to the Fraud Alert, the OIG stated that "[r]outine waiver of deductibles and co-payments by charge-based providers, practitioners or suppliers is unlawful because it results in 1) false claims, 2) violations of the Anti-Kickback Statute, and 3) excessive utilization of items and services paid for by Medicare." According to the OIG, a "provider, practitioner or [physician] who routinely waives Medicare co-payments or deductibles is misstating its actual charge. For example, if a [physician] claims that its charge for a [service] is $100, but routinely waives the co-payment, the actual charge is $80. Medicare should be paying 80 percent of $80 (or $64) rather than 80 percent of $100 (or $80). As a result of the [physician's] misrepresentation, the Medicare program is paying $16 more than it should for this item."

It is the government's position that routinely waiving Medicare co-pays and deductibles is a violation of the FCA. Because the physician is misrepresenting the actual charge, as noted above from the special Fraud Alert, it is the government's view that the physician is knowingly submitting a claim for payment that is false or misleading. Because knowledge is a requirement under the FCA, the government will assert that the physician knows he or she is submitting a false or misleading claim since they have actual knowledge of the waiver of the co-pay or deductible.

The waiver of Medicare co-pays and deductibles also implicates the AKS if it were proven that the waiving of the co-pay or deductible was intended to encourage the Medicare beneficiary to continue to use the practice's services.

Routine waiver of Medicare co-pays and deductibles also implicates the civil monetary penalties law. The civil monetary penalties law is violated if the physician knew or should have known that by waiving a patient's Medicare co-pay or deductible that such act would likely influence the patient to seek services from that physician or practice. The civil monetary penalties law, however, does permit the waiving of Medicare co-pays and deductibles as long as (1) the waiver is not advertised; (2) the waivers are not routine or customary; and (3) there are good faith determinations of financial need or failed reasonable collection efforts.

In the OIG's Compliance Program Guidance for Individual and Small Group Physician Practices, the OIG stated, under the AKS, that "a physician's regular and consistent practice of . . . waiving otherwise applicable co-payments for services rendered to a group of persons . . . would not implicate the Anti-Kickback Statute so long as membership in the group . . . does not take into account . . . any group member's ability to refer to, or otherwise generate federal health care program business for, the physician." The OIG stated, in the Guidance, that the civil monetary penalties law would also be implicated if the waiver was not made based upon financial need. The OIG did not clarify the application of the FCA except by stating that any particular facts and circumstances regarding the waiver or a co-pay or deductible would need to be evaluated based upon the totality of circumstances.

Waiving of co-pays or deductibles may also violate the practice's contract with insurance companies. If the patient is required to pay a co-pay, many insurance contracts require the payment of the co-pay by the patient as a prerequisite for the insurance company being obligated to pay its portion of the payment for the service rendered by the practice. Stated simply, if the patient does not pay the co-pay, the insurance company is not required to pay the practice the payment that otherwise would be required by contract. Similar to the false claims analysis above, if the physician or practice waives any portion of the deductible, and still bills the insurance company the full amount, the bill submitted by the practice could overstate the actual charge, thereby creating possible insurance fraud. This is the same example cited above from the special Fraud Alert where the payment should have been $64 instead of $80 due to the physician's waiver of the $20 co-pay for the $100 service.

Because of the concerns under the fraud and abuse laws, many providers were using aggressive collection tactics to collect co-pays and
deductibles from patients. Some providers believed that if they did not
collect the amount that was due, and instead wrote off the amount
due, the provider would run risk of violating various fraud and abuse
laws. Recognizing the ability to waive co-pays and deductibles due to
financial hardships, the OIG, on February 2, 2004, which was amended
on June 18, 2007, reminded the medical community that as long
as the waiver of co-pays and deductibles are as a result of financial
hardship or need, such waiver would not violate fraud and abuse laws.
Thus, it is a best practice for physician practices to adopt a charity
care policy and apply the charity care policy by waiving co-pays and
deductibles when warranted. Depending upon the size of the physician
practice, the extent to which financial hardship is documented will
vary. At a minimum, physicians should have a good faith belief that
the patient is experiencing a financial hardship prior to waiving
Medicare co-pays or deductibles.

2.6.7.3   *Professional Courtesy*

Professional courtesy is steeped in tradition in the medical field.
Professional courtesy is the act of providing free or discounted medical
services to fellow physicians and members of their family. However,
professional courtesy also raises fraud and abuse concerns.

Because physicians to whom professional courtesy is offered are referral
sources for the medical practice, it could be inferred that professional
courtesy is offered in order to encourage future referrals or to reward or
thank the physician for past referrals. As stated previously in this book,
under the AKS, it is a criminal violation to offer anything of value with
the intent to induce referrals. Thus, offering professional services could
implicate the AKS if the necessary intent to induce or reward referrals
could be proven.

Not all statutes and regulations prohibit professional courtesy. Under the
Stark Law, designated health service entities, like hospitals or ambulatory
surgery centers, can provide professional courtesy as long as the following

conditions are met: (1) the professional courtesy was offered to all physicians on the entity's bona fide medical staff or in the local community without regard to the volume or value of referrals or other business generated between the parties; (2) the items and services were of a type routinely provided by the entity; (3) the entity's professional courtesy policy was in writing and approved in advance by the entity's governing body; (4) the professional courtesy was not offered to any federal health care beneficiary unless there was a good faith showing of financial need; and (5) the arrangement did not violate the Anti-Kickback Statute. Thus, even though entities that have a bona fide medical staff may, according to the Stark Law exception, offer professional courtesy, the AKS could still be implicated if the requisite intent to induce referrals could be proven.

Further, because professional courtesy is the provision of either free or reduced medical services, all of the issues described above regarding the waiver of co-pays and deductibles are also applicable to professional courtesy.

Because of the implication of the AKS and the issues raised in connection with the waiver of co-pays and deductibles, except in the case of financial need and hardship, professional courtesy should generally be discouraged.

2.6.7.2   *Payments to Physicians for Consulting and Other Nonclinical Services*

In 2006 Lincare, a respiratory products supplier, agreed to pay $10 million and to enter into a 5-year CIA to resolve its civil liability for AKS and Stark law violations.[107] At the time, this was the OIG's largest CMP Law settlement ever. The OIG alleged that Lincare paid kickbacks to physicians "disguised as payments pursuant to purported consulting agreements," as well as sporting and entertainment event tickets, gift certificates, rounds of golf, golf equipment, fishing trips, meals, advertising expenses, office equipment, and medical equipment.[107]

In 2007 Advanced Neuromodulation Systems, Inc, a manufacturer of spinal stimulation devices, agreed to pay $2,950,000 and to enter into a 3-year CIA to resolve its liability for allegedly paying kickbacks. The

OIG alleged that the manufacturer paid kickbacks to physicians for ordering their products, including a number of physicians who were paid $5000 for every 5 new patients tested with the company's products under a program that did not have any significant clinical value and was merely a marketing device.[108]

In 2007 Bristol-Myers Squibb and its generic division, Apothecon, paid $515 million to settle various allegations related to the marketing and pricing of name-brand and generic drugs.[109] The charges included allegations that the drug company paid kickbacks to physicians in the form of consulting fees and expenses in connection with consulting programs.

In 2007 Zimmer, Inc, Depuy Orthopaedics, Inc, Biomet Inc, and Smith & Nephew, Inc, manufacturers of hip and knee surgical implant products, agreed to pay $310 million to settle claims that from at least 2002 through 2006, these companies used consulting agreements with orthopedic surgeons to induce the purchase of their devices.[110] The government's investigation found that the firms paid surgeons hundreds of thousands of dollars a year for consulting contracts and lavished them with trips and other expensive perquisites in exchange for using the companies' products exclusively. In addition to the civil settlements, the 4 companies executed deferred prosecution agreements requiring new corporate compliance procedures and the appointment of monitors selected by federal prosecutors to review their compliance with these procedures.

In connection with a broader prosecution of the University of Medicine and Dentistry of New Jersey that also resulted in a deferred prosecution agreement and submission to oversight by a monitor selected by federal prosecutors, a number of cardiologists were accused of accepting payments in return for referrals to the cardiac surgery program at an affiliated hospital, disguised as salaries for teaching services.[111] One cardiologist who pled guilty agreed to pay $560,000 to settle his civil liability, which was twice what he received in salary. Another who did not plead guilty agreed to pay $1.4 million to settle his civil liability, which was 2½ times what he received in salary. This is another case in which the physicians accused of receiving kickbacks from a large institution were prosecuted, in addition to the institution that paid them.

2.6.7.5   *Payments for Clinical Services*

In OIG advisory opinion 05-08, the OIG considered a clinical laboratory's proposal to pay physicians who drew blood in their offices an amount in the range of $3 to $6 per patient, to be negotiated between the physician and the laboratory.[112] At the time, Medicare paid physicians about $3 per patient for drawing blood in their office. The OIG's reasoning for its negative opinion included the following analysis:

> There is a substantial risk that the Lab would be offering the blood draw remuneration to the physicians in exchange for referrals to the Lab. Under the Proposed Arrangement, the physicians could receive up to twice the $3 amount Medicare pays for blood specimen collection, plus any necessary blood-drawing supplies free of charge. Particularly when viewed in the aggregate, this compensation provides an obvious financial benefit to the referring physician, and it may be inferred that this benefit would be in exchange for referrals to the Lab. Where a laboratory pays a referring physician to perform blood draws, particularly where the amount paid is more than the laboratory receives in Medicare reimbursement, an inference arises that the compensation is paid as an inducement to the physician to refer patients to the laboratory, particularly in the circumstances presented here."[112]

This may have been an example of an advisory opinion requested in the hope of receiving a negative response, in an attempt to deter physicians from requesting payments and competing laboratories from making them.

2.6.7.6   *Swapping*

In 1999 the OIG issued advisory opinion 99-2,[113] warning that an arrangement in which an ambulance company would give a nursing home and skilled nursing facility a discount for certain services might be a violation of the AKS. The discount was 50% off the company's charges to Medicare for similar services. The company asserted that the discount was justified by higher costs it incurred in connection with services for which it received payment from the Medicare program, but the OIG was unconvinced and wrote:

> In evaluating whether an improper nexus exists between a discount and referrals of federal business in a particular arrangement, we look for indicia that the discount is not commercially reasonable in the absence of other, non-discounted business. In this regard, discounts on [services that a skilled nursing facility (SNF) is obligated to provide for its Medicare Part A inpatients] that are particularly suspect include, but are not limited to:
>
> ■ discounted prices that are below the supplier's cost, and
>
> ■ discounted prices that are lower than the prices that the supplier offers to a buyer that (i) generates a volume of business for the supplier that is the same or greater than the volume of Part A business generated by the PPS [the Prospective Payment System used by the Medicare Part A Program to pay for inpatient hospital and SNF services that cover a variety of services and supplies with a single payment that are dependent on the patient's condition and not by the quantity of services or supplies that the hospital or SNF provided to the patient] SNF, but (ii) does not have any potentially available Part B or other Federal health care program business.
>
> This is an illustrative, not exhaustive, list of suspect discounts; other arrangements may be equally suspect. Each of the above pricing arrangements independently gives rise to an inference that the supplier and the SNF may be "swapping" discounts on Part A business in exchange for profitable non-discounted Part B business, from which the supplier can recoup losses incurred on the discounted business, potentially through overutilization or abusive billing practices.[113]

In 2003 the OIG reported that an ambulance company agreed to pay $10,000 to resolve its civil liability for paying kickbacks to a hospital in the form of deep discounts on all ambulance transports of inpatients for which the hospital was financially responsible in return for the hospital's promise to refer other ambulance business, for which the company could receive payment from Medicare.[104]

The OIG's warnings about swapping arrangements clearly have not eliminated swapping and may not even have significantly curtailed it. The pressure on hospitals and nursing facilities to reduce their costs, and the pressure on ambulance companies (as well as other companies that provide services that are covered by Part A and Part B) to compete for hospital and nursing home business is intense. In 2007 the OIG reported that an ambulance company agreed to pay the United States over $2.5 million and enter into a CIA to resolve its civil liability for providing illegal inducements to hospitals in exchange for referrals.[104] The company provided or offered inducements to hospitals in the form of contracts that gave the medical facilities discounts on transports of inpatients in exchange for the referral of all or some of the ambulance transports of Medicare patients being discharged from the hospitals.

2.6.7.7   *Joint Ventures*

Joint ventures involving referral sources and referral recipients present some of the most difficult cases to analyze under the AKS. Joint ventures that are carefully structured generally involve a genuine attempt to direct capital, some or all of which is provided by the referral sources, toward a business that provides an actual service. However, joint ventures may also generate returns in the form of profits distributed to referral sources that *could* be used to induce their referrals to the joint venture or to the other participants in the joint venture. In many instances, it is clear from the outset that the joint venture could not survive without referrals from investors. In the absence of a safe harbor, the question becomes whether the parties' intent in establishing the joint venture was purely to engage in the business (or other purposes that do not conflict with the AKS) or whether the parties intended the arrangement to induce referrals.

For many years, the OIG has warned that joint ventures with referral sources as investors may violate the AKS. Joint ventures were the subject of a 1989 OIG special fraud alert and a 2003 OIG special advisory bulletin, which addressed *contractual joint ventures*—ie, joint ventures that do not necessarily involve investment in a new legal entity. The guidance provided by these warnings is supplemented by a number of advisory opinions that concern joint ventures, a few of which are discussed below.

In OIG advisory opinion 04-17, the OIG found significant risk of an AKS violation in what could be described as a turnkey lease and management services arrangement under which a laboratory management company affiliated with a laboratory would provide facilities and services to physician group practices.[114] The management company would enter into agreements with the practices to furnish all management and administrative services, equipment leasing, subleasing, technical, professional, and supervisory pathology services, and billing services for each practice to operate a pathology laboratory, in return for a combination of flat, monthly fees and per-specimen fees. For billing and collection services, which were optional, the practices would pay a percentage of the collections for laboratory services. The management company would establish up to 5 independent and self-contained laboratories within a single building, but each laboratory would have sufficient equipment to perform its own services and the laboratories would not share space or equipment. The pathologists and technical laboratory personnel provided by the management company would rotate among the laboratories but would provide services only on behalf of one practice's laboratory while located in that practice's laboratory. The OIG's analysis included the following analogy to the contractual joint ventures described in its 2003 special advisory bulletin:

> By agreeing effectively to provide services it could otherwise
> provide in its own right for less than the available reimbursement,
> the Requestor would potentially be providing a referral source—a
> Physician Group—with the opportunity to generate a fee and a profit.
> If the intent of the Proposed Arrangement were to give the Physician
> Groups remuneration through the Path Labs in return for referrals to:
> (i) the Path Labs; or (ii) the Requestor's Affiliated Lab, the anti-
> kickback statute would be violated.

The OIG's analysis also included a refutation of the assertion that the flat fees payable by the practices represented a meaningful business risk demonstrating the bona fides of the arrangement, because "[the practice] would have complete control over the amount of business it would send to the Path Lab and could make substantial referrals to the Path Lab." Continuing in this vein, the OIG wrote: "In fact, while our conclusion would be the same even absent the historical correlation, by basing the Monthly Fee for each Physician Group on historical utilization data for that Physician Group, the parties can easily ensure that the business generated by the Physician Group would be sufficient to meet or exceed the Monthly Fee."[114]

In OIG advisory opinion 04-08, a physician group proposed forming a limited liability company (LLC) to establish a physical therapy center.[115] This center would lease space, equipment, and a staff therapist to the physicians in the group as well as other physicians with patients who require physical therapy services. The center would be located in the same building as the group and all of the other physicians who might utilize its services.

The LLC maintained that it would not bill Medicare, Medicaid, or any other third-party payer for services provided in the center. Instead, the physician would bill the appropriate health insurance provider for services rendered at the center to their patients. Each physician would sign a 1-year lease with the LLC and pay a monthly rental fee for unlimited use of the center. Those using the therapist would pay a higher monthly rental fee. The rental fee would be calculated by totaling the monthly rental value of all space, equipment, and administrative services and dividing by the total number of physicians. This would ensure that each physician would pay the same amount for the services of the LLC regardless of actual usage. The fee would be verified and audited by an independent appraisal firm to ensure that it is consistent with fair market value. The OIG posited that this arrangement constituted a source of referrals between the group's physicians and the other outside physicians who would enter into a lease with the LLC. In fact, the OIG stated that the formula used to calculate the monthly rental fee for each physician lessee was designed to "guarantee a desired maximum income stream" instead of basing it on actual usage of the center and, as such, could compensate for referrals. Finally, the OIG maintained that this arrangement did not come under a safe harbor. As the OIG viewed this agreement, the center would be available to physicians only on an "as-needed basis," and, therefore, the leases were actually part-time leases. Pursuant to the safe harbor requirements, "periodic, sporadic, or part-time leases must specify precisely the timing and duration of the rental periods and the compensation charged for each rental period." Since these leases did not specify this information, the arrangement was not protected by a safe harbor.[115]

In OIG advisory opinion 08-10, the OIG opined that "there is a significant risk that the [following] Proposed Arrangement would be an improper contractual joint venture that would be used as a vehicle to reward . . . Urologist Groups for their referrals [for intensity-modulated radiation therapy (IMRT) and] might violate the Anti-Kickback Statute."[116] The proposed arrangement involved a physician group practice that provided cancer treatment services in a free-standing facility, including IMRT. The practice decided to enter into an agreement with some of the urologists who refer prostate cancer patients to the practice, but who themselves do not perform IMRT, under which the urologists would lease, on a part-time basis, the space, equipment, and personnel services necessary to perform IMRT. The OIG's analysis included the following:

> By agreeing effectively to provide services it could otherwise provide in its own right for less than the available reimbursement, the Requestor and its Radiologists would potentially be providing a referral source – a Urologist Group – with the opportunity to generate a fee and a profit. If the intent of the Proposed Arrangement were to give the Urologist Groups remuneration through the IMRT to induce referrals to the Requestor, the anti-kickback statute would be violated.[116]

With the exception of investments in ambulatory surgery centers (ASC), which were the subject of several advisory opinions and are now the subject of an OIG safe harbor regulation, the OIG's guidance has provided little comfort that a joint venture that relies on physicians who are referral sources for its profitability will not be a target for prosecution under the AKS.

Physician investments in ASC hold a special place under the federal anti-kickback law. Physician-owned ASC usually cater largely or exclusively to the physician investors' patients, and often generate rates of return that are far higher than typical passive investment opportunities. In general, an investment with these features would be suspect under the AKS.[1]

Since the adoption in 1999 of the safe harbor regulation for physician investments in ASC (the OIG's ASC Safe Harbor)[2], such investments have legal protection from prosecution under the AKS, **but only if** they meet all of the requirements of the regulation. However, even when they do not meet *all* of the OIG's ASC Safe Harbor requirements, physician investments in ASC generally are thought to hold a special place *vis á vis* the AKS.

In 1998 (prior to the adoption of the OIG's ASC Safe Harbor) the OIG issued Advisory Opinion 98-12, stating that it would not prosecute an arrangement in which 3 orthopedic surgeons and 2 anesthesiologists specializing in pain management invested in and established an ASC, although the arrangement may potentially violate the AKS. To obtain the favorable opinion, the physicians certified the following:

- Distributions and voting rights would be allocated according to the amount of capital contributions, and although not all physicians would be making the same capital contribution, the

---

[1]"The AKS makes it a criminal offense to knowingly and willfully offer, pay, solicit, or receive any remuneration to induce or reward referrals of items or services reimbursable by a federal health care program." 42 USC § 13200–76(b) AKS violations may be, and frequently are, grounds for charges under a variety of other federal health care statutes, including the FCA, and the Health Care Fraud Statute. These charges carry significant civil and criminal penalties, and FCA charges can be brought by private whistleblowers who are entitled to share in any award or settlement.

Although certain types of arrangements may be said to be suspect or likely to attract scrutiny, an arrangement only violates the AKS when a party intends for the arrangement to induce or reward referrals.

Prior to the publication of the OIG's ASC Safe Harbor (defined infra), the OIG regulatory safe harbors for investments in health care joint ventures was limited to ventures that were not dominated by physician investors. *See,* Advisory Opinion 98-12.

[2]42 C.F.R. §1001.952(r); 64 F.R. 63518.

amount of capital contributions would not be based on any expected volume of referrals to other physician-investors;

- They each derived at least 40% of their aggregate medical practice income from ASC procedures[3];

- They would each perform a majority of the ASC procedures at this particular ASC;

- All ancillary services performed at the ASC would be integrally related to the primary procedure;

- They estimated that Medicare reimbursement would account for only 5% of the ASC revenue; and

- They would provide their patients with a written disclosure of their ownership in the ASC.

Other than the estimate that only 5% of the ASC's revenue would be Medicare reimbursement, these certifications (or variations of them) appear as requirements in the OIG ASC Safe Harbor. In addition, the physicians certified that they would make a significant amount of capital contributions in the ASC, and personally guaranty the payments under the lease for the ASC premises. The OIG ASC Safe Harbor has the additional requirement that neither the ASC nor any investor can loan funds to, or guarantee a loan for an investor if the investor uses any part of such loan to obtain the investment interest, which presumably was not a significant concern. The OIG ASC Safe Harbor also allows for physicians to jointly invest in ASC with hospitals. For such physician-hospital joint ventures, the requirements applicable to physician investors are the same as they are for all-physician ASC investments, and hospital investors must not be in a position to refer patients to the ASC (although, as described below, the OIG has approved of arrangements where hospital investors are in a position to refer patients, but certify, in effect, that they will not take any advantage of this position).

---

[3] "ASC Procedures" are defined in the Advisory Opinion and in the OIG ASC Safe Harbor as Medicare-covered surgical and other medical procedures included on the applicable list of ambulatory surgical center covered procedures established by HCFA (now CMS) in the Federal Register.

A subtle but very substantive difference between the certifications in the Advisory Opinion 98-2 and the OIG ASC Safe Harbor is that the physicians certified that the *amount of capital contributions* by each physician would not vary based on expected volume of referrals *to the other physician-investors*, while the OIG ASC Safe Harbor requires that "[t]he *terms on which an investment interest is offered* to an investor must not be related to the previous or expected volume of referrals, services furnished, or the amount of business otherwise generated from that investor *to the [ASC]*." This distinction could be read to imply that in preparing the Advisory Opinion, the OIG was not concerned with whether or not capital contributions varied with expected volume or value of referrals to the ASC—ie, that physicians could be offered differing numbers of shares based on the volume or value of procedures that they were expected to bring to the ASC[4]—although some would expect that such a linkage of referrals to financial interests would be seen as undesirable by the OIG, or would at least have been of interest and would have merited attention in the Advisory Opinion.

The OIG ASC Safe Harbor provides a somewhat muted message on whether or not, if the price and distribution rights for each share are equal, shares can be allocated among physician investors from the outset based on their expected referrals to the ASC. However, the language of the safe harbor can easily be interpreted as excluding such volume or value–based allocations.

The OIG has issued several advisory opinions concerning physician investments in an ASC since the safe harbor regulation went into effect. In these advisory opinions, the OIG has indicated that they

---

[4]Linkage of share allocations based on referrals is often seen as very desirable when trying to develop a successful ASC. Since it is assumed by most (including the OIG) that physicians who invest in an ASC are likely to perform a high percentage of their outpatient procedures there, a physician who performs a high volume of profitable outpatient procedure practice is obviously a desirable investor for competing ASCs. Such a physician (if he or she is a rational investor) would be expected to weigh the anticipated economic returns when choosing among different ASC investment options.

would not prosecute ASC investment arrangements that deviated from the OIG ASC Safe Harbor for the following reasons:

- Hospital investors were in a position to refer patients, but certified that their employed physicians would not refer patients to the ASC and do not encourage or track their medical staff's referrals to the ASC or the physician-investors.

- Some physician-investors did not derive at least 1/3 of their medical practice income from ASC procedures, but they did derive at least one-third of their medical practice income from surgical procedures performed in either an ASC or a hospital setting, which is significant considering the desirability of many spine surgeons as investors since they can perform low numbers of very expensive procedures at an ASC. In one instance, the requestor certified that the hospital-based surgeons would not make pain management referrals to other investors.

- Physician investors did not individually own their shares in the ASC, but owned them as pass-through investments through a holding entity.

- The return on all investments would not be proportional to the investors' capital investment because a hospital investor purchased its shares from the ASC at a per share price that was higher than the capital investment of the physician investors, but the parties certified that the price paid by the hospital was the fair market value of the shares purchased by the hospital, and the difference in price was a result of the timing of the purchases and reflected appreciation in the value of the ongoing ASC. However, in a subsequent advisory opinion, the OIG declined a request for protection from AKS prosecution related to a sale (certified by the requestor to be at a fair market value price) where the hospital was purchasing appreciated shares from some, but not all, of the physician-investors.

The OIG has also twice issued advisory opinions declining protection from AKS prosecution in which some of the ASC investors were optometrists or physicians who were referral sources for the other investors or the ASC, but did not derive substantial income from surgery or invasive procedures in any setting.

2.6.8   Self-referral Law Violations

Unless a statutory or regulatory exception applies, the Stark Law prohibits a physician, or an immediate family member of the physician who has a direct or indirect financial relationship with an entity, from making any referrals to that entity for the furnishing of designated health services (DHS) for which payment otherwise may be made by the Medicare or Medicaid programs.[117,118] DHS include the following services:

1. clinical laboratory services
2. physical therapy, occupational therapy, and speech-language pathology services
3. radiology and certain other imaging services
4. radiation therapy services and supplies
5. durable medical equipment and supplies
6. parenteral and enteral nutrients, equipment, and supplies
7. prosthetics, orthotics, and prosthetic devices and supplies
8. home health services
9. outpatient prescription drugs, and
10. inpatient and outpatient hospital services.[119,120]

An entity that furnishes DHS pursuant to prohibited referrals under the Stark Law is barred from billing or submitting a claim for payment for that DHS.[121]

The CMS regulations and commentary that interpret the Stark law and attempt to make it comprehensible are vast and dense. Comparisons to the Internal Revenue Code are only slight hyperbole. The passage of a third phase of regulations in 2007 has both increased and decreased the confusion that the law creates. Nonetheless, prosecutions related to Stark Law violations are likely to become more frequent as the phase III regulations (in combination with the revisions to the Medicare

Anti-Mark-Up Rule) have partially filled some of the cracks left
open in prior years (eg, by restricting the use of per click and percentage compensation and "under arrangements") and reinforced the
government's ability to use technical violations to support prosecutions
that result in relatively small, but increasingly large, settlements.

On March 24, 2009, the OIG published another open letter to health
care providers, narrowing the scope of its provider self-disclosure protocol
so that providers will no longer permitted to report Stark Law violations
that are not also AKS violations. "Although we are narrowing the scope
of the [self-disclosure protocol] for resources purposes," the OIG stated
in this letter, "we urge providers not to draw any inferences about the
Government's approach to enforcement of the physician self-referral law."
(www.oig.hhs.gov/fraud/docs/openletters/OpenLetter3-24-09.pdf)

The following examples of Stark Law prosecutions focus on cases where
the absence of a written agreement required under the Stark Law
appears to have been important in determining the outcome. While in
each case there were also allegations of AKS violations, the technical
violation under the Stark Law may be enough to convince the defendant
to agree to pay a significant amount to settle the charge.

In 2009 a hospital entered into a settlement agreement with the OIG
to pay $21,025.62 in civil penalties for violations of the AKS and Stark
Law.[122] The hospital had recruited a physician for a medical director
position. As part of the agreement, the physician received the use of
hospital space for private benefit and the utilization of various hospital
personnel to assist with clerical duties related to the physician's private
practice, without a contractual entitlement to do so.

After it self-disclosed conduct to the OIG, in 2008 a hospital agreed to pay
$391,500 to resolve its liability under the CMP Law related to kickbacks.[123]
The OIG alleged that the hospital had compensation arrangements with
employed physicians that failed to comply fully with the Stark Law's
restrictions on productivity bonuses. Specifically, the physicians were
compensated for services that were not personally performed by them.

In 2008 a hospital agreed to pay $350,000 to resolve its liability under
the CMP Law related to physician self-referrals.[135] The OIG alleged that

the hospital made physician salary guarantee payments to 3 orthopedic specialists without entering into written physician recruitment agreements with the recruited physicians.

After it self-disclosed conduct to the OIG, in 2008 a hospital agreed to pay $780,000 for allegedly violating the CMP Law provisions applicable to kickbacks.[136] The OIG alleged that the hospital provided information technology resources to nonemployee physician groups without written contracts in place. Specifically, the hospital reported that it failed to document information technology agreements with 10 different physician practices/groups and also failed to bill and collect for those information technology resources.

In *United States ex rel Kosenske v Carlisle HMA, Inc*, Blue Mountain Anesthesia Associates, PC, a group of 4 physicians who practiced anesthesiology, signed an anesthesiology services agreement in 1992 with a hospital that established an exclusive service arrangement under which the group would provide all anesthesia services required by the hospital's patients.[124] In return, the hospital agreed to provide the space, equipment, and supplies reasonably necessary and economical for the group to provide these anesthesia services, at no charge, and would not permit any other physicians to provide anesthesia or pain management services at the hospital. The group agreed that its physicians would not provide anesthesia or pain management services elsewhere.[125]

While the group did not provide pain management services at the hospital when the agreement was signed, it did so 12 months later. There was no dedicated space at the hospital to provide pain management services at the time the agreement was signed, and the group saw patients in space used for other hospital purposes. In 1998, the hospital built a stand-alone facility that included a pain clinic, and the group began providing pain management services at this facility. The agreement (now 6 years old) was not amended, and the hospital did not charge the group rent for the space and equipment or a fee for the support personnel it provided.[126]

The lower court dismissed the case, finding that the 1992 agreement established the hospital's agreement to provide the group with both anesthesia and pain management facilities at no charge in a fair market value exchange for the group's agreement to provide services at the hospital.

However, the US Third Circuit overturned the dismissal, finding that the 1992 agreement did not cover pain management services and could not have constituted a fair market value exchange since the parties did not know when they signed the agreement before the clinic was built what the value of the pain management facilities would be.

2.6.9   Inducements to Beneficiaries

The CMP Law provides that a person who offers or transfers to a Medicare or Medicaid beneficiary any remuneration that the person knows or should know is likely to influence the beneficiary's selection of a particular provider, practitioner, or supplier of Medicare or Medicaid payable items or services may be liable for CMPs of up to $10,000 for each item or service.[127] *Remuneration* includes, without limitation, waivers of co-payments and deductible amounts (or any part thereof) and transfers of items or services for free or for a price lower than fair market value.

In 2008 the Los Angeles police uncovered a scheme orchestrated to defraud the Medicare and Medicaid program of millions of dollars.[128] Private medical centers worked with patient recruiting operations that identified homeless people from the streets and brought them, with fake medical diagnoses, to the hospitals. These homeless "patients," some with Medicare eligibility, received small sums of money, usually $20 to $30, to stay at a hospital for a short period of time. Patients sometimes received other inducements, such as food or cigarettes, as an incentive to remain in the hospital. These patients would receive treatment for conditions that did not exist and the treatments were then billed to Medicare.[128] In 2009, a hospital's chief executive and the operator of a homeless service center pleaded guilty to health care fraud and other crimes.

In OIG advisory opinion 07-02, the OIG warned that the following arrangement might be subject to prosecution under the CMP Law.[129] Some patients of a large nonprofit hospital were transferred by ambulance to the hospital from other facilities outside of the hospital's local area. The local Medicare carrier previously paid claims for these ambulance services, but the carrier began refusing to pay the full amount of these claims, citing Medicare requirements that limit ambulance benefits to local ambulance transportation only, except where nonlocal transportation is necessary to take the patient to the nearest institution with appropriate facilities. The hospital proposed to contract with various air and ground ambulance suppliers to transport patients to the hospital from hospitals located outside its locality. The hospital would pay the transport companies a negotiated fee and would be entitled to seek payment for the ambulance services from payers, including Medicare and Medicaid. The hospital would not advertise the arrangement.

The OIG concluded that this arrangement would be an improper inducement to beneficiaries because "the payment or subsidy of an expense that would ordinarily be borne by a patient constitutes remuneration to the patient." Further, the OIG deemed it likely that this compensation would influence patients to order services reimbursable by Medicaid or Medicare and induce the patient to choose this specific hospital for hospital services. The OIG deemed the hospital's assurance that it would not advertise the services insufficient to alleviate its concerns, because the patients' physicians would know of the services and would inform their patients of this option. Providing the subsidy would generate business for the hospital and, as a direct result, more costs for Medicare and Medicaid.[129]

2.6.10   Employing Excluded Persons

HHS is required to exclude individuals or companies who are convicted of certain serious criminal offenses from participating in federal health care programs and has the authority to exclude others for committing certain lesser (although still serious) offenses.[130] In fiscal year 2008 the OIG excluded over 3000 individuals and organizations for fraud or abuse against federal health care programs or their beneficiaries.[59]

In addition, no "federal health program payments may be made with respect to items or services (even administrative and management services) that are furnished by an excluded individual."[131] If a physician or entity submits claims to Medicare or Medicaid for services rendered by an excluded individual, that physician or entity may be liable under the FCA. A finding of such liability can subject the liable individual or entity to mandatory reimbursement as well as $5500 to $11,000 for each false or fraudulent claim filed.

In 2008 alone, the OIG reported on more than 15 settlements with providers that had employed individuals who they knew or should have known were excluded from participation in federal health benefit programs. These settlements included payments ranging from a little more than $1000 to $562,000. In 2005 one hospital agreed to pay $2 million to resolve its liability for employing 2 excluded individuals.

2.7 Legal Compliance Programs

The OIG encourages all health care entities to maintain a legal compliance program to avoid violations of fraud and abuse laws. A compliance program is an organization's systematic approach to complying with applicable laws, and an attempt to avoid the liability and expense that can result when laws are broken or when an organization is accused of violating laws. Its central function is to bring conduct within the organization that is legally questionable to the attention of management. Once an issue is in management's hands, it can decide how to proceed: if the conduct is clearly inconsistent with management's goals for the organization, it can be stopped; if the issue is more nuanced, management can evaluate the risks and take measures to limit potential liability. For large organizations, it is hard to see how management could maintain control over a widespread staff of employees and representatives without a system for compliance. For smaller organizations, compliance programs can help the managers discipline themselves and their staff to keep abreast of legal developments. In the event that a serious criminal violation does occur, the existence of a compliance program can also be a mitigating factor in determining the level of culpability and the penalty.

For small physician practices, the OIG has suggested 7 components for a legal compliance program:

- Conducting internal monitoring and auditing
- Implementing compliance and practice standards
- Designating a compliance officer or contact

- Conducting appropriate training and education
- Responding appropriately to detected offenses and developing corrective action
- Developing open lines of communication
- Enforcing disciplinary standards through well-publicized guidelines.[132]

The OIG offers other variations on these steps in compliance guidance to other types of health care firms listed in the following section. However, the volume of health care laws can easily overwhelm a compliance program, so whatever process is used to develop a compliance program, management should try to identify and control the biggest problems first, and not let the program get bogged down in issues that are not germane to the organization.

When establishing a compliance program, it is a good idea to also develop a protocol for responding to subpoenas and governmental investigations—eg, what to do when an OIG or Federal Bureau of Investigation agent shows up at the door. This is important to avoid breaking laws that prohibit impeding a government investigation, and also to give the organization's attorneys the opportunity to exert some control to protect the organization's rights in connection with the investigation process and perhaps work with prosecutors to control the damage.

2.8 Published Physician Compliance Guidance

The OIG has published several compliance program guidelines for providers of all different sizes, as listed below:

- Compliance Program Guidance for Individual and Small Group Physician Practices, *65 Fed Reg 59434 (Oct 5, 2000)*. Available at: http://oig.hhs.gov/authorities/docs/physician.pdf.
- Compliance Program Guidance for Nursing Facilities, *65 Fed Reg 14289 (Mar 16, 2000)*. Available at: http://oig.hhs.gov/authorities/docs/cpgnf.pdf.

- Compliance Program Guidance for Hospitals, 63 *Fed Reg* 8993 (1998). Available at: http://oig.hhs.gov/authorities/docs/cpghosp.pdf.

- Supplemental Compliance Program Guidance for Hospitals, 70 *Fed Reg* 4858 (*Jan 31, 2005*). Available at: http://oig.hhs.gov/fraud/docs/complianceguidance/012705HospSupplementalGuidance.pdf.

In addition to compliance program guidelines, the OIG has a wealth of information regarding fraud and abuse on its Web site accessible to the public. Health care professionals should take the time to review the OIG fraud alerts and advisories (http://oig.hhs.gov/fraudalerts.html#2), the OIG advisory opinions (http://oig.hhs.gov/fraud/advisoryopinions/opinions.html), and the OIG semiannual report (http://oig.hhs.gov/publications/semiannual.html).

Besides the OIG, there are several other published resources on compliance guidance that providers may wish to review:

- Evaluating and Improving a Compliance Program: A Reference Guide for Healthcare Board Members, Healthcare Executives and Compliance Officers; Health Care Compliance Association, April 2003.

- The Compliance Effectiveness Study: A Study of the Relationships Between the Sentencing Guidelines' Compliance Program Provisions and Effective Compliance; Lori S. Richardson Pelliccioni, Doctoral Dissertation, University of California, Los Angeles, 2002.

2.9   The Office of Inspector General's Annual Work Plan

Each year, the OIG publishes a work plan,[133] which highlights the specific areas of fraud and abuse on which the agency intends to focus. The OIG identified the following investigative and audit areas for physicians and other professionals in its 2009 work plan:

- Place of service errors
- Evaluation and management services during global surgery periods

- Medicare practice expenses incurred by selected physician specialties
- Outpatient physical therapy services provided by independent therapists
- Medicare payments for colonoscopy services
- Physicians' Medicare services performed by nonphysicians
- Appropriateness of Medicare payments for polysomnography
- Long-distance physician claims requiring a face-to-face visit
- Geographic areas with a high density of independent diagnostic testing facilities
- Patterns related to high utilization of ultrasound services
- Medicare payments for chiropractic services billed with the acute treatment modifier
- Physician reassignment of benefits
- Medicare payments for unlisted procedure codes
- Laboratory test unbundling by clinical laboratories
- Variation of laboratory pricing
- Clotting factor furnishing fee
- Medicare billings with modifier GY.

2.10   Conclusion

Health care fraud and abuse is a significant problem that has plagued the nation for decades. Over the last decade, the government has utilized a number of tools at its disposal to combat fraud and abuse. As the federal health care programs continue to consume an increasingly large percentage of the federal budget, the government has increased efforts to reduce fraud and abuse of the health care system. In so doing, the government has, with increased fervor, targeted health care providers. Such increased scrutiny from the government has forced health care providers to develop compliance programs to assist them in avoiding fraudulent and abusive acts, saving the provider from criminal and civil penalties.

Physicians should look closely at their actions and take stock of the examples set out above while developing their own compliance programs. Physicians should periodically reevaluate their practices and relationships and root out all potential situations that could result in fraud and abuse claims in order to avoid drawing the ire of the government watchdogs. Again, to be clear, there are very severe penalties for any violation.

In any event, it is important to remember that health care fraud enforcement is, or at least should be, a tool to help properly defend the integrity of the health care system to permit the health care provider to continue to provide health care to patients. To the extent that health care fraud or abuse inappropriately diverts resources that otherwise would be available for appropriately patient care, we are all harmed.

References

1. Henry F. Kaiser Family Foundation. U.S. healthcare costs: background brief. www.kaiseredu.org/topics_im.asp?imID=1&parentID=61&id=358.

2. *United States v. Forest Laboratories*, 03-10395, US District Court, District of Massachusetts. United States filed complaint against Forest Laboratories for allegedly violating the False Claims Act: pharmaceutical company allegedly marketed drugs for unapproved pediatric use and paid kickbacks. US Attorney, District of Massachusetts (February 25, 2009). www.usdoj.gov/usao/ma/Press%20Office%20-%20Press%20Release%20Files/Feb2009/ForestPR.html.

3. Public Law 95-142.

4. *18 USC §1347.*

5. *18 USC §1341.*

6. *18 USC §287.*

7. *42 USC §1320a-7b(a).*

8. *42 USC §1320a-7a.*

9. *42 USC §1320-7b(b).*

10. *42 USC §1395nn.*

11. *31 USC §3729.*

12. *31 USC § 3729(a)(1).*

13. *31 USC § 3729(a).*

14. *United States ex rel Schmidt v Zimmer, Inc, 386 F3d 235 (3rd Cir 2004).*

15. *United States ex rel Schmidt v Zimmer, Inc, 386 F3d 237 (3rd Cir 2004).*

16. *United States ex rel Schmidt v Zimmer, Inc, 386 F3d 240 (3rd Cir 2004).*

17. *31 USC § 3729(b).*

18. *42 USC § 1320a-7c(a).*

19. Dept of Health and Human Services, Dept of Justice. Health care fraud and abuse control program annual report for FY 2007. November 2008. www.oig.hhs.gov/publications/docs/hcfac/hcfacreport2007.pdf; p 4.

20. *42 USC § 1320a-7c(b).*

21. Centers for Medicare and Medicaid Services. www.cms.hhs.gov/.

22. US Dept of Health and Human Services, Office of Inspector General. www.oig.hhs.gov/.

23. US Dept of Justice. www.usdoj.gov/.

24. *31 USC § 3730(b).*

25. *42 USC § 1396b.*

26. *42 USC § 1395ddd(b)(1).*

27. *42 USC § 1395ddd(b)(2), (3).*

28. *42 USC § 1320a-7b(a).*

29. *42 USC § 1320a-7b(b).*

30. *18 USC § 287.*

31. *18 USC § 1035.*

32. *18 USC §§ 1341 and 1343.*

33. *18 USC § 1347.*

34. *42 USC § 1518.*

35. *USSG § 1B1.1*

36. *42 USC § 1320a-7a.*

37. *42 CFR §1003.102.*

38. *31 USC § 3729(7).*

39. *42 USC 1320a-7.*

40. US Dept of Health and Human Services, Office of Inspector General. Integrity agreement between the Office of Inspector General of the Department of Health and Human Services, and Candita Catucci, MD and Juan Carlos Acosta, Corporate Integrity Agreements Document List (March 20, 2007). www.oig.hhs.gov/fraud/cia/agreements/acosta_juan_carlos_03202007.pdf.

41. Harris G. Crackdown on doctors who take kickbacks. *New York Times.* March 3, 2009. www.nytimes.com/2009/03/04/health/policy/04doctors.html?_r=1&scp=1&sq=lew%20morris%20kickback&st=cse.

42. US Dept of Health and Human Services, Office of Inspector General. Protecting public health and human services programs: a 30 year retrospective. April 4, 2007. http://oig.hhs.gov/publications/docs/retrospective/AnniversaryPub.pdf.

43. *42 USC § 1395y(a)(1)(A).*

44. *42 USC 1320a-7a(1)(E).*

45. *42 USC §1395y(l)*

46. *United States ex rel Gayeski v Bland,* No. 04-14349 (February 5, 2007). www.usdoj.gov/usao/fls/PressReleases/Attachments/070726-01.NatureofAction.pdf.

47. US Attorney, Southern District of Florida. Neurosurgeon and hospital pay $1,275,000 settlement for medically unnecessary spinal surgeries. July 26, 2007. www.usdoj.gov/usao/fls/PressReleases/070726-01.html.

48. US Dept of Justice. Three Miami physicians and three medical workers charged with $10 million Medicare fraud scheme. February 13, 2009. www.usdoj.gov/opa/pr/2009/February/09-crm-122.html.

49. Office of the Attorney General of Florida. Miami-Dade husband and wife arrested for $200,000 Medicaid fraud. April 26, 2007. http://myfloridalegal.com/newsrel.nsf/newsreleases/D642D2C44C2D33E8852572C9005714D6.

50. *42 USC §1320a-7a(a)(1)(A)*.

51. *United States v Awad*, 551 F3d 930, 934 (9th Cir 2009).

52. *United States v Awad*, 551 F3d 935 (9th Cir 2009).

53. *United States v Awad*, 551 F3d 930 (9th Cir 2009).

54. US Dept of Justice, Northern District of Illinois. Two area physicians among four defendants charged in three separate federal health care fraud schemes. January 30, 2009. http://chicago.fbi.gov/dojpressrel/pressrel09/jan30_09.htm.

55. *United States v Rousseau*, 534 F2d 584 (CA Miss 1976).

56. *United States v Rousseau*, 534 F.2d 585 (CA Miss 1976).

57. *United States v Augustine Medical, Inc*, 2004 WL 256772, 1 (D Minn 2004).

58. *United States v Augustine Medical, Inc*, 2004 WL 256772, 2 (D Minn 2004).

59. US Dept of Health and Human Services, Office of Inspector General. Semi-Annual Report, to Congress Spring 2008 http://oig.hhs.gov/organization/oi/highlights.asp.

60. Washington G2 Reports. California AG investigating clinical labs. January 2009. www.g2reports.com/issues/GCR/2009_1/1619071-1.html.

61. *42 USC § 1395g*.

62. *42 CFR § 413.20(a), (b)*

63. *42 CFR § 413.9(c)(3)*.

64. *United States v Bourseau*, 531 F3d 1159, 1162 (9th Cir 2008).

65. *United States v Bourseau*, 531 F3d 1159, 1164 (9th Cir 2008).

66. US Dept of Health and Human Services, Office of Inspector General. False and Fraudulent Claims Archive. August 12, 2005.

67. *United States v Collins*, 596 F2d 166, 167 (6th Cir 1979).

68. *United States v Collins*, 596 F2d 168 (6th Cir 1979).

69. *United States ex rel Geisler v IMED Corp*, 1997 WL 769456, 1 (ND Ill 1997).

70. *United States v Alemany Rivera*, 781 F2d 229 (1st Cir 1985).

71. *United States v Alemany Rivera*, 781 F2d 231 (1st Cir 1985).

72. *United States v Cabrera-Diaz*, 106 F Supp 2d 234, 236 (DPR 2000).

73. *United States v Cabrera-Diaz*, 106 F Supp 2d 237 (DPR 2000).

74. US Dept of Health and Human Services, Office of Inspector General. Review of Medicare outlier payments at Brigham and Women's Hospital for fiscal year 1999. December 7, 2001. www.oig.hhs.gov/oas/reports/region1/10100516.pdf.

75. US Dept of Justice. Tenet Healthcare Corporation to pay US more than $900 million to resolve False Claims Act allegations. June 29, 2006. www.usdoj.gov/opa/pr/2006/June/06_civ_406.html.

76. Washington in Brief. Health care firm to pay $265 million to US *Washington Post.* June 16, 2006; A07.

77. *42 USC § 1320a-7b(a)(3).*

78. *31 USC §3729(a)(7).*

79. US Dept of Health and Human Services, Office of Inspector General. OIG compliance program for individual and small group physician practices. October 5, 2000. 65 FR 194. www.oig.hhs.gov/authorities/docs/physician.pdf.

80. US Attorney Central District of California. Nebraska hospital pays $4 million to resolve lawsuit alleging that it failed to return overpayments from government health insurance programs. www.usdoj.gov/usao/cac/pressroom/pr2006/149.html.

81. US Dept of Health and Human Services, Office of Inspector General. OIG enters into $2 million civil monetary penalty settlement with radiology practice. www.oig.hhs.gov/publications/docs/press/2009/WestValley-ImagingA.pdf.

82. Provider self-disclosure protocol. 63 Fed Reg 58,399 (October 30, 1998).

83. US Dept of Health and Human Services, Office of Inspector General. An Open Letter to Health Care Providers. April 15, 2008. http://oig.hhs.gov/fraud/docs/openletters/OpenLetter4-15-08.pdf.

84. US Dept of Health and Human Services, Office of Inspector General. False and Fraudulent Claims Archive. November 28, 2005.

85. *United States v Singh*, 390 F3d 168, 176 (2nd Cir 2004).

86. *United States v Singh*, 390 F3d 168, 178 (2nd Cir 2004).

87. *Minnesota Association of Nurse Anesthetists, United States ex rel v Allina Health System Corp*, 276 F3d 1032 (8th Cir 2000).

88. Allina Health System settlement reaffirms government's view of providers' affirmative duty to report overpayments. *Law Watch*. February 12, 2002. www.foley.com/files/tbl_s31Publications/FileUpload137/681/law_watch_2002v06.pdf

89. Miletich S. UW med school failed to address overbilling problems, panel says. *Seattle Times*. July 21, 2005.

90. US Dept of Health and Human Services and Dept of Justice. Health care fraud and abuse control program annual report for FY 2006. November 2007. www.oig.hhs.gov/publications/docs/hcfac/hcfacreport2006.pdf, pp 13–14.

91. *United States ex rel Aranda v Community Psychiatric Centers of Oklahoma, Inc*, 945 F Supp 1485 (WD Okl 1996).

92. *United States ex rel Aranda v Community Psychiatric Centers of Oklahoma, Inc*, 945 F Supp 1488 (WD Okl 1996).

93. *United States ex rel Aranda v Community Psychiatric Centers of Oklahoma, Inc*, 945 F Supp 1487 (WD Okl 1996).

94. Dept of Justice. US gets $750,000 for fraud claims against Oklahoma hospital. February 11, 1997. www.usdoj.gov/opa/pr/1997/February97/062civ.htm.

95. *42 USC § 1320a-7b*.

96. *United States v Rutgard*, 116 F3d 1270 (9th Cir 1997).

97. *United States v Rutgard*, 116 F3d 1287 (9th Cir 1997).

98. *Ecclesiastes*, Chapter 1, Verse 9.

99. US Dept of Health and Human Services, Office of Inspector General. Advisory opinions. www.oig.hhs.gov/fraud/advisoryopinions.asp.

100. *42 CFR §1001.952(a)*.

101. *42 CFR §1001.952(b), (c), (d)*.

102. *In re Lupron Marketing and Sales Practices Litigation*, 2005 WL 2006833 (D Mass 2005).

103. US Dept of Health and Human Services and Dept of Justice. Health Care Fraud and Abuse Control Program Annual Report For FY 2003. http://oig.hhs.gov/publications/docs/hcfac/hcfacreport2003A.htm.

104. US Dept of Health and Human Services, Office of Inspector General. Kickback and physician self-referral archive. http://oig.hhs.gov/fraud/enforcement/cmp/kickback_archive.asp.

105. US Dept of Health and Human Services, Office of Inspector General. Letter re: complimentary local transportation program. December 9, 2002. http://oig.hhs.gov/fraud/docs/alertsandbulletins/LocalTransportation.pdf.

106. US Dept of Health and Human Services, Office of Inspector General. Advisory Opinion 08-05. http://oig.hhs.gov/fraud/docs/advisoryopinions/2008/AdvOpn08-05B.pdf.

107. US Dept of Health and Human Services, Office of Inspector General. OIG settles largest ever civil monetary penalty case. May 15, 2006. www.oig.hhs.gov/publications/docs/press/2006/Lincare051506.pdf.

108. US Dept of Health and Human Services, Office of Inspector General. OIG settles civil monetary law case against medical device manufacturer. July 2, 2007. http://oig.hhs.gov/publications/docs/press/2007/ANS%20Press%20Release.pdf.

109. US Dept of Health and Human Services, Office of Inspector General. OIG semi-annual report to Congress, October 1, 2007 to March 31, 2008. http://oig.hhs.gov/publications/docs/semiannual/2008/semiannual_spring2008.pdf.

110. Artificial joint maker settles kickback case. *New York Times*. September 28, 2007.

111. Cardiologists linked to UMDNJ kickback scheme settle civil suits. *Newark Star Ledger*. May 7, 2008.

112. US Dept of Health and Human Services, Office of Inspector General. Advisory Opinion 05-08. http://oig.hhs.gov/fraud/docs/advisoryopinions/2005/ao0508.pdf.

113. US Dept of Health and Human Services, Office of Inspector General. Advisory Opinion 99-2. http://oig.hhs.gov/fraud/docs/advisoryopinions/1999/ao99_2.htm.

114. US Dept of Health and Human Services, Office of Inspector General. Advisory Opinion 04-17 (December 10, 2004). www.oig.hhs.gov/fraud/docs/advisoryopinions/2004/ao0417.pdf.

115. US Dept of Health and Human Services, Office of Inspector General. Advisory Opinion 04-08 (June 23, 2004). www.oig.hhs.gov/fraud/docs/advisoryopinions/2004/AdvOp04-08B.pdf.

116. US Dept of Health and Human Services, Office of Inspector General. Advisory Opinion 08-10 (August 19, 2008). www.oig.hhs.gov/fraud/docs/advisoryopinions/2008/AdvOpn08-10A.pdf.

117. *42 USC § 1395nn et seq.*

118. *42 CFR § 411.353 et seq.*

119. *42 USC § 1395nn(h)(6)(B).*

120. *42 CFR § 411.351.*

121. *42 USC § 1395nn(a)(1)(B).*

122. US Dept of Health and Human Services, Office of Inspector General. Kickback and physician self-referral archive (January 27, 2009). www.oig.hhs.gov/fraud/enforcement/cmp/kickback.asp.

123. Dept of Health and Human Services, Office of Inspector General. Kickback and physician self-referral archive (December 3, 2008). www.oig.hhs.gov/fraud/enforcement/cmp/kickback.asp.

124. *United States ex rel Kosenske v Carlisle HMA, Inc*, 554 F3d 88 (3rd Cir 2009).

125. *United States ex rel Kosenske v Carlisle HMA, Inc*, 554 F3d 91 (3rd Cir 2009).

126. *United States ex rel Kosenske v Carlisle HMA, Inc*, 554 F3d 93 (3rd Cir 2009).

127. *42 USC § 1320a-7a(a)(5).*

128. Dimassa CM, Winton R. FBI raids three Southern California hospitals in probe of Medicare fraud. *Los Angeles Times*. August 7, 2008.

129. US Dept of Health and Human Services, Office of Inspector General. Advisory Opinion 07-02 (March 7, 2007). www.oig.hhs.gov/fraud/docs/advisoryopinions/2007/AdvOpn07-02E.pdf.

130. *42 USC § 1320a-7.*

131. US Attorney's Office, District of New Hampshire. Wentworth-Douglass Hospital and Wentworth-Douglass Physician Corporation agree to pay $340,000.00 to resolve allegations related to their employment of individuals who were excluded from federal health care programs (December 11, 2008). www.justice.gov/usao/nh/press/december08/ JF_WentworthDouglas.html.

132. US Dept of Health and Human Services, Office of Inspector General. OIG compliance program for individual and small group physician practices. 65 FR 59434. October 5, 2000.

133. US Dept of Health and Human Services, Office of Inspector General. Work plan. http://oig.hhsgov/publications/workplan.html#1.

134. 42 CFR § 424.535.

135. Dept of Health and Human Services, Office of Inspector General. Kickback and physician self-referral archive (Novemebr 4, 2008). www.oig. hhs.gov/fraud/enforcement/cmp/kickback.asp.

136. Dept of Health and Human Services, Office of Inspector General. Kickback and physician self-referral archive (May 10, 2008). www.oig.hhs. gov/fraud/enforcement/cmp/kickback.asp.

CHAPTER 3

Best Practices for Avoiding Fraud and Abuse Liability

Robert A. Wade, Esquire

3.1 Where Does a Physician Practice Begin Developing an Effective Compliance Program?

We read about it all the time. Hospitals, pharmaceutical companies, large health systems, device manufacturers, durable medical equipment companies, home health agencies, and yes, even physicians, are investigated and in egregious cases are prosecuted for medical fraud and abuse. Sometimes, from the press reports, it seems that the medical provider intentionally tried to game the system for financial gain. Sometimes the news reports will indicate that a physician either intentionally upcoded medical procedures or performed procedures that were not medically necessary.

However, there are always 2 sides to a story. Did the physician really perform medically unnecessary procedures or did the physician unintentionally bill for a procedure that did not meet Medicare's strict medical necessity requirements? Did the physician perform a service but bill under the wrong code, from which the government has alleged that a service did not occur because of the use of the wrong code? The claimed *intentional act* could have stemmed from a physician not fully documenting the procedure performed or the medical condition of the patient that caused the physician to perform the service. Physicians did not go to medical school to learn how to create squeaky clean documentation to support medical services. Physicians choose the medical profession to help patients with their medical issues. However, despite lofty ambitions, like quality of patient care, documentation and adherence to billing requirements are necessary to defend reimbursement received if the performance of and billing for a medical service is ever questioned by a third-party payer or the Department of Justice.

It is against this background that physicians must decide whether, and to what extent, to implement a compliance program. As shown in this chapter, there are various components of an effective compliance program that should be considered. Implementing these components will utilize both financial and staff resources. The expenditure of these resources, however, will be worthwhile if the practice is ever investigated for inappropriate activity.

In addition to the prevention of fraud and abuse, an effective compliance program can make the payment of claims more efficient, while simultaneously minimizing billing mistakes. This means that, through the implementation of an effective compliance program, the practice may generate additional revenue. If, through the compliance program, those involved in the reimbursement process, including physicians, document the services performed more completely, the practice will be able to bill more accurately for those services. Many physician practices unintentionally undercode out of fear of overcoding for procedures. A compliance program can move a practice to the point where it is performing medically necessary services, those services are accurately documented, and the services provided are accurately billed and paid for by third-party payers. Implementing an effective compliance program can also reduce the possibility that the practice will be audited for inappropriate billing activity.

At the outset, it should be emphasized that compliance programs are voluntary. Unless the practice is under a corporate integrity agreement, which is a mandatory compliance program imposed by the Office of Inspector General (OIG) of the Department of Health and Human Services, the practice has the option of deciding whether to implement a compliance program. This chapter will assist in identifying the areas that the practice needs to focus on when choosing to implement a compliance program, with practical suggestions on how to implement these various components.

Chapter 1 explained the various fraud and abuse laws that apply to physicians. Many of these laws impose high fines and penalties, and in egregious cases where financial incentives are offered to induce referrals, criminal liability can be assessed. Some of these laws, like the Stark Law, have very prescriptive requirements to meet an applicable exception. If a practice conducts activities that are covered by any of these laws, strict adherence to the technical requirements is required. Ignorance is no defense. Many physicians have been investigated regarding these laws, and some have been criminally prosecuted for violating the laws. Some physicians have even spent time in jail for violations of these laws, such as the anti-kickback statute (AKS). Obviously, criminal prosecution of a physician occurs only when the government is able to show intentional wrongdoing.

Regardless of the size of a physician practice, it is imperative to develop an effective compliance program. Through such a program, many of the real-life examples in this book, including the top 10 identified in Chapter 2, could potentially be avoided. This does not mean that by implementing a compliance program all aspects of fraud and abuse can be effectively identified and eliminated. The rules and regulations covering the medical industry are far too complex and far-reaching for an effective compliance program to identify all errors. Because of this complexity, errors, most of which are not intentional, may occur. Physicians, however, cannot simply throw their hands in the air in frustration and a sense of futility because of the complexity of the medical regulations. Physicians must show a good-faith effort to implement an effective compliance program if they want the benefits of a compliance program.

There is no single model compliance program that can apply to all physician practices. The scale and scope of the compliance program will depend on (1) the type of practice, (2) the number of physicians affiliated with the practice, (3) whether the practice is a single specialty or a multispecialty practice, (4) the financial ability of the physician practice to dedicate resources to a compliance program, and (5) the past history of the physician practice dealing with fraud and abuse issues. A solo practitioner's compliance program will look drastically different from a compliance program for a multispecialty and multioffice physician practice with a couple hundred physicians.

When developing a compliance program, creativity and resourcefulness are helpful. The practice can either develop a compliance program from scratch or look to other resources for assistance in development of the program. Physician practices can participate in other providers' compliance programs, such as a hospital at which the physicians are on the medical staff. A practice can also combine with other physician practices in the area to collaborate in the development and implementation of a compliance program.

Trying to implement simultaneously all aspects of a compliance program can be overwhelming. A better plan is to start simply with one component, and as time and resources become available, continue to add other components to the compliance program. As discussed later, if the practice's staff has never received training or education, that may be the best place to start. If the practice may have a high risk for billing issues, the auditing and monitoring components of an effective compliance program may be an appropriate starting point. Once one component of the compliance program is successfully established, move to another component, continuing in this manner until all aspects of the compliance program are fully implemented and functional.

The OIG has provided substantial guidance on the implementation of compliance programs. On October 5, 2000, the OIG posted the Compliance Program for Individual and Small Group Physician Practices in the Federal Register (65 Fed. Reg. 59434). The OIG has also provided guidance for other health care areas, including hospitals, nursing homes, pharmaceutical companies, and home health agencies. This compliance guidance can be found at the OIG's web site at www.oig.hhs.gov/. This web site can be a valuable resource for a physician practice; in addition to the compliance guidance, the site also contains a plethora of other resources, including opinion letters, fraud alerts, and open letters from the OIG to the health care industry. In addition to the OIG web site, there are other web sites that can provide guidance on the implementation of a compliance program. If a practice's specialty has a national institute or academy, these can be valuable resources to consult when developing a compliance program.

Many consulting and law firms provide assistance to physicians regarding the implementation and monitoring of effective compliance programs. When selecting a consultant, the practice should ensure that the firm and persons chosen have extensive experience in health care compliance and have previously implemented effective compliance programs. Consultants who are quick to produce a booklet or binder containing the compliance program should be avoided. The advisor should ask many questions about the practice in an effort to get to know its culture and determine the appropriate methodology for implementing the compliance program. The advisor should interview key influencers within the practice as well as others, including physicians, nurses, registration staff, billers, and coders, in order to determine the most appropriate component to begin and possible cultural impediments with respect to the compliance program implementation. The advisor should be encouraged to be open and honest regarding his or her impression of the practice, as many physicians have failed to implement effectively a compliance program because of cultural issues. For example, if a key influencing physician will speak critically about the compliance program or has exhibited intentional disregard for billing, coding, and documentation rules, the practice may need to begin with focusing on altering this physician's reactions and adherence to billing and coding requirements before implementing a program. If the practice does not deal with these cultural issues at the outset, it can potentially waste substantial resources trying to implement an effective compliance program around these naysayers.

In addition to a cultural assessment, the advisor should review all other areas of the physician practice in building an appropriate compliance program. For example, past training should be reviewed, the billing system should be analyzed to ensure that it has all applicable components, the practice's documentation standards should be reviewed, and past correspondence with third-party payers questioning reimbursement received needs to be analyzed. In addition, any documentation provided as a result of such correspondence needs to be reviewed. In this way, the advisor will be able to determine whether the practice is currently under investigation, thus making the auditing and monitoring component of the program the first area of focus.

After the advisor has conducted a preliminary assessment, a plan regarding the process and order of implementation of the compliance program components should be presented, reviewed, and approved. Prior to any official commencement of the compliance program, key leadership within the practice needs to communicate their support for and endorsement of the implementation of the compliance program and pledge to resolve any issues identified as a result of the program. This emphasis and support from key management cannot be overemphasized or overlooked. Many compliance programs have failed when leaders overtly or indirectly discredit or intentionally choose not to correct identified problems and concerns. If employees believe that key leaders will not support a compliance program or the findings that result from the program, the practice will not be able to implement an effective compliance program regardless of how many resources the practice dedicates to the compliance program. Just as President Harry Truman had a sign on his desk in the Oval Office that read, "The Buck Stops Here," key leadership within the practice are the persons who are primarily responsible for the effective implementation of the compliance program. In effect, the compliance buck stops with key leadership.

In the Compliance Program for Individual and Small Group Physician Practices, the OIG noted that compliance programs contain "seven components that provide a solid basis upon which a physician practice can create a voluntary compliance program:

- Conducting internal monitoring and auditing;
- Implementing compliance and practice standards;
- Designating a compliance officer or contact;
- Conducting appropriate training and education;
- Responding appropriately to detected offenses and developing corrective action;
- Developing open lines of communication; and
- Enforcing disciplinary standards through well-publicized guidelines."

Each of these components needs to be implemented to have an effective compliance program.

The remaining portions of this chapter will explore these 7 components with practical guidelines and recommendations on how to implement each of them effectively. As stated previously, strict adherence to all proposals and recommendations contained in this chapter may not work for a given physician practice as each practice is different, especially from a cultural perspective. The recommendations should be used only as practical guidance, as they are best practices that have worked for other physician practices in the country.

3.2 Designation of a Compliance Officer for the Practice

If a practice is choosing to implement a voluntary compliance program, it will need to formally designate a person who will be responsible for the oversight and implementation of the various components of the compliance program. The person in charge of the compliance program is typically known as the practice's *compliance officer* (also may be called an *integrity officer* or *ethics officer*). It is important to emphasize, however, that it is not only the compliance officer's responsibility to ensure that the practice implements and monitors an effective compliance program. Every person affiliated with the practice is responsible for ensuring compliance. The compliance officer should be the person who assists the consultant and those affiliated with the practice with the implementation and maintenance of the program.

Who should be selected to be the compliance officer? Effective compliance officers exemplify the following characteristics:

- Approachable
- High ethical standard
- Able to ask tough questions
- Able to effect change
- Capable of advocating for an issue
- Well organized
- Attention to detail
- Capable of explaining complex issues
- Able to dedicate time to compliance initiatives
- Able to allocate resources on the basis of priority of issues.

An effective compliance officer is able to receive concerns, investigate whether the concerns are legitimate, and determine whether the concerns expose the practice to risk. If risk is identified, the compliance officer should be able to develop and recommend corrective actions and monitor any corrective action once implemented.

A compliance officer cannot be that in name only, but must have compliance functions as part of his or her core job responsibility and must dedicate sufficient time to the performance of compliance initiatives. A form with the job description for a compliance officer is included as Figure 3-1. An effective compliance officer needs to be capable of multitasking and performing compliance risk assessments. Multitasking is extremely important, as the compliance officer will need to keep track of all of the activities of the compliance program. This will include maintaining documentation regarding the compliance program's implementation and tracking the status of compliance investigations, including auditing, monitoring,

Job Title: Compliance Officer		
Reports to **(Supervisor's Title):**	**Human Resource** **Approval:**	**Date:**

Purpose of Position

The purpose of the position of the physician practice's compliance officer is to develop, implement, revise, and oversee the physician practice's compliance program. The compliance officer shall be responsible for maintaining the expanding visibility of the compliance program at all levels within the physician practice. The compliance officer is responsible for overseeing the development and implementation of training regarding the physician practice's compliance program through all levels of the physician practice. The compliance officer shall regularly report on compliance activities to the physician practice's board of directors. The compliance officer shall be responsible for evaiuating the effectiveness of the compliance program and for modifying components of the compliance program to make it more effective. The compliance officer shall regularly seek out information regarding all statutes, rules, regulations, and requirements of third-party payers that Impact the physician practice in order to understand such requirements and to implement change when the requirements are modified from time to time. The compliance officer will provide oversight regarding any investigation, including reviews and audits conducted by payers, including Medicare/Medicaid. The compliance officer will also provide oversight regarding any disciplinary action or enforcement involving employees, agents, and inde-pendent contractors of the physician practice.

Major Accountabilities

1. Provide oversight and leadership regarding the development and implementation of the physician practice's compliance program.

FIGURE 3-1 | Compliance Officer Job Description

2. Advise the physician practice's employees, especially key leadership, regarding the implementation of the components of the physician practice's compliance program.

3. Serve as an expert to the physician practice with respect to statutory, regulatory, and third-party payer requirements, including Medicare/Medicaid, as they impact the operation of the physician practice.

4. Consult with external experts, such as health care attorneys and accountants, with respect to matters where the expertise of an external resource is deemed to be reasonably necessary.

5. Oversee the reporting process to generate a culture within the physician practice of encouraging employees to bring compliance concerns to the attention of the physician practice. Consistent with the physician practice's policy on problem reporting and nonretaliation, the compliance officer shall encourage employees to bring issues to the attention of their supervisors, key leadership, directly to the compliance officer, and through the physician practice's anonymous reporting process. As a result of any issues reported through the reporting mechanisms, the compliance officer shall be responsible for overseeing a thorough and complete investigation regarding any reported compliance concerns.

6. Be responsible for the investigation and enforcement of the physician practice's nonretaliation policy.

7. Develop and implement training and education regarding the physician practice's compliance program and job-specific training to ensure that all employees understand the compliance requirements of their positions.

8. Be responsible for coordinating the compliance program functions through the physician practice's compliance committee.

Created [date]   [electronic file name and path]   page 2 of 3

FIGURE 3-1 | Compliance Officer Job Description (Continued)

9. Serve as the liaison with the board of directors regarding any compliance activities within the physician practice. This reporting responsibility shall include compliance concerns that have been reported, status of training and education, status and results of any internal investigation, results of internal auditing and monitoring activities, and any external audit, review, or investigation, including from Medicare, Medicaid, or any of their contractors.

Qualifications

1. Significant experience in the health care industry with compliance program experience.
2. Knowledge regarding statutes, rules, regulations and requirements of third-party payer programs, including Medicare and Medicaid, that may impact the physician practice's operations.
3. Excellent written, oral, and presentation communication skills.
4. Exemplify the following: (1) approachable; (2) high ethical standard; (3) able to ask tough questions; (4) able to effect change; (5) capable of advocating for an issue; (6) well organized; (7) attention to detail; (8) capable of explaining complex issues; (9) able to dedicate time to compliance initiatives; and (10) able to allocate resources based on priority of issues.

FIGURE 3-1 | Compliance Officer Job Description (Continued)

and other internal investigations. A form report to key leadership regarding the compliance initiative is provided as Figure 3-2. The compliance officer will also need to triage issues as they arrive to quickly assess what issues being reported through the compliance mechanisms are being made in good faith and potentially expose the practice to risk. If the compliance officer believes that any of these reported issues pose risk to the practice, he or she needs to allocate resources effectively to review these issues, determine whether corrective action is warranted, implement the corrective action, and monitor the issue in the future to prevent its recurrence. Because of these demands, the designated person must have excellent organization skills and have refined the art of diplomacy.

The compliance officer should also be capable of remaining calm even as complex and multifaceted issues are being brought to his or her attention. The compliance officer should remain neutral until all of the facts are investigated and known. He or she should not easily jump to conclusions or immediately act on any and every concern brought to his or her attention. This role requires that the designated person be very fact-oriented. The old adage "trust but verify" needs to be employed by the compliance officer. If people within the physician practice are representing that certain facts are true, the compliance officer needs to receive documentation to validate that the representations being made are in fact true. This means even though the compliance officer may have personal relationships and friendships with other employees affiliated with the physician practice, he or she needs to obtain sufficient information and documentation to confirm facts or allegations. Acting quickly on allegations, without a full and complete understanding of the facts, can lead to disastrous outcomes. Thus, the role requires great discernment and objectivity.

The practice's compliance officer must also ensure the compliance and integrity of the practice's operations. The compliance officer is responsible for ensuring organizational compliance, not the individual or personal ethical standards or beliefs of all of the employees. Everyone affiliated with the practice needs to understand that the compliance officer is there to protect the organization like an organizational ombudsman. The lines between personal ethical standards and organizational standards should be

Key Leadership Report from: __________ [Date] through: __________ [Date]

ON TARGET ALERT

I. EDUCATION - _______________ ***[Organization Name]****'s* ***COMPLIANCE PROGRAM*** *mandates that each employee, on an annual basis, complete education regarding (1) the* ***COMPLIANCE PROGRAM*** *generally, including the code of conduct; and (2) compliance with statutes, rules, and regulations applicable to his/her duties and responsibilities. The annual period is from __________ [Month] to __________ [Month]. The following is the status of education for __________* ***[Organization Name]****'s employees.*

➢ **New Employee COMPLIANCE PROGRAM Training**

1. Number of new employees during quarter
2. Percentage of new employees deficient more than 90 days %

Annual COMPLIANCE PROGRAM Training %

➢ **Annual Compliance Education (Due __________ [Month, Day, and Year])**

1. Number of employees
2. Percentage of employees completing education (Beginning __________ Month, Day, and Year) %

II. COMPLIANCE PROGRAM COMMITTEE - _______________
[Organization Name] *has a Compliance Committee.*

➢ **COMPLIANCE COMMITTEE**

1. Number of members on compliance committee
2. Percentage of members attending compliance committee meetings %
3. Number of meetings this quarter

Created [date] [electronic file name and path] page 1 of 3

FIGURE 3-2 Compliance Report

III. ANONYMOUS REPORTING PROCESS

1. Number of anonymous reports during quarter
   a. Anonymous reports related to human resource issues
2. Number of anonymous reports closed during quarter
3. Number of anonymous reports substantiated with appropriate corrective action

IV. COMPLIANCE ISSUES Reported to Compliance Officer

1. Number of issues open during quarter
2. Number of issues closed during the quarter

V. COMPLIANCE PROGRAM POLICIES - _____ [Organization Name]'s COMPLIANCE PROGRAM requires the development, implementation, and monitoring of policies to ensure _____ [Organization Name] conducts business in compliance with applicable statutes, rules, and regulations.

1. Number of COMPLIANCE PROGRAM policies
2. Number of new policies implemented during the quarter

VI. BILLING AND CODING REVIEWS - _____ [Organization Name] is required to review its billing/coding compliance. _____ [Organization Name] will conduct reviews as part of scheduled audits or to investigate concerns.

1. Number of reviews open during quarter
2. Number of reviews closed during quarter
3. Number of reviews requiring repayment/processing of claims

Created [date]   [electronic file name and path]   page 2 of 3

FIGURE 3-2 | Compliance Report (Continued)

VII. GOVERNMENT INVESTIGATIONS - *It is* _____
[Organization Name]'s policy to cooperate with all government investigations. Due to the sensitive nature of government investigations, an oral report will be made by the Compliance Officer regarding any known government investigations.

FIGURE 3-2 | Compliance Report (Continued)

well specified. Otherwise, employees will believe that the compliance officer represents all employees, not the practice as an organization.

The compliance officer must also be capable of effectively explaining the activities of the compliance program within the physician practice. For example, if an allegation regarding inappropriate billing has been made and the compliance officer has suspended billing because of the allegation, the officer must be able to explain why he or she believes the suspension of claims is appropriate as a result of the allegation. Further, if the compliance officer is investigating a particular physician or department, he or she needs to conduct the investigation on an impartial basis to find the root cause of any infraction or error. Frequently, errors occur because of lack of resources, including lack of effective training and education. If the root cause of an error is lack of training and education, the compliance officer needs to delegate resources to provide the necessary training. The compliance officer must do all of this while maintaining a conducive working relationship with those affiliated with the physician practice.

The compliance officer likewise needs to keep in mind that the practice's primary objective is to provide patient care. For example, if a problem is suspected regarding reimbursement for a particular procedure, it would be inappropriate to cease providing the procedure, as this will materially impact the patient care provided by the practice. Alternatively, it would be better for the compliance officer to suspend claims regarding the procedure, lifting the suspension only after a thorough investigation has been performed and appropriate corrective action has been implemented, if warranted.

The practice likewise needs to cloak the compliance officer with sufficient authority to carry out effectively his or her duties and responsibilities. Using again the example of a suspected billing irregularity, the compliance officer will have effective authority if he or she is able to suspend claims until the allegation has been thoroughly investigated. If the compliance officer has to obtain approval through a substantial chain of command in order to suspend claims, he or she may have insufficient authority to execute effectively the responsibilities of the position. The compliance officer will still have effective authority if concurrence of the financial officer was required prior to suspending claims. If the financial officer is required to approve of such suspension of claims, the compliance officer will need to provide sufficient documentation showing that the alleged billing irregularity is probable, the concern was brought to his or her attention in good faith, and the risks, including false claims, that the practice may face if it does not take immediate action. It is appropriate for the compliance officer to work collaboratively with key stakeholders in the practice, but the compliance officer should not be so low in the practice's hierarchy that it would take many approvals to effect a change if the compliance officer believes that immediate action is required.

Although no one should be ruled out as a potential compliance officer, certain individuals who perform key roles for the physician practice may be perceived to have a conflict of interest due to their other assigned roles. Such roles and potential conflicts are as follows:

Role	Possible Conflict of Interest
Financial officer	Would favor the financial performance of the physician practice over correcting compliance irregularities
Majority owner	May favor financial performance and practice expansion and affiliations over correcting compliance irregularities
Legal officer	May try to cover compliance concerns with the attorney-client privilege instead of investigating and correcting compliance irregularities with transparency.

Even though these potential conflicts of interest exist, and perceptions regarding such conflicts could permeate a physician practice, appropriate safeguards can be implemented to decrease the potential conflicts. For example, if a billing irregularity is brought to the attention of the financial officer who also serves as the compliance officer, an independent third party could be engaged to review the issue. Likewise, if the legal officer is the compliance officer, the legal officer's role as compliance officer would take precedence in regard to any compliance initiative. In these events, outside counsel should be used for the review of and advice related to legal issues.

The physician practice needs to ensure that the compliance officer is well trained. Just as continuing medical education is provided by the practice for its physicians, the physician practice should ensure that sufficient resources exist for the compliance officer to receive periodic training regarding compliance issues that impact the practice. The compliance officer should be sent to national or regional compliance conferences, or participate in Web-based or audio conferences, to stay current on compliance issues. Because statutes and regulations in the health care industry change with great frequency, keeping the compliance officer knowledgeable about all changes will assist the practice in remaining compliant with all such changes. The training received by the compliance officer should be focused on the practice's area of specialty.

It is very important that the compliance officer also be easily accessible within the practice. The compliance officer must have sufficient office hours that employees can talk to him or her about any compliance concern. Employees should know how to contact the compliance officer to address any concerns or to answer any questions that arise on a daily basis. Employees should be encouraged to address concerns and to question the compliance officer regarding any compliance issue. Top management of the practice needs to emphasize the open lines of communication with and accessibility to the compliance officer.

The practice should also provide resources to the compliance officer to assist in the implementation of the compliance program. The compliance officer should have access to legal counsel knowledgeable about compliance issues that impact the practice. The compliance officer should be able to engage auditors and certified coders to assist with the auditing and monitoring function of the practice. For financial irregularities, access to accountants, including forensic accountants, may be appropriate. Further, it is also possible that the compliance officer will need access to private investigators to assist with issues.

If the practice does not have an individual capable of fulfilling the role of compliance officer, or if the available resources are insufficient to have one person affiliated with the practice designated as the compliance officer, other alternatives exist. The compliance function can be divided among various employees within the practice as long as, in the aggregate, the entire compliance function has appropriate oversight. If this method is chosen for the physician practice, all persons to whom a compliance function has been delegated need to meet periodically to ensure that, as a whole, the compliance program is operating effectively. For example, one employee could be designated as being responsible for preparing and maintaining the policies and procedures, while another employee is responsible for the periodic auditing and monitoring functions. All of these roles should report to the key management within the physician practice. If the compliance function is divided among many employees, one employee should be designated as the person to whom compliance concerns need to be reported. This person needs to have the attributes noted above regarding the selection of the compliance officer.

Another alternative is to outsource the compliance officer to a compliance consultant or lawyer. The outsourced compliance officer can serve as the compliance officer for more than one entity. If the practice chooses to outsource its compliance officer function, the employees need to have sufficient interaction with such external person that this person understands how the practice operates, and employees should be encouraged to bring issues to the outsourced compliance officer's attention. If the practice uses an outsourced compliance officer, one person within the practice should be designated as the key liaison between the compliance officer and the practice. Although outsourcing the compliance officer function may make the designation of a compliance officer more affordable, the practice will need to consider the limitations of using an outsourced compliance officer. Such limitations include lack of accessibility, lack of understanding of how the practice operates, and possible unavailability if the person is serving several practices and is working on a crisis situation for one of the other clients. The outsourced compliance officer should make frequent reports, preferably no less frequently than quarterly, to key management regarding the compliance officer's activities as they relate to the practice.

The selection of the compliance officer, and persons who are to be involved with the compliance program, needs to be made with special care and attention. Just as key leadership within the physician practice can prevent the effective implementation of a compliance program if they speak negatively about the program, choosing the wrong person to be the compliance officer can have a significant negative impact on the development and implementation of the program. If the selected compliance officer is not very well organized, the practice may not be able to use its compliance program as a defensive strategy if it is ever investigated by the OIG or the Department of Justice. If the practice asserts that is has an effective compliance program, the compliance officer needs to have documentation that supports its vibrant implementation and constant monitoring of all aspects of the compliance program. Likewise, if the compliance officer is not approachable, employees will not bring compliance causes to the officer's attention.

The role of compliance officer can be both challenging and rewarding. As long as the compliance officer has sufficient support from the physician practice, the officer can implement an effective compliance program and appropriately respond to issues as they arise. The role is also intellectually stimulating, as the compliance officer will need to know and understand the legal and regulatory requirements that are imposed on the practice. Alternatively, if the practice names a compliance officer, but does not support the compliance officer's role or does not designate sufficient resources, the compliance officer will be ineffective in implementing and monitoring an effective compliance program. Many compliance officers have resigned out of frustration because their physician practice did not support their role or dedicate sufficient resources. If this occurs with the practice, the program may be deemed to be ineffective and be more of a liability than a benefit.

3.3 Training and Education

Educating employees on the general components of the compliance program, and the statutory and regulatory requirements of each employee's job function, is the backbone of an effective compliance program. Most employees desire to do the right thing. Many times compliance issues occur simply because the employee did not understand the legal and regulatory requirements of his or her job function.

Further, physician practices experience turnover of employees from time to time. If employees are not educated regarding their position at the beginning of their tenure, the practice will be exposed to heightened compliance risks. Because of these issues, the practice must be proactive in providing educational opportunities for employees regarding their role in ensuring that the practice complies with all applicable legal and regulatory requirements.

The first area of focus of the practice's training program should be the structure and scope of the compliance program. A sample agenda of a training program is included as Figure 3-3. All aspects of the compliance program must be communicated to the employees through an educational program both at the commencement of the compliance program and periodically thereafter. It is highly recommended that training regarding the general components of the compliance program occur at least annually to ensure that the employees understand the importance and the various components of the compliance program. Annual training will also keep the program at the top of employees' minds.

The general compliance program training should begin with an overview of the practice's code of conduct. The code of conduct should be tailored to the practice to emphasize the practice's mandate to adhere to all applicable policies, procedures, rules, and regulations. The code of conduct should be written in a manner that fits with the culture of the employees, and it should be generally understandable by the practice's employees. The code of conduct should not contain legalese, and it is advisable to keep the language at a seventh-grade level or below.
A short and concise code of conduct is better than a multipage one that covers all of the minutia of the compliance program. Education of employees on the compliance program should emphasize the code of conduct and adherence to it.

As noted previously, it is very important for employees to know who the compliance officer is and how to contact the officer if they have

Compliance Program Basic Training Agenda

I. Introduction of Compliance Officer

II. Key Leadership Statement of Why a Compliance Program Is Important

III. What Is a Compliance Program?

IV. What Are the Components of the Compliance Program?

1. Conducting internal monitoring and auditing

2. Implementing compliance and practice standards

3. Designating a compliance officer or contact

4. Conducting appropriate training and education

5. Responding appropriately to detected offenses and developing corrective action

6. Developing open lines of communication

7. Enforcing disciplinary standards through well-publicized guidelines.

V. Reporting Compliance Concerns

VI. Code of Conduct

VII. Questions and Answers

Created [date]   [electronic file name and path]   page 1 of 1

FIGURE 3-3 | Compliance Program Basic Training Agenda

any questions or would like to raise any compliance issues. Ideally, general training regarding the compliance program should occur at the commencement of the program and annually thereafter. This training should include an opportunity for the compliance officer to address the employees and emphasize his or her personal commitment to dedicate the resources for the practice to ensure compliance with all applicable rules and regulations. By involving the compliance officer in this training, the practice's emphasis on compliance will be more than mere words, as the compliance officer will provide a face for the program. The training should make the employees feel as if they are important team members, with the compliance officer, in ensuring the compliance and integrity of the practice.

It is extremely important for the practice to educate the employees regarding policies and procedures, including how to access such policies and procedures. A list of all applicable compliance policies and procedures should be provided with detailed discussion regarding each policy and procedure so that the employees understand their purpose and how to comply. As policies and procedures change or are updated, or if new policies and procedures are adopted, additional education should be provided so that employees stay up to date regarding the compliance program's policies and procedures. A best practice would be to include all of the policies and procedures on the practice's intranet so that employees can gain access to them if they have any questions or wish to review them in order to comply with their requirements.

In addition to general training regarding the compliance program, each employee should be trained in his or her job-specific requirements at least annually. For example, if an employee serves in a coding or billing function, training should be provided regarding the applicable policies, procedures, statutes, and regulations related to how to code and bill for procedures performed and billed by the practice. The physician practice should be proactive in identifying job-specific compliance training to ensure that each employee has adequate training regarding how his or her function impacts the practice's compliance program. For coding and billing training, the OIG, in the Compliance Program for Individual and Small Group Physician Practices, provided the following examples of items that could be covered in coding and billing training:

- Coding requirements
- Claim development and submission processes
- Signing a form for a physician without the physician's authorization
- Proper documentation of services rendered
- Proper billing standards and procedures and submission of accurate bills for services or items rendered to federal health care program beneficiaries
- The legal sanctions for submitting deliberately false or reckless billings.

It is very important that the practice require its physicians to participate in compliance training. Physicians should be required, as a condition of employment, to participate in both general and job-specific training on a periodic basis. Thus, when developing the practice's training and education program, special emphasis should be given to the physicians' participation. As noted previously in this chapter, if the practice focuses solely on nonphysician providers and other staff members, it will send a message that the compliance program does not apply to the physicians. Physicians, however, are extremely important to the practice, and if physicians understand and adhere to the legal, statutory, and regulatory requirements, the practice will experience significantly lower risk. A best practice is to use one of the physicians as a lead trainee and internal champion for the compliance program. Another method is to use an external physician to provide some compliance training. Training with the physicians should also include the involvement of the compliance officer.

Compliance training for the physicians may need to be structured differently from training for other staff members affiliated with the practice. Because of unique pressures placed on physicians, compliance training may need to occur outside of normal business hours and even abbreviated sessions may need to be considered, depending on the physicians' past compliance training and adherence to legal, statutory, and regulatory requirements.

There are various methods of providing education to the employees. The practice could train its employees by using other employees who are knowledgeable regarding the subject matter. The compliance officer should provide the training regarding the general components of the practice's compliance program. There are also other methods that the practice can employ to carry out job-specific training. Various companies provide audio conferences, Web-based training, and training on CDs that the employees can access as time permits. There are also numerous local, regional, and national conferences that focus on compliance education and can provide the necessary job-specific training for the employees. Further, there are numerous periodicals that focus on specific medical specialties that can provide valuable periodic training for the employees. If the practice subscribes to any periodical, a best practice would be to require each of the employees to review the periodical and to document their review and adherence to the issues discussed.

If the practice is large enough, compliance articles in the employee newsletter should be considered. Other educational methods used by physician practices include monthly emails regarding compliance issues, screen savers, and even compliance education through fun-to-read picture strips. Because compliance education is considered to be dry, the practice needs to adopt training methods that fit within its culture and will engage everyone affiliated with the practice to be actively involved in the program.

It is also important to document the effectiveness of the compliance training and education. Many practices are conducting periodic testing of compliance issues to ensure that the compliance training was effective. Sometimes, this periodic testing can occur as part of the practice's training sessions. Some practices conduct testing on an annual basis outside of the formal training sessions. If testing occurs, the practice will need to establish a minimum pass rate. If an employee does not meet the minimum pass rate, additional remedial training will need to be provided with further follow-up testing to ensure that the employee understands the issues missed during prior testing.

Documentation of the training and education provided by the practice needs to be maintained so that the practice will be able to prove that it provided necessary compliance training and education. Documentation regarding employees' participation in compliance training and education ideally will be tracked through the human resources database. If the human resources database does not have a tracking mechanism, a tracking mechanism will need to be established that is specific for compliance education. To accomplish this objective, the practice can create its own compliance education database so that all compliance education taken by the employees is documented, including any testing results if the practice decides to test its employees. If the practice does not have the necessary resources to establish an electronic database for compliance education, paper documentation can be maintained to document employee participation.

As discussed later, if the practice adopts an auditing and monitoring program, this can be an extremely important educational opportunity, especially for the physicians. All results of all audits and reviews should be shared with the physicians and other employees, where appropriate, so that training regarding the appropriate documentation, billing, and coding will occur in the future. If internal resources are insufficient to provide the necessary education as a result of the auditing and monitoring functions, external resources should be located and engaged to provide the training. Ideally, after each auditing and monitoring activity, those involved in the auditing and monitoring activity should sit down with the physicians and explain their findings. Coding and billing manuals, including program guidance, should be shared with the physicians so that they understand the written requirements imposed by applicable third-party payers. For example, if the issue relates to a medical necessity determination, either national or local medical determinations should be provided.

When auditing and monitoring results are used with physicians as an educational opportunity as part of the practice's compliance education and training, the physicians' view should also be considered. If a physician reasonably disagrees with the outcome of the auditing and monitoring function, additional research can be performed and additional resources located to assist with the documentation, coding, or billing discrepancy. A collegial exchange of opinion, backed by supporting resources, should occur until any disagreement over compliance require-ments is satisfactorily resolved.

Implementing effective education and training for the employees requires a dedication of resources. The practice will need to find appropriate compliance training and education opportunities, as well as selecting methods of education that will work within the culture of the practice. Successful compliance training educates the employees regarding why the issue is important and how to comply. A fun, engag-ing educational opportunity will be more effective than a dry, boring presentation. Thus, sufficient preparation must occur to ensure that the employees will participate and be engaged. The resources committed to provide effective education will help ensure that the employees under-stand their role in the practice's compliance program and that they have the necessary training regarding their job function to ensure that their performance adheres to all compliance requirements.

3.4   Policies and Procedures

A central component of a physician practice compliance program is the standards and policies and procedures by which the practice will oper-ate. As noted by the OIG in the Compliance Program for Individual and Small Group Physician Practices, policies and procedures "help to reduce the prospect of erroneous claims and fraudulent activity by identifying risk areas for the practice and establishing tighter inter-nal controls to counter those risks, while also helping to identify any aberrant billing practices." Thus, the physician practice will need to identify applicable risk areas and to develop standards and policies and procedures around those risk areas to reduce the potential for violations occurring. The OIG has identified 4 potential risk areas that physician practices should focus on when developing its standards and policies and procedures: (1) coding and billing, (2) reasonable and necessary services, (3) documentation, and (4) improper inducements, kickbacks, and self-referrals. Although these identified risk areas are not exhaustive or complete, they generally will apply to most physician practices. There are other risk areas on which the practice may desire to focus in light of the practice's complexity and past history.

For coding and billing, the OIG has identified the most frequent subjects of investigations related to physician practices as follows:

- Billing for items or services not rendered or not provided as claimed
- Submitting claims for equipment, medical supplies, and services that are not reasonable and necessary
- Double billing resulting in duplicate payment
- Billing for noncovered services as if covered
- Knowing misuse of provider identification numbers, which results in improper billing
- Unbundling (billing for each component of the service instead of billing or using an all-inclusive code)
- Failure to properly use coding modifiers
- Clustering
- Upcoding the level of service provided.

If any of these are potential risk areas for a given physician practice, a comprehensive policy and procedure regarding each applicable risk area should be developed. As noted previously, training regarding each of these risk areas, including any adopted policy and procedure, should occur with all applicable employees, including physicians.

Medical necessity is also a high-risk area for many physician practices. Although physicians can order any test or service that they believe is medically necessary based on the patient's medical condition, Medicare, as well as other third-party payers, has established its own definition of what services it deems to be reasonable and necessary based on a patient's condition. Physician practices need to actively evaluate all services ordered by a physician to determine whether, on the basis of the patient's condition, the test will meet the reasonable and necessary standards by the applicable third-party payer. Many physicians evaluate the medical necessity criteria through booklets or payer Web sites, and some physician practices have purchased medical necessity screening software that will evaluate the patient's documented medical condition to determine whether such documented condition meets the payers' criteria.

Medical necessity documentation usually focuses on the provider's documentation of the patient's medical condition, which establishes the reason for ordering the test or service. Some of the medical necessity criteria are based on comorbidities experienced by the patient. Thus, it is very important that the practice's policies and procedures related to medical necessity documentation emphasize that the medical record must document all of the patient's applicable medical conditions, including comorbidities, which may justify the ordering of a test or procedure.

One of the most important compliance issues facing physician practices relates to the documentation of the diagnosis and treatment. Such documentation will establish the reason the physician ordered a test or procedure. Medical record documentation can also be used to (1) identify the provider, (2) determine whether the services provided were medically necessary, (3) determine the accuracy of the claim billed, and (4) identify the location where the provider provided the service. The OIG has provided internal documentation guidelines that physician practices might use to ensure the accuracy of medical record documentation, which include the following:

- The medical record is complete and legible.
- The documentation of each patient encounter includes the reason for the encounter; any relevant history; physical examination findings; prior diagnostic test results; assessment; clinical impression or diagnosis; plan of care; and date and legible identity of the observer.
- If not documented, the rationale for ordering diagnostic and other ancillary services can be easily inferred by an independent reviewer or third party who has appropriate medical training.

- Current Procedural Terminology and International Classification of Diseases, Ninth Revision, Clinical Modification codes used for claims submission are supported by documentation and the medical records.
- Appropriate health risk factors are identified. The patient's progress, his or her response to treatment, and any changes in treatment and any revision in diagnosis are documented.

As emphasized above, it is important that the practice's policies and procedures focus on obtaining appropriate documentation that is consistent with the care provided and that conforms to the third-party payers' requirements. For medical record documentation, the practice should focus on how to improve documentation to be consistent with the care provided and third-party requirements. The physicians' coding frequency can be compared to that of other similarly situated physicians to determine whether the distribution of services provided by the physician is consistent with national or regional norms. However, just because the physicians' coding distribution is not consistent with the average coding distribution for the specialty does not necessarily mean that the coding is incorrect or that the physician is not providing appropriate services. The physicians' coding distribution needs to be consistent with the patients under the physicians' care and the medical ailments treated by the physicians. The policies and procedures regarding medical record documentation can assist in ensuring that the physicians' medical records support the services provided and claims submitted for reimbursement.

The policies and procedures should also cover the proper completion of the Centers for Medicare and Medicaid Services (CMS) Form 1500. On the form, the diagnosis code for evaluation and management services selected needs to be consistent with the reason for the visit or service. All applicable modifiers should be included. Further, the practice needs to provide CMS with information regarding a beneficiary's other possible insurance coverage under the Medicare Secondary Payer Policy.

Another significant area for the physician practice relates to improper inducements, kickbacks, and self-referrals. The practice needs to establish policies and procedures and strict adherence to the require-ments under the AKS and Stark Law to ensure that any financial arrangement between the physicians, including the physician practice, and other providers, including designated health service enti-ties such as hospitals, are consistent with all legal requirements. The practice needs to establish, through its policies and procedures, docu-mentation requirements for all financial arrangements with other medical providers to ensure that all financial arrangements are commer-cially reasonable and at fair market value. A best practice would include having all such financial arrangements evaluated by a knowledgeable health care attorney or health care consultant who is familiar with the type of financial arrangement sought and the compensation arrangement proposed.

As noted previously in this book, the risks for violating the AKS and Stark Law are high and can subject the practice to significant investiga-tion costs, fines, and penalties if a violation occurs. Further, even being investigated can have severe financial repercussions on the practice. It is because of these risks and potential costs that the physician prac-tice needs to establish, by policy and procedure, an effective process to evaluate all financial arrangements that could possibly implicate the AKS and Stark Law. If the practice is large enough and has sufficient resources, all such financial arrangements should be reviewed and approved by a centralized committee within the practice. This commit-tee should include, as a member, the compliance officer. If the practice is not large enough to have sufficient resources to establish an approval committee, simply having the proposed financial arrangements reviewed by a knowledgeable and experienced health care attorney is sufficient. Many physicians rely on the opinions expressed by the party with whom they desire to enter into a financial arrangement, such as a hospital. However, if the hospital is not receiving adequate advice, such reliance will be at the practice's peril. It is better to commit the resources up front to evaluate the financial arrangement to ensure compliance with all applicable statutes and laws, including the AKS and Stark Law, than have the financial arrangement be investigated and reviewed by entities such as the OIG or the Department of Justice and found to be inappropriate.

There are numerous other areas about which the physician practice may desire to adopt a formal policy and procedure. Other areas on which the practice may desire to focus include the following:

- Appointment scheduling
- Employee orientation
- Nonretaliation policy
- Disciplinary actions
- Evaluation and management coding
- Procedure coding
- Credit balances
- Billing
- Documentation standards
- Collections
- Office registration
- Medicare secondary payer
- Advanced beneficiary notices
- Code of conduct
- Nonphysician providers
- Patient privacy
- Patient security
- Patient supervision
- Fee schedules
- Modifiers
- Multiple procedures
- Unbundled procedures
- Laboratory
- Radiology
- Patient relations
- Marketing and public relations

- Medical record retention
- Financial management and accounting
- Patients who speak a foreign language.

The process of writing a policy and procedure should not be rushed. The first step is to understand the risk area; second, to determine how the risk area impacts the practice; third, to determine how the risk area can be managed within the physician practice; fourth, to determine what safeguards need to be established to identify, minimize, or eliminate the risk; fifth, to determine who within the physician practice needs to be accountable for the risk area; and sixth, to determine how the risk area is to be monitored. Step 7 is to draft the policy and procedure on the basis of steps 1 through 6. After the policy and procedure are drafted, they should be shared with those involved in the activity to determine whether the policy and procedure can be implemented effectively within the physician practice. Once there is appropriate buy-in regarding the policy and procedure, all applicable employees will need to be trained regarding the policy and procedure. Thereafter, the practice will need to monitor the risk area to ensure that the policy and procedure are being followed.

The policies and procedures implemented by the practice should be dynamic, meaning that they apply specifically to the unique practice. As operations change, the policies and procedures applicable to the practice should likewise change to be consistent with the change in operations. When the practice reviews risk areas, if an operational change is required to further reduce or eliminate the risk, the policies and procedures will need to be modified. Frequently, as a result of annual compliance training and education, recommendations will come from the employees regarding a proposed change in operations to ensure compliance. These recommendations need to be evaluated to determine whether such proposed changes can be made effectively and will further efforts to reduce risk within the physician practice. These comments can also come through other reporting mechanisms, including direct recommendations to the compliance officer.

It would be a mistake to draft policies and procedures and not monitor the operations to ensure that they are consistent with the policies and procedures. It is likewise a mistake to draft a policy and procedure and never reevaluate them to see whether changes are required. Thus, the practice needs to be diligent in continuing to monitor and modify the policies and procedures as a performance improvement function.

The good news about policies and procedures is that the practice may not have to draft them from scratch. Many third-party companies offer template policies and procedures that can be modified to conform to the practice's operation. Further, other similar practices may be willing to share their policies and procedures, which can be adapted. The compliance officer can network with other compliance officers affiliated with similar physician practices to obtain prototype policies and procedures that can be evaluated. This is another reason to commit the resources to have the compliance officer attend national and regional meetings with other physician practice compliance officers so that compliance best practices can be shared. At these meetings and conferences, compliance officers can freely share practices and discuss what works and does not work, thereby improving the practice's own policies and procedures.

If another similar physician practice is attempting to develop policies and procedures, such policies and procedures could be jointly developed. In this way the costs related to the development can be shared, reducing the amount of resources each practice will need to dedicate in the development of the compliance program's policies and procedures.

There are risks associated with the development of the practice's policies and procedures. If a policy and procedure are developed and not followed, and the lack of strict adherence causes an inappropriate claim for reimbursement to be submitted, the policy and procedure can be used against the practice in an associated investigation. For example, if the practice establishes a policy to have all tests ordered assessed with the medical necessity determination of applicable third-party payers, and the practice does not carry out this policy, the practice could be faulted with lack of adherence to its own policies and procedures.

At the commencement of many governmental investigations, the investigating entity, such as the OIG or Department of Justice, will ask the physician practice to provide copies of all of its compliance policies and procedures. If strict adherence to the practice's policies and procedures is not met, and the government believes that such lack of strict adherence resulted in inappropriate reimbursement, the government may allege that the lack of strict adherence was intentional. As noted previously in this book, if the government can prove knowledge, it can bring claims under the False Claims Act (FCA) for inappropriate reimbursement received by the practice. This is especially true if the lack of strict adherence was systemic, instead of just an isolated infraction. This possible risk emphasizes the reason to continuously train the employees regarding the compliance policies and procedures and periodically reevaluate the policies and procedures to determine whether any changes are required because of changes in either operations or payer requirements.

Even though there is possible risk connected with the lack of strict adherence to policies and procedures, it is still a best practice to develop them around risk areas that impact the practice.

3.5   Review and Monitoring

Physician practices should have a strong review and monitoring program as a component of their compliance program. This review and monitoring component should apply to (1) the medical necessity determination for tests and procedures, (2) medical record documentation, (3) codes billed, and (4) reimbursement received. The review and monitoring program will assess all of these components to ensure that the claims made by the physician practice and reimbursement received can be defended on the basis of the medical condition of the patient and the documentation in the medical record. This is a documentation-intensive analysis that requires a review of all supporting documentation to ensure that such documentation is appropriate with respect to the reimbursement paid for the services provided. Many physician practices operate on a paper medical record basis. As a result, when the medical record documentation is reviewed and monitored, the paper medical record must be assessed and evaluated. Many physician practices are implementing, and many have already implemented, an electronic medical record. For those practices, the review and monitoring will be based on the electronic medical record developed by the practice.

For those physician practices that have a paper medical record, it is imperative that the practice maintain a full and accurate copy of the medical record and that all medical record documentation requirements are followed. Paper medical records, by their nature, require the practice to assemble all applicable paper records and maintain such paper records in each patient's medical record file. This means that all progress notes, tests ordered, procedure results, and analysis must be obtained and such documentation must be assembled in the patient's medical record file. If a practice gets behind in its assembly of paper documentation, a review and monitoring program can be compromised due to the lack of documentation in a patient's medical record to support the service provided. Thus, it is imperative that physician practices keep current with all medical record documentation so that each patient's medical record can be maintained in a complete, current, and accurate status. If a physician falls behind in dictation, this will have a severe negative impact on the practice's review and monitoring program.

Electronic medical records are easier to review and monitor, as all applicable documentation is maintained within the practice's computerized electronic medical record system. Electronic medical records, however, are not without risk. Many electronic medical records establish templates regarding the physician-patient encounter. As long as the electronically generated template conforms with the evaluation and assessment by the physician, such a template will make the physician's documentation function easier than with a paper medical record. However, because the electronic templates are selected as options by the physicians, through the selection of the template encounter, a procedure or evaluation and management code is generated. If the electronic template selected does not conform with either the medical condition of the patient or the service provided by the physician, an inappropriate code will be generated. Thus, for physician practices that utilize an electronic medical record, the review and monitoring program must include the ability to determine whether the template description of the service provided or medical condition of the patient as selected by the physician is accurate.

When physician practices begin a review and monitoring program as a component of their compliance program, they should begin with a baseline review of the claims reimbursed by federal and state agencies and managed care companies to determine the compliance level of the practice's documentation, coding, and billing with respect to the applicable requirements. Once a baseline review has been performed, periodic reviews can focus on the areas where errors were discovered during the baseline review.

The baseline and periodic reviews do not require a 100% review of each medical record. The practice could commence with a 10% review of records, with the selected records representing a cross section of the type of services the practice provides. It is recommended that a certified coder perform the payment review, as coders have the requisite training to perform a claims review. The certified coder could either be employed by the physician practice or be an independent contractor hired by the practice. Even if the physician practice has a certified coder on its staff, it is a best practice, both at the commencement of the review program and periodically thereafter, to have the practice's claims reviewed by an independent reviewer to validate the accuracy of the internal reviews. Independent reviews are less likely to be influenced by internal pressure within the practice. It is important to evaluate the qualifications and certification of the coder selected to ensure that he or she has the requisite knowledge and expertise in the practice's specialties.

When a prospective third-party coder is evaluated, a review of the coder's training and experience is required. The practice needs to evaluate the coder's certification to ensure that the coder is certified to review claims in the practice's specialties. Other clients of the coder should also be contacted to determine whether the prospective coder is a correct fit to conduct the review and audit of the practice. In addition to the prospective coder's certification and training in the practice's area of specialty, determining whether the coder's personality fits with the culture of the practice is important. Although it is important to have a coder who is well trained in the practice's specialties, it is equally important to have one who can conduct the audit and review in a manner that has minimal impact on the practice's normal operation and patient care services. The practice will also want to select an independent coder who will be impartial and provide review results that can be defended on the basis of third-party requirements.

Once a baseline review has been conducted and periodic reviews have been performed according to the issues identified in the baseline review, the physician practice can become more proactive with respect to other high-risk areas that may impact it. If a payer continuously seeks additional documentation for a particular procedure, the practice may want to perform a review focusing on this procedure to ensure that the procedure is being performed, and sufficient documentation is being obtained, to support the payment received for the procedure. Further, if the practice is aware that other practices are being reviewed for a particular procedure that the practice provides, a procedure-specific review can be performed to ensure that the performance of the procedure conforms with all requirements. Such awareness can be obtained either through the networking of the compliance officer or through a review of periodicals that are specific to the practice's area of specialization. This is one reason why it is important for the practice to be involved in any association that is specific to the practice's specialties.

Ideally, all reviews should be performed on a prospective basis. This means that the claims are reviewed prior to billing. If, as a result of the prospective review, errors or deficiencies are noted, the claim can be modified before it is billed. By conducting a prospective review, if errors are identified and claims modified before billing, the practice will not have review results that indicate that it has received reimbursement that, on the basis of the practice's review, it is not entitled to retain. As a result of performing prospective reviews, the practice is not identifying reimbursement received that could be potentially determined to be false claims. Thus, it is a prudent process to begin, if possible, with a prospective review rather than a retrospective one.

By contrast, if a retrospective review is performed and errors are identified, the practice will be required to repay such errors as it now has actual knowledge, through the performance of the retrospective review, that it has received reimbursement that is not supported by the medical record or through the medical necessity determination process.

As noted above, the results of all reviews can be shared with all physicians and employees involved as an educational opportunity and to ensure that any errors identified are not repeated.

If, as a result of performing a prospective review, an error has been identified that appears to be systemic in nature, or it is believed that the error has occurred over a long period of time, a retrospective review may be required. In a retrospective review, the practice will be reviewing the documentation and claims that have already been paid by third parties. Any errors identified in a retrospective review may require repayment to the payer. Typically, these repayments are based only on the claims reviewed. However, if the error is systemic and has existed for a long time, the error rate may have to be extrapolated over the claims paid during that period of time. For example, if the practice decides to conduct a retrospective review and an error rate of 20% is identified by reviewing a small subset of records, a statistically valid sample may need to be identified and reviewed. A certified coder can assist the practice in determining the number and types of claims that will need to be reviewed to generate a statistically valid review. If, as a result of performing a statistically valid review, the error rate is confirmed, such error rate may need to be extrapolated over the claims paid by all applicable payers. For example, if the error rate in the statistically valid review is 20% and the practice has received $10,000 from a payer, the extrapolated repayment may be $2000 ($10,000 × 20% error rate = $2000).

When errors are identified for claims that have already been paid, the practice will need to determine how and to whom to make the repayment. Depending on the nature of the results, a simple reprocessing of claims may be warranted. If the error is a result of a systemic problem or is determined through an extrapolation process, a repayment to the payer outside of the claims process may need to occur. Health care legal counsel should be consulted when making a repayment, especially outside of the claims reprocessing process, to ensure that the repayment is appropriately made and all necessary disclosures are provided.

Due to the complexity of the health care reimbursement system, repayment of claims based on reviews conducted by physician practices is commonplace. In fact, those physician practices that have developed effective compliance programs typically have a history of making repayments through either the claims reprocessing process or direct repayments to third-party payers. It is highly probable that some errors will occur in every physician practice. However, if physician practices implement an effective compliance program, which includes a review in monitoring program, such errors will be identified and corrected. If the practice has never made a repayment, it is because the practice (1) does not have an effective review and monitoring program, (2) has conducted reviews and has not determined that there are any claims paid that are not supported by the medical record, or (3) has identified claims that are not supportable but has chosen not to make any repayment. If the practice falls into the last category, it is incurring substantial risk, which may include possible criminal liability. It is because of these risks that implementing a review program as part of the practice's compliance program is imperative.

Another review area on which the practice should focus is its financial arrangements with referral sources. As noted previously in this book, financial arrangements with referral sources are a target area for the government. The practice will want to ensure that each financial arrangement with a referral source conforms to the AKS, the Stark Law, and all other applicable laws, rules, and regulations. One of the primary issues related to the financial arrangements with referral sources is to ensure that each arrangement is commercially reasonable and at fair market value. It is important for the practice to review each financial arrangement and have sufficient documentation by which it can defend the arrangement as being commercially reasonable and consistent with market values.

In conducting a review of the financial arrangements, it is important to review the source of the payments and determine whether such payment can be defended on the basis of the documentation maintained by the physician practice. All financial payments paid to and received from referral sources or entities to which the physicians refer patients should be identified. The practice should determine whether a written agreement exists that sets forth the specifics regarding the financial arrangement the practice has with the referral person or entity. The practice will then need to determine whether it has sufficient documentation to support the services rendered or, if the arrangement is an ownership or investment interest, whether such ownership or investment interest, and the return therefrom, is consistent with the investment made and the applicable requirements under the AKS and Stark Law. For example, if any of the physicians have a medical directorship with a designated health service entity, such as a hospital, the practice needs to determine whether it has sufficient documentation supporting the hours paid for such medical directorship. Typically, these hours will be documented through monthly time records. A form for the time record is included as Figure 3-4. It is important for the protection of the physician practice that these time records be maintained to defend any payment made by such entity to the physician practice. The hourly rate received for such services must be fair market value and commercially reasonable on the basis of the services performed and the tenure and expertise of the physician performing the services. This is a critical monitoring aspect of the practice's compliance program to ensure adherence to the AKS and Stark Law. Audit forms to review physician financial arrangements are included as Figure 3-5.

As noted above, auditing and monitoring must begin with a baseline assessment of the physician practice. Once the baseline assessment is determined, the practice can implement a more detailed and rigorous review and monitoring program of its documentation, coding, billing, and reimbursement received. When errors or irregularities are identified, corrective action is required. Such corrective action may include

Organization Name

PHYSICIAN: MEDICAL DIRECTOR OF:

«FirstName» «LastName», «Title»   _____

PAY PERIOD: _____   «JobTitle»

For a complete listing of duties please refer to the Medical Director Agreement.

Please indicate time in half-hour increments.

DUTIES	1	2	3	4	5	6	7	8	9	10	11	12	13	14	15	16	17	18	19	20	21	22	23	24	25	26	27	28	29	30	31
A. Providing program assistance, guidance, and recommendations																															
B. Providing medical guidance and direction																															
C. Providing educational in-services and/or conferences																															

Created [date]   [electronic file name and path]   page 1 of 2

FIGURE 3-4   Physician Pay Period Chart

140

D. Administrative duties																																			
E. Discussing and reviewing treatment																																			
F. Acting as physician liaison																																			
G. Meeting regularly with clinic staff. Attending meetings as requested																																			
H. Other																																			

(a) GRAND TOTAL: _____

Approved by: _____

«FirstName» «LastName», «Title»   Date

* In addition to the above, please generally describe the services performed this month.

Created [date]   [electronic file name and path]

page 2 of 2

FIGURE 3-4 | Physician Pay Period Chart (Continued)

141

[Physician Practice Name]

DOCUMENT PRODUCTION CHECKLIST

The following is a list of documents that are required to be copied and assembled in the order they appear on this checklist. If the document is located and copied, place a checkmark before the description of the document. If the document either is not applicable or could not be located, insert N/A in the space before the document description.

Contract Party: _____

Contract Type:

☐ Leases in MOB

☐ Employment - Medical Administration

☐ Employment - Teaching

☐ Independent Contractor - Clinical

☐ Physician Recruitment

☐ Other

☐ Leases - Other Than MOB

☐ Employment - Clinical

☐ Independent Contractor
 - Medical Administration

☐ Independent Contractor
 - Teaching

☐ Hospital-Based Group

Created [date]   [electronic file name and path]   page 1 of 4

FIGURE 3-5 | Document Production Checklist

List and Description of Documents	
	Executed copy of contract and all amendments
	Fair market value documentation supporting the financial arrangement in the contract
	Minutes of meeting where contract was discussed and approved
	List of all payments made to and from contract party related to the contract
	Legal review of contract (both internal and external)
	Time sheets submitted by contract party
	Productivity data if any portion of compensation is based on productivity
The following documents apply only to recruitment arrangements:	
	Community need analysis
	For income guarantees, financial documentation relied on for payment of income guarantee, including incremental expenses
	Documentation relied on supporting the reasonableness of amount of income guarantee or forgivable loan
	If contract does not specify, state where physician moved from, and when: Relocated from: _____ 　　　　　　　City　　　　　　　　　　State Date physician relocated: _____

FIGURE 3-5　|　Document Production Checklist (Continued)

[Physician Practice Name]

CONTRACT REVIEW CHART

Contract Type:	4. Employment (Clinical)	8. Independent Contractor (Teaching)
1. Lease in MOB	5. Employment (Teaching)	9. Hospital-based Group
2. Lease Other than MOB	6. Independent Contractor (Medical Administration)	10. Physician Recruitment
3. Employment (Medical Administration)	7. Independent Contractor (Clinical)	11. Other (Please Specify)

CONTRACTING PARTIES:

[Physician Practice Name] & _____, M.D.

ISSUE	FILE COMPLETE	REVIEWER COMMENTS
Executed Copy and All Amendments		***Agreement Name:*** ***Term:***
FMV Documentation Supporting Arrangement		***Compensation:*** ***Time:*** ***FMV Justification:***

Created [date]   [electronic file name and path]   page 3 of 4

FIGURE 3-5   Document Production Checklist (Continued)

Meeting Minutes with Discussion and Approval		***Committee Minutes:***
List of Payments to and from Party		***Aggregate Amounts:*** ***2008:*** ***2009:*** ***2010:***
Legal Review		
Time Sheets Submitted		
Productivity Data		
ADDITIONAL COMMENTS:		

FIGURE 3-5 | Document Production Checklist (Continued)

repayment or reprocessing of reimbursement received by the practice. As noted above, this is a normal function of a physician practice that has an effective compliance program. The practice's review and monitoring program should cover all third-party payers, including Medicare, Medicaid, and managed care companies. In addition to analyzing the reimbursement received by the practice, all financial arrangements between the practice and the physicians affiliated with it should be evaluated to ensure compliance with the AKS and Stark Law. As noted in Chapter 1, the Stark Law has strict "bright line" requirements that must be adhered to if the Stark Law is involved. Enhanced review and investigation regarding the Stark Law will occur, and it is imperative for all physician practices to ensure strict adherence to an applicable exception if any of its financial arrangements come under the Stark Law.

Because of the risks under the FCA, Stark Law, and AKS, physician practices should establish a strong review and monitoring program as part of their compliance program.

3.6 Responding to Compliance Issues

The physician practice should encourage its employees to report, in good faith, all suspected compliance concerns. By establishing a culture of encouraging employees to question the practice's adherence to compliance principles, the practice will be better able to investigate, on its own terms, any alleged compliance irregularity. It is better for the practice to receive good-faith concerns from employees than to have such employees report the concerns to other parties directly, such as the OIG or the Department of Justice. If the practice has a culture of open dialogue regarding suspected compliance issues, it is less likely that employees will feel as if the only way to have the issues addressed and resolved is to report their concerns to the government. To encourage employees to report suspected compliance concerns, the physician practice must have a policy against retaliation against those who bring

Physician Practice	POLICY/PROCEDURE	
Subject: **PROBLEM REPORTING and NONRETALIATION**	Eff. Date: 1/1/08	Revised: 1/1/09

Reporting and Nonretaliation

Purpose

The physician practice understands that a critical part of its compliance program is the promotion of a culture that seeks to prevent, detect, and resolve conduct that either does not conform, or is believed not to conform, with any federal, state, and private payer requirements, as well as the physician practice's policies and procedures. To promote this culture, the physician practice establishes a reporting process and a strict nonretaliation policy to protect employees and others who report problems and concerns in good faith from retaliation. The physician practice understands that any retaliation or retribution, whether overt or covert, can undermine the problem reporting process and sever the open lines of communication for reporting compliance concerns.

Policy

1. All employees are required, and have an affirmative duty and responsibility, to report perceived misconduct, including actual or potential violations of laws, regulations, policies or procedures, or the physician practice's code of conduct.

2. Key leadership within the physician practice will encourage employees to report problems and concerns through ordinary reporting channels.

FIGURE 3-6 | Reporting and Nonretaliation

3. Employees are encouraged to use the physician practice's reporting process. The physician practice has established a process that employees can use to remain anonymous, which includes [insert anonymous reporting process].

4. If an employee, once making a good-faith report, does not believe that the issue has been sufficiently investigated and resolved, the employee is encouraged to report the issue up the chain of command, including reporting the issue to the physician practice's compliance officer.

5. Any form of retaliation against any employee who reports a perceived problem or concern in good faith is strictly prohibited.

6. Any form of retaliation will be subject to discipline, including up to termination.

7. Employees cannot use the reporting process to exempt themselves from consequences if they were participants in the activity being reported. However, self-reporting may be taken into account in determining the appropriate corrective action.

Procedures

The following procedures apply to all employees:

1. Any actual knowledge of facts that would be an actual, potential, or perceived violation of law, regulation, policy, procedure, or the physician practice's code of conduct must be immediately reported to the employee's supervisor, to the physician practice's compliance officer, or through the physician practice's anonymous reporting process.

2. If any employee knows that a violation of this policy has occurred, such violation must be reported to the physician practice's compliance officer or through the physician practice's anonymous reporting process.

FIGURE 3-6 | Reporting and Nonretaliation (Continued)

3. Employees may also report any problems or concerns, including potential compliance concerns, to the physician practice's human resource officer.

4. If an employee reports a compliance concern to his or her supervisor or another person in key leadership, and the issue has not been satisfactorily resolved, the employee is required to report the concern to the physician practice's compliance officer.

5. Key leadership of the physician practice are required to support this policy and encourage the good-faith reporting of problems and concerns through the mechanisms described in this policy. At a minimum, supervisors should (1) meet with their direct reports to discuss the main objectives of this policy and (2) provide access to a copy of this policy to all members of the department.

6. The physician practice's compliance officer is responsible for investigating any reported retaliation against an employee who reported a compliance concern in good faith.

7. The physician practice's compliance officer will report the results of any investigation regarding suspected retaliation to the physician practice's board of directors.

FIGURE 3-6 | Reporting and Nonretaliation (Continued)

compliance issues to the practice's attention. The nonretaliation policy should be in writing and also should be exemplified through practice. A sample nonretaliation policy is included as Figure 3-6. If any employee suspects retaliation because he or she, in good faith, brought a compliance concern to the practice's attention, such allegation of retaliation must be thoroughly investigated.

Investigations regarding possible retaliation are challenging. The employee who suspects retaliation must be interviewed to determine the basis of such belief. Many times, the alleged retaliation will be in the form of discipline regarding job performance. For example, if the employee was given a written reprimand for poor job performance, the employee may allege that such written reprimand was motivated by retaliation due to his or her report of a compliance concern, especially if the concern involved the employee's supervisor or superior. Next, the supervisor who provided the written reprimand will need to be interviewed and the basis on which the written reprimand was given needs to be analyzed to determine whether such written reprimand was warranted despite the employee's compliance allegation. It is important to have someone with human resources or employment law experience assist the practice on these type of investigations to assist in making the determination regarding whether the written reprimand was warranted. If the allegation of retaliation is correct, disciplinary action must be taken against the individual who retaliated. If the practice determines that no retaliation has occurred, this should be communicated to the employee who alleged retaliation, including providing the employee with information regarding the results of the investigation. Frequently, if the result of the investigation is a determination that no retaliation has occurred, the employee will disagree with the conclusion. Therefore, it is very important to have maintained full and complete documentation regarding the investigation and the facts that were relied on in making the final determination that no retaliation occurred.

If the practice is large enough, it is important for the compliance officer to have a list of those employees who have brought compliance concerns to the attention of the practice. If any type of disciplinary action is taken against any of these individuals, the compliance officer should be notified so that the he or she can make a determination as to whether the disciplinary action could have been motivated by retaliation. It is better to be proactive in this area instead of waiting to see if any such employees are going to assert a retaliation claim.

All legitimate compliance concerns should be thoroughly investigated. It is important, however, not to jump to the conclusion that the concern being reported is true and accurate. The person receiving compliance concerns, usually the compliance officer, needs to document the facts as being alleged by the employee bringing the compliance concern to the attention of the practice. The purpose of the investigation is to review the facts to assess whether the compliance concern has merit and whether the facts will prove that corrective action is necessary.

After a compliance concern has been reported, and the practice believes that the concern was reported in good faith, an internal investigation should begin. The investigation could be performed by the practice's compliance officer, another employee within the practice, or an independent third party. Compliance investigations need to review the nature of the compliance concern, including potential interviews of individuals involved with the issue. It is important to emphasize to employees that their participation in a compliance investigation is required for their continued employment by the practice. If a third party is brought in to perform the investigation, especially if that third party is an attorney, it is important that the third party emphasize that it does not represent the employees individually, and all issues identified through the investigation process will be communicated to the appropriate individuals within the practice.

Compliance investigations must be carried out in an intentional and structured format. The investigation should define what facts are known and what facts need to be reviewed to determine the accuracy of the concern. After the structure of the investigation is drafted, the investigation should proceed to obtain all necessary facts. This could include the generation of billing reports, if the concern relates to a possible billing problem. If the concern deals with a possible violation of law, or billing regulation, such law or regulation needs to be researched to ensure that the practice has sufficient documentation regarding the required standard. This may result in the engagement of a health care attorney or a third-party coder or auditor to assist with the investigation.

Interviews, as part of an investigation, also need to be highly structured. The types of questions to be asked and the facts to be reviewed should be carefully documented before any interview is conducted. Ideally, 2 persons representing the practice should conduct the interview, with 1 person being an observer. Meticulous notes should be taken regarding the issues discussed during the interview. After the interview, a memorandum regarding the facts discussed or identified during the interview should be drafted. If an attorney is one of the interviewers, any legal conclusions drawn from the interview should be documented in a separate written instrument, apart from the fact-based memorandum, protected by the attorney-client privilege.

All information and records regarding the investigation should be maintained in a separate centralized file. Depending on the nature of the investigation, such documentation may need to be locked with limited access or even stored at an offsite facility, such as the office of the practice's legal counsel.

At the conclusion of the investigation, the facts and applicable statutes and regulations need to be analyzed to determine whether the compliance concern was validated through the internal investigation. An official report regarding the results of the investigation needs to be made to key leadership with a recommendation regarding possible corrective action, if warranted.

If a compliance concern is validated, appropriate corrective action must be taken. If the issue pertains to billing, repayment may be warranted. If the issue is a human resource one, appropriate disciplinary action may be required. It is important to "talk the talk and walk the walk." If the organization is going to encourage adherence to compliance principles, then it must be prepared to implement corrective action if compliance concerns are determined to be valid. If a compliance concern has been validated and the practice does not take appropriate corrective action, not only could there be legal consequences for inaction, but the cultural emphasis the practice has placed on compliance will be negatively impacted. The emphasis on compliance must begin at the top with those individuals who are the key managers of the physician practice. If, as a result of a thorough investigation, the compliance concern is not validated, then this determination, along with supporting documentation, should be provided to the individual who brought the concern to the practice's attention. It is important to close the investigation with the reporting person, if known, so that the person will understand that the practice took the concern seriously, conducted a thorough investigation, and concluded the investigation with sound reasoning obtained from the review of the facts and applicable legal and regulatory requirements.

Employees should also be rewarded for their participation in compliance initiatives. Compliance investigations can be emotional, and rewarding employees for being involved in compliance investigations furthers the practice's emphasis on a strong and effective compliance program. Such awards could be logo items such as shirts or even public recognition for the employee *doing the right thing*. The emotional aspect of an internal investigation cannot be overstated. Those involved in an internal investigation, especially those who may have been accused of a compliance breach, may feel as if their personal integrity has been challenged. It is important to emphasize to such employees that internal investigations are merely one component of an effective compliance program. Frequently, errors occur because of a lack of education or resources. If the investigation does not identify anyone with actual intent to do wrong, the investigation will probably conclude with further dedication of resources and more training regarding the conduct that led to the compliance breach. It is because of this emotional component of internal investigations that employees involved in such investigations need to be supported and encouraged as well as given positive reinforcement at the conclusion of the investigation.

All documentation regarding the investigation results should be maintained by the practice. These documents will show the efforts and resources committed by the practice to review suspected issues and to implement appropriate corrective actions.

If the practice has an effective compliance program, it will have a history of appropriately responding to compliance concerns. Responding to compliance concerns is a tangible way to show the employees in the practice that it is serious about operating a compliant practice.

3.7   Open Lines of Communication

It is extremely important to establish open lines of communication and encourage employees to bring compliance concerns to the attention of the practice. As noted previously, if employees are bringing compliance concerns to the practice's attention, the practice will be able to investigate the compliance concern and implement appropriate corrective actions. Alternately, if employees feel that open lines of communication do not exist, their only recourse to correct compliance concerns would be to bring the issue to the attention of the government. If the government initiates an investigation against the practice, the practice will be placed in a defensive posture and will have to respond to the government's structure and timing of the investigation, instead of conducting the investigation within its own structure and allocation of resources.

Responding to a government-initiated investigation can be very damaging to the practice. Government-initiated investigations substantially disrupt the normal operation of a physician practice. Instead of focusing on providing quality patient care, the practice will need to dedicate resources to producing information and corresponding with the lead investigators from the government. If the government is in control of the investigation, not only will they have every right to access the practice's medical and financial records, but they also have the right to interview the staff, physicians, and patients. All of these interviews by government investigators can have a huge emotional and public relations impact on the practice. For example, if a government investigator interviews a patient and the patient is handed a business card that has the title "Fraud Investigator" on it, the patient may perceive that the physicians and practice are involved in fraudulent activity. This can also create challenges for the physician and practice to continue to provide necessary medical treatment if patients believe that fraud may have occurred within the practice.

Responding to government investigations can also be costly from a financial prospective. The practice will need to hire expert legal and other consultants who are knowledgeable about responding to governmental investigations. These professionals not only will interact with the government investigators, but also will need to review and approve all documentation being submitted as part of the government investigation.

Because of the cost and disruption the practice will face if it is involved in a government investigation, it is highly advisable to encourage and solicit feedback and concerns from employees through open lines of communication.

As stated previously, encouraging open lines of communication begins with the top leadership of the practice. Key leaders need to overtly encourage employees to bring compliance concerns to the practice's attention. Further, when an employee does bring up a compliance concern, the employee should be encouraged and thanked for making the report. Nothing will terminate the open lines of communication more quickly than an employee being reprimanded or criticized for expressing concern. If one employee is the recipient of discipline or criticism for reporting a compliance concern, other employees will use that person as an example and will decide not to report issues within the structure of the compliance program. If employees believe that open lines of communication do not exist, they will choose not to discuss the issues, resign from their positions, or, as noted above, bring the issue to the attention of the government or a *qui tam* realtor. As discussed previously in this book, if an employee becomes a *qui tam* realtor, any recovery can be shared with that person.

Besides establishing a culture of reporting compliance concerns, the practice needs to adopt a structure through which employees can bring these concerns to the attention of the practice and compliance officer.

If the practice is large enough, an anonymous reporting process should be implemented. This is typically accomplished through a hotline, usually monitored and operated by an independent third party. There are many third-party providers of anonymous hotlines; the price will vary depending on the size of the practice and the type of services being requested from the third-party hotline provider. However, if the practice is not large enough to engage the services of a third-party hotline, it can implement an internal hotline through which employees can report compliance concerns anonymously. The internal hotline can be simply a telephone extension that immediately rings into voicemail on which employees can report their concern. The greeting on the voicemail must be carefully crafted so that the employee is encouraged to leave a message, and the greeting should emphasize the practice's policy against retaliation. If the telephone system is capable of monitoring the number of calls and the number of calls made for which a voicemail message was not left can be determined, the practice may need to analyze the hotline greeting to determine whether it is encouraging the reporting of compliance concerns.

If the practice is not large enough to have either an external or anonymous internal hotline, then it should at least establish a box in which employees' compliance concerns can be deposited in writing. The box should be locked and be accessible only by the compliance officer. A sample compliance issue request is included as Figure 3-7.

Another approach that can be used to protect the anonymity of the employees is to encourage employees who desire to bring a compliance concern to the attention of the practice on an anonymous basis to establish a free Web-based e-mail account. Once the e-mail account is established, employees can e-mail their compliance concerns to the compliance officer's attention for review and investigation. If the identity of the employee is anonymous, the compliance officer can respond to the employee's blind e-mail account to confirm receipt of the compliance concern and communicate the status of the investigation and corrective action taken as a result of the investigation and analysis of the alleged facts.

Another critical aspect of establishing open lines of communication is for the practice to encourage employees to bring compliance concerns

COMPLIANCE CONCERN REPORT

Please describe below, using as much detail as possible, the suspected compliance issue and background information regarding the issue/concern:

Compliance issue: _____

_____

Why is this a compliance concern/risk? _____

_____

_____

Documents to be reviewed: _____

_____

_____

Persons involved/knowledgeable of issue: _____

_____

_____

Name (Optional - You can remain anonymous if you leave this area blank):

_____

_____

If you provide your name, we will be able to contact you for other information/ documentation and to update you regarding status of review.

Created [date]   [electronic file name and path]   page 1 of 1

FIGURE 3-7 | Compliance Concern Report

to the attention of the compliance officer. As noted previously in this chapter, as long as the compliance officer is approachable, and if employees genuinely believe that the compliance officer will ensure that the practice remains compliant, direct access through the compliance officer may be the best avenue through which employees will bring these concerns to the attention of the practice.

All compliance concerns brought to the attention of the practice, regardless of the avenue used, should be documented. The date and time, and the avenue through which the employee brought the compliance concern, should be tracked. As noted above, if there is a good-faith belief that the allegation has merit, a thorough investigation should occur. The results of the investigation of a compliance concern should be documented in a file. Separate files should be kept on each good-faith reported compliance concern. All documentation related to the compliance concern and the results of each investigation should be kept in each compliance file.

Providing feedback to those reporting compliance concerns is very important in fostering open lines of communication. If reports are made and no feedback is provided, and if tangible corrective action is not made, the employee may believe that the practice intentionally chose to do nothing about the reported concern. In fact, the practice may have conducted a thorough investigation and concluded that no breach occurred. If an independent third party is used to monitor the hotline, typically a process is provided for the anonymous caller to call back and receive information regarding the results of the investigation of the hotline report. Typically, these employees are given an identifying number assigned to their issue that they can use when they call back in to the hotline to receive updates regarding the investigation and the ultimate outcome of the investigation. If the practice is using an internal hotline, it will be difficult to provide anonymous feedback to the caller regarding the status and outcome of the investigation. Likewise, if the practice is using a compliance suggestion box, feedback will be impossible unless the individual was identified in his or her statement.

All good-faith compliance concerns, and the avenue of the reporting of such concerns, should be communicated to the leadership of the physician practice.

The leadership should monitor the existence of compliance concerns, the avenues through which the compliance concerns are being reported, and the nature of the investigations, and ensure that appropriate cor-rective action and closure regarding all compliance concerns have been performed. Further, any monitoring related to the corrective actions should likewise be reported to the leadership of the physician practice so that they can be assured that any corrective action taken is being appropriately implemented. Frequently, these reports will be made at meetings of the key leadership, like the meetings of the board of directors. During these meetings, the compliance officer should be in attendance and be able to answer any questions regarding the reported compliance concerns and investigation status. If a reporting avenue is not being utilized, the leadership of the practice should investigate why compliance concerns are not being reported through such an avenue. For example, if the practice has established an external hotline and no hotline calls have been received, a survey of the employees should be conducted to determine whether they fear retaliation for bringing com-pliance concerns forward. If the result of the survey indicates a fear of retaliation, the practice's nonretaliation policy should be further rein-forced. Despite well-written nonretaliation policies, many employees will fear retaliation. Because of this fear, the practice must be very vigi-lant to investigate all allegations of retaliation.

Open lines of communication can also be encouraged through the annual and periodic training and education, and periodic compliance reinforcement included in employee newsletters, posters promoting the practice's reporting processes, computer screen savers, and other promo-tions from the compliance officer and compliance department.

Employees generally want to do the right thing and to work for a practice that desires to operate in compliance with all applicable rules and regulations. If the practice promotes compliance and a culture of no retaliation, employees will bring compliance issues to the atten-tion of the practice. The primary purpose of emphasizing open lines of communication is so that the employees will bring compliance concerns directly to the attention of the practice instead of reverting to reporting the concerns to the government or a *qui tam* attorney.

3.8   Disciplinary Action

Most government guidance on the development and implementation of effective compliance programs state that a component of a compliance program needs to involve disciplinary actions taken against individuals who violate a physician practice's compliance program or applicable statutes, rules, and regulations. It is preferred, however, to talk in terms of accountability. Accountability means holding the physicians and employees responsible for adherence to the compliance program, including code of conduct and all applicable statutes, rules, and regulations. Accountability has 2 sides. The first is to recognize and reward employees for doing the right thing. Thus, it is important that the compliance program consider how it will reward employees who are actively involved in the program and seek to adhere to and promote it. This includes recognizing employees with token awards or annual evaluation credit for their adherence to the practice's compliance program.

The other side of accountability is disciplinary. If individuals have been involved in compliance breaches, appropriate disciplinary action must be taken. Depending on the nature of the compliance breach, simple warnings can be issued, and in egregious cases, termination of the employee may be warranted. As part of the compliance program, the practice should adopt a policy that generally delineates between severity of compliance breaches and resulting disciplinary action that may be taken for compliance violations.

Typically, employees want to do the right thing. Compliance breaches are usually a result of ignorance or lack of resources, especially lack of education regarding job-specific functions. If the compliance breach was the result of such ignorance or lack of education, the employee should be provided appropriate education with a warning that if further compliance breaches regarding the same issue occur in the future, heightened disciplinary action may be taken. If, however, an intentional breach occurs, aggressive disciplinary action should occur. This is especially true with respect to physician documentation and coding practices. If the practice determines that a physician is ordering medically unnecessary services or is intentionally upcoding procedures to increase reimbursement, aggressive disciplinary action must be taken. Alternatively, if a physician is a champion for the practice's compliance program, he or she should be appropriately rewarded and encouraged. For example, if a physician is performing consistently with all requirements, or has improved his or her compliance with billing and documentation requirements, he or she should be recognized with a token award or public recognition.

Disciplinary action for compliance issues should also be monitored to ensure that compliance breaches of equal severity receive substantially equivalent disciplinary action. Documentation regarding all disciplinary action taken as a result of compliance breaches should be monitored, documented, and tracked by the person who is responsible for the human resources function of the physician practice. If certain individuals are given less severe disciplinary action for substantially equivalent compliance breaches, problems with the enforcement of the compliance program will occur, and possible legal action can be taken by individuals who receive more severe discipline than other similarly situated employees for substantially similar compliance breaches. For example, if a physician and a registration clerk commit substantially similar compliance breaches, but the registration clerk is disciplined more harshly than the physician, an inequitable result will occur and the physicians, because of their status within the physician practice, will be presumed by the nonphysician employees to be above the compliance program. A class of individuals within the physician practice cannot be given more favorable treatment. Otherwise, the culture within the physician practice would indicate that there is a double standard with respect to adherence to the terms and conditions of the compliance program. Simply stated, if physicians are allowed to commit compliance breaches without discipline, it will be perceived that physicians do not need to adhere to the compliance program, thereby destroying the effectiveness of the compliance program across the physician practice. No one should be above the practice's compliance program. All employees, regardless of their status or position within the physician practice, must adhere to all of the requirements of the compliance program. Disparate treatment of compliance breaches will tend to undermine the effectiveness and support for the compliance program.

A sample disciplinary policy is attached as Figure 3-8.

Physician Practice	POLICY/PROCEDURE	
Subject:	Eff. Date:	Revised:
ENFORCEMENT AND DISCIPLINE	**1/1/08**	**1/1/09**

Enforcement and Discipline

Purpose

The physician practice's obligation to operate consistently with all applicable statutes, rules, regulations, policies, procedures, and the physician practice's code of conduct will be consistently enforced through appropriate disciplinary mechanisms, including, as appropriate, discipline of individuals responsible for the failure to detect an offense. The physician practice will develop guidelines for disciplinary action. The type of discipline imposed in each case will be determined on the basis of the specific facts. All infractions that are substantially similar should receive substantially the same type of disciplinary action.

Policy

1. All employees, as a condition of their continued employment by the physician practice, have an obligation to comply with all applicable statutes, rules, regulations, and private payer health care program requirements, as well as the physician practice's code of conduct.

2. As a result of an investigation into a compliance concern, if inappropriate activity occurred, the employees involved in the inappropriate activity, and the employees who had knowledge of the inappropriate activity and failed to correct such activity, will receive disciplinary action.

FIGURE 3-8 | Enforcement and Discipline

3. The type of disciplinary action will be based on how egregious the action or inaction was that led to the compliance infraction. Disciplinary action can include verbal reprimand, written reprimand, temporary suspension, and, in egregious cases, termination.

4. Employees who *knowingly* acted or failed to act, or employees who have committed multiple compliance infractions, will be disciplined more harshly than employees who did not know that their conduct was in violation of a compliance standard, or are involved in their first compliance infraction.

5. The physician practice will strive to issue disciplinary action consistent with the type of infraction regardless of the position the employee holds within the physician practice.

6. All disciplinary action will be taken consistent with the physician practice's human resources policies and procedures.

7. All employees will be required to report conduct of another employee or agent of the physician practice that a reasonable person should know violates any of the physician practice's compliance standards or policies, including code of conduct, or a violation of statute, rules, regulations, or third-party payer programs.

Procedures

1. Disciplinary action will be taken against individuals who commit compliance infractions through either their action or their failure to act.

2. Disciplinary action will be imposed after a thorough investigation of a compliance issue.

3. Prior to issuing disciplinary action, the type of compliance infraction will be evaluated to determine the severity of the compliance breach,

FIGURE 3-8 | Enforcement and Discipline (Continued)

including the potential risk imposed on the physician practice for the compliance breach.

4. The physician practice's compliance officer should be consulted with respect to determining the type of disciplinary action to be imposed.

5. As a general rule, disciplinary action shall be more severe for conduct that is a knowing, intentional, or willful violation of the law, or of the physician practice's standards, procedures, or code of conduct.

6. The physician practice's compliance officer shall be notified of all disciplinary actions involving compliance violations and shall be consulted prior to termination or suspension of an employee for a compliance violation.

7. The compliance officer shall keep a record of all disciplinary actions for compliance violations and the specific grounds for those actions.

8. Through the physician practice's compliance education and training program, all employees will be educated about the disciplinary process.

9. A supervisor or physician of the physician practice may be subject to discipline if it is determined, in consultation with the compliance officer, that the supervisor or physician was negligent in the supervision of employees or agents under his or her control or direction.

10. All agents and independent contractors of the physician practice shall be required, as a term of their contractual relationship, to comply with all applicable statutes, rules, regulations, and the physician practice's policies, procedures, and code of conduct. Failure to comply with such requirements shall be grounds for termination of the contractual relationship of such agents and independent contractors.

Created [date]   [electronic file name and path]   page 3 of 3

FIGURE 3-8 | Enforcement and Discipline (Continued)

3.9 Conclusion

Compliance programs in physician practices need to be tailored to the size of the practice, the history of compliance issues related to the practice, and the type of risks the practice faces based on the complexity of services provided. No one compliance program will fit all physician practices. The most important part of developing an effective compliance program for the practice is to establish a culture of compliance so that everyone affiliated with the practice understands and can trust that the practice will adhere to all compliance requirements, regardless of the cost. This should start with the leadership of the practice, as they need to set the expectation regarding the performance of all aspects of the practice.

Implementing an effective compliance program requires a dedication of resources. These resources, however, will save the physician practice in the long run if appropriate procedures have been put in place to detect and correct compliance issues or irregularities. It is better to invest the resources in the development of an effective compliance program than to pay these resources in fines, penalties, and investigation expenses if compliance allegations are alleged against the practice.

Two of the most important aspects of implementing an effective compliance program within the physician practice are to keep it simple and to make it fun. The code of conduct, policies and procedures, and training and education must be able to be understood and followed by the physicians and employees. A compliance program and policies and procedures that are full of legalese will not be understood or appreciated by everyone within the physician practice. Although health care lawyers can assist in the development and documentation of the compliance program, they need to understand that their audience is not attorneys. The practice needs to engage the use of external resources, if appropriate, to assist in the development of the compliance program. These external attorneys and consultants need to understand how to take complex compliance issues and make then understandable for the individuals affiliated with the practice. The objective of an effective physician practice compliance program is to take all of the necessary requirements that apply to the practice and boil them down to an understandable format and training.

Likewise, the compliance program needs to be made enjoyable to encourage participation. Compliance issues, especially the myriad of statutes, rules, and regulations that apply to physician practices, can be highly technical and at times both contradictory and confusing. For example, at compliance training, door prizes and other fun rewards can be offered for both participation and correct responses. The practice could sponsor a compliance week where the compliance program is emphasized by means of incentives and rewards.

The physician practice should be flexible, intentional, and responsive in developing and implementing its compliance program. The program will be successful and effective if it has appropriate buy-in from all levels of the practice, including physicians, and if the employees can see that the practice is striving to be compliant in all aspects of its operations regardless of the cost.

CHAPTER 4

What To Do If The Practice Gets Into Trouble

Paul W. Shaw, Esquire

4.1 Voluntary Disclosure of Overpayments

4.1.1 Introduction

All health care providers, from individual physicians to large hospital systems, periodically receive incorrect payments from Medicare, Medicaid, and other health care insurers. Most frequently these incorrect payments are in fact overpayments because there was an error in how the service was coded or billed. While most overpayments are resolved in the ordinary course of business by a physician's billing staff through voluntary refunds or payment adjustments, there are occasions where a billing problem is systemic and has continued for a number of years without the knowledge of the physician.

Systemic overpayment problems are frequently uncovered during the course of a routine internal review of billing practices. The question becomes whether a pattern of willful misconduct has occurred. In such a case, the physician (with guidance from experienced health care counsel) must assess the situation to determine if it is in the physician's best interests to make a voluntary disclosure and agree to a settlement of the case. Even if voluntary disclosure is in the physician's interests, there is the additional question of the type of settlement that can be reached with the government. The primary goal is to resolve any ensuing investigation in an administrative or civil manner and avoid a criminal investigation and potential prosecution.

After the physician practice has conducted an independent investigation of the facts, the practice is faced with the question of how to proceed. If there are problematic facts, should the practice "fall on its sword" or "circle the wagons?" While there are no definitive answers to this question, a physician or practice should consider a number of factors in deciding whether to self-disclose, as the potential benefits of a voluntary disclosure must be weighed against the very real risk that a disclosure could result in an investigation of the practice.

Regardless of the decision to make a voluntary disclosure, it is critical that the physician or practice stop any further billing errors or violations once he or she becomes aware of the problem. Doing so not only demonstrates good faith but corroborates the physician's position that the error was unintentional. Continuing to incorrectly bill after becoming aware of the issue could subject the physician or practice to a criminal investigation.

4.1.2   Legal Obligation to Disclose Overpayments

Both Medicare and Medicaid regulations make any health care provider responsible for any overpayments made by the program. Additionally, under federal law, it is a felony for whoever has knowledge of the occurrence of any event affecting the initial or continued right to any Medicare benefit or payment to conceal or fail "to disclose such event with an intent fraudulently to secure such benefit or payment either in greater amount than is due or when no such benefit or payment is authorized" (42 USC §1320a-7b[a][3]). While this statute is ambiguous at best as to whether it requires a health care provider, such as a physician, to report every instance of an overpayment, it is the government's position that this law obligates all health care providers to make a voluntary disclosure and refund an overpayment once a physician or practice becomes aware that he or she is retaining funds that should not have been paid to begin with. The knowing retention of such funds, even if the payment did not result from any intentional misconduct, could expose the physician or practice to potential criminal investigation.

The federal civil False Claims Act (FCA) provides for a civil penalty of between $5,500 and $11,000 per violation, as well as up to three times the actual damages sustained by the government. The FCA is most often used when a physician or other health care provider bills for services that are not actually rendered or otherwise makes an affirmative false claim to the government. As a result of recent amendments to the FCA, health care providers who retain overpayments made by the federal government are also subject to the "reverse" false claims provisions of the FCA. These amendments include an obligation to return all overpayments made by the government. Thus, a violation of the FCA now occurs when an overpayment is knowingly and improperly retained, even in the absence of an affirmative false claim or statement. This includes credit balances that result from duplicate payments from both a primary and secondary insurer (such as Medicare) or payments in excess of the allowable charges.

4.1.3   OIG'S Program Guidance for Physician Practices

In today's health care environment, physicians and all other providers are expected to police themselves for billing flaws and discrepancies. In October 2000, the Office of Inspector General (OIG) issued Compliance Guidance for Individual and Small Group Physician Practices. The document provides guidance to assist physician practices in complying with federal health care programs. The OIG readily acknowledged that billing mistakes will occur. The OIG explicitly stated that innocent billing errors or even negligence in connection with billing practices will not subject a physician to criminal, civil, or administrative penalties. The OIG also stated that it was very mindful of the difference between innocent errors ("erroneous claims") on the one hand, and reckless or intentional conduct ("fraudulent claims") on the other. The OIG counseled that "[w]hen physicians discover that their billing errors, honest mistakes, or negligence result in erroneous claims, the physician practice should return the funds erroneously claimed, but without penalties. In other words, absent a violation of civil, criminal or administrative law, erroneous claims result only in the return of funds claimed in error."

4.1.4   OIG'S Protocol for Provider Self-Disclosure

Apart from the Compliance Guidance for Individual and Small Group Physician Practices, the OIG has also issued a Provider Self-Disclosure Protocol in which the OIG expresses its position that "health care providers have an ethical and legal duty to ensure the integrity of their dealings with [government] programs." If a provider discovers a pattern of internal billing flaws, the OIG sets out a system of self-disclosure that may lead to government leniency regarding reported misbillings or overpayments. Included in this protocol is the recommendation that providers engage in either claim-by-claim review or statistical sampling of the claims affected by the incorrect billings.

It is important to emphasize that this self-disclosure protocol is designed only for situations where a provider, such as a physician, believes a potential violation of law may have occurred, that is, the practice engaged in fraud or intentional misconduct. In a recent open letter to the health care community, while urging providers to self-disclose improper conduct, the Inspector General stated that matters that involve overpayments or errors that do not indicate violations of the law should be brought directly to the attention of the Medicare carrier or other entity responsible for claims processing and payment.

4.1.5   Considerations to Voluntary Disclosure

Apart from the guidance provided by the OIG, the criminal statute regarding fraudulent concealment of overpayments, and potential liability under the civil FCA, there are a number of considerations a physician practice should take into account in deciding whether to make a voluntary disclosure. First, there are a number of benefits to self-disclosure:

- Administratively, the OIG has stated that physicians who promptly self-disclose improper conduct to the government may be eligible for favorable treatment in the resolution of their cases.

- In the civil context, the federal FCA provides that a voluntary disclosure will reduce any damages to twice the amount of damages instead of the potential three times damages. However, to be granted this advantage, the disclosure must be made to the US Attorney within 30 days after the provider first becomes aware of the violation. The provider must also fully cooperate with the investigation and must not have actual knowledge of the existence of any investigation by the government. In addition, the voluntary disclosure of improper billing practices on a timely basis can potentially shield the physician practice from a whistleblower within the practice filing a civil false claim action against the practice.

- A self-disclosure before any investigation has been initiated will influence whether the US attorney will bring a civil or criminal action. Quite often, the government will not proceed with a criminal action against a physician practice where the practice has voluntarily disclosed the inappropriate conduct, has taken prompt corrective actions to prevent the conduct from occurring in the future (including disciplinary actions against the responsible individuals within the practice), cooperates fully with any investigation conducted by the government, and complies with any additional remedial measures negotiated with the government.

At the same time, physicians should be aware of the risks involved in self-reporting to the government. First and foremost is the consideration that the issue may never be discovered or reported to the government, thereby needlessly exposing the physician practice to a minimum of repayment and the very real potential of additional sanctions and punishment. In addition, to gain the benefits from cooperation with the government, the physician practice may be exposed to a more expansive investigation; that is, even if the reported overpayment is of a relatively small amount of money, the physician practice could be subject to a much larger audit. For example, while the disclosure to the government may involve the inappropriate use of a particular billing code, the government may initiate a full audit of the physician's billing practices across the full range of services billed to Medicare.

Physicians should be aware that making a disclosure and repayment to a Medicare contractor or state Medicaid program does not remove the potential that the matter will be referred to the OIG or state Medicaid Fraud Control Unit (MFCU) for further investigation if it is suspected that the physician or practice engaged in fraud or intentional misconduct. In the event of such a referral, the OIG has cautioned that it "cannot reasonably make firm commitments as to how a particular disclosure will be resolved or the specific benefit that will enure to the disclosing entity."

However, it is generally the case that if the physician practice has a relatively clean track record with Medicare/Medicaid, and the overpayment was not the result of intentional misconduct, it is best to make a disclosure.

4.1.6   Making a Self-Disclosure

Determining the entity to which the disclosure of an overpayment should be made depends on the nature of the overpayment itself. Unless the overpayment was the result of intentional misconduct, the OIG advises that the physician practice should make the disclosure to the Medicare/Medicaid entity that processed the claims and issued the payment, such as the Medicare carrier. As stated above, a disclosure to the OIG should be made pursuant to the Self-Disclosure Protocol only if there is suspected fraudulent conduct.

If the overpayment involves only a few discrete claims, then the physician's billing staff can administratively handle the repayment by refunding the monies directly to the Medicare carrier, Medicaid, or other health insurance payer. For example, the Medicare program has a standard Part B Voluntary Refund Form for use in making refunds (see Figure 4-1).

If it is found that a billing issue has persisted for an extended period of time and involves a potentially large amount of money, it is recommended that the practice involve experienced health care counsel in drafting the disclosure. Involving counsel is important because it will not be possible to make a large refund to the Medicare carrier or Medicaid without a detailed explanation describing the circumstances in which the practice learned of the issue and the methodology employed by the practice to determine the amount of the overpayment. Indeed, Medicare carriers generally will make the following inquiries whenever a voluntary disclosure is made:

- Why was the voluntary refund made?
- How was it identified?
- What sampling techniques were used to identify the refund?
- What steps were taken to ensure that the issue leading to the overpayment was corrected?
- On what date was the corrective action implemented?
- What claims and claim information were involved in the inappropriate payments?
- What methodology was used to arrive at the amount of the refund?
- Was a full assessment performed to determine the entire time frame and the total amount of refund for the period during which the problem existed that caused the refund?

Because Medicare and Medicaid will be seeking the answers to these questions, the practice should hire an auditor or coding specialist to properly evaluate the extent of the error and the amount involved. In addition, it is equally important that the practice ensure that appropriate corrective actions are taken to prevent the error from recurring in the future. Once all the facts have been determined, the attorney or practice can then submit a detailed disclosure to the Medicare carrier or Medicaid (see Figure 4-2).

★ **National Government Services**
A CMS Contracted Agent

Medicare

Overpayment Recovery Unit Part B Voluntary Refund Form

To Be Completed By Medicare Contractor

Date: _____ Contractor Deposit Control #: _____

Date of Deposit: _____ Contractor Contact Name: _____

Phone #: _____ Contractor Fax: _____

Contractor Address: _____

To Be Completed By Provider/Physician/Supplier, Or Other Entity

Please complete and forward to your Medicare contractor. This form, or a similar document containing the following information, should accompany every unsolicited/voluntary refund so that receipt of check is properly recorded and applied.

Physician/Supplier or Other Entity Name: _____

Address: _____

PTAN #: _____ NPI #: _____ Tax ID #: _____

Contact Person: _____ Phone #: _____

Amount of Check $: _____ Check #: _____ Check Date: _____

Refund Information

For each claim, provide the following:

Patient Name: _____ HICN: _____

Date of Service: _____ Medicare Claim Number: _____

Claim Amount Refunded $: _____

Reason Code for Claim Adjustment: _____ (Reason codes are listed below. Use one reason per claim.) (Please list all claim numbers involved. Attach separate sheet, if necessary)

Note: If specific patient/Health Insurance Claim (HIC)/claim #/claim amount data not available for all claims due to statistical sampling, please indicate methodology and formula used to determine amount and reason for overpayment: _____

Note: If specific patient/ HIC/claim # information is not provided, no appeal rights can be afforded with respect to this refund. Providers/physicians/suppliers, and other entities who are submitting a refund under the Office of the Inspector General's (OIG's) Self-Disclosure Protocol are not afforded appeal rights as stated in the signed agreement presented by the OIG.

For Institutional Facilities Only: Cost report year(s): _____ (If multiple cost report years are involved, provide a breakdown by amount and corresponding cost report year.

For OIG Reporting Requirements

Do you have a Corporate Integrity Agreement with OIG? ☐ Yes ☐ No
Are you a participant in the OIG Self-Disclosure Protocol? ☐ Yes ☐ No

Reason Codes

Billing/Clerical
01 – Corrected date of service
02 – Duplicate
03 – Corrected CPT Code
04 – Not our patient(s)
05 – Modifier add/remove
06 – Billed in error

MSP/Other Payer involvement
07 – MSP group health plan insurance
08 – MSP no-fault insurance
09 – MSP liability insurance
10 – MSP, Workers' Comp. (including Black Lung)
11 – Veterans Administration

Miscellaneous
12 – Insufficient documentation
13 – Patient enrolled in HMO
14 – Services not rendered
15 – Medical necessity
16 – Other – Be specific

Mail Completed Form To

Connecticut Providers–
National Government Services, Inc.
J 13 Part B Carrier
P. O. Box 26308
New York, New York 10087-6308

Indiana Providers–
National Government Services, Inc.
Part B Carrier
P. O. Box 660066
Indianapolis, Indiana 46266-0066

Kentucky Providers–
National Government Services, Inc.
Part B Carrier
P. O. Box 660077
Indianapolis, Indiana 46266-0077

New Jersey Providers–
National Government Services, Inc.
Part B Carrier – New Jersey
P. O. Box 13081
Newark, New Jersey 07188-3081

Downstate New York Providers–
National Government Services, Inc.
J 13 Part B
P. O. Box 13897
Newark, New Jersey 07188-3897

Upstate New York Providers–
National Government Services, Inc.
J 13 Part B
P. O. Box 26394
New York, New York 10087-6394

Queens Co. New York Providers–
National Government Services, Inc.
J 13 Part B
P. O. Box 26254
New York, New York 10087-6254

National Government Services, Inc.
Page: 1 of 1
Form #19056

CMS/
CENTERS for MEDICARE & MEDICAID SERVICES

FIGURE 4-1 Medicare Voluntary Refund Form

Law Firm No.1

Boston,
MA 01251

Tom Jones

Direct Dial: (555) 555-8555
Email: xxx@yyy.com

November 6, 2007

VIA MESSENGER DELIVERY

_____, Esq.
Second Deputy General Counsel
Executive Office of Health and Human Services
One Ashburton Place – 11ᵗʰ Floor
Boston, MA 02108

  Re: ABC Pediatrics, Inc.
    Boston, MA
    (Medicaid Provider No. 12345)

    Notice of overpayment

Dear Ms. _____:

  I am counsel to ABC Pediatrics, Inc. ("ABC"), of Boston, MA. I am writing to disclose an overpayment situation that was discovered during an internal review of claims that had been submitted on behalf of ABC to the MassHealth program.

  ABC is a group medical practice that was incorporated as a not-for-profit corporation in 1992. ABC is composed of a number of pediatricians and pediatric specialists who practice at the XYZ Hospital ("XYZ"). Prior to August 7, 2000, ABC had offices separate from XYZ at 2 Main Street in Boston. All outpatient care was rendered at that location as well as at the hospital. On August 7, 2000, ABC relocated from Main Street to XYZ, and all outpatient services have thereafter been rendered in the outpatient clinics of the hospital.

  From August 2000 through September 2007, ABC outsourced its billing to a third-party billing company, Ability Systems, Inc. ("AS"), of Boston, MA. In connection with a recent review of billings to the MassHealth program for services rendered by the ABC physicians, ABC discovered that AS had billed MassHealth with an incorrect place of service designation (Item No. 24B) on Form 5. For a period of time, claims had a "place of service" designation of "office, facility, business location" (Code 01) when the claims should have specified "outpatient hospital" (Code 04) as the place of service. As a result, ABC was incorrectly paid at the higher differential payment for these claims. While ABC regularly received and reviewed the remittance advices issued by MassHealth for claims submitted by AS, these documents only reflected the CPT codes that had been used. ABC had no knowledge that AS used an incorrect place of service designation.

page 1 of 2

FIGURE 4-2 | Sample Voluntary Disclosure Letter

When ABC discovered the problem in late September 2007, it immediately contacted AS, who determined that the incorrect place of service designation was inexplicably used during the three-year period from August 2003 through August 31, 2006. Upon inquiry, AS informed ABC that it had billed all services from September 1, 2006 to date with a correct designation of "outpatient hospital." AS never informed ABC of the prior error or why it corrected the place of service designation after August 2006. It was only when ABC made inquiry that AS provided the foregoing information. ABC has ceased using AS as its billing agent.

On September 26, 2007, ABC requested AS provide the billing data for all claims submitted during AS's tenure so that it could compute the number of claims that had been submitted to MassHealth with an incorrect place of service. AS provided this data on October 24, 2007, and ABC was able to isolate the claims that involved an incorrect place of service designation, which is contained on the enclosed Excel spreadsheet. From this data, ABC has determined that the total overpayment paid by MassHealth during this three-year period amounts to $112,935.40.

I would appreciate your giving me a call to discuss this matter in greater detail. Please be assured that ABC will cooperate fully in any follow-up inquiry.

Very truly yours,
LAW FIRM NO. 1.

By: _____
Tom Jones

TJ:jag
Enclosure (Excel spreadsheet)

cc: ABC Pediatrics, Inc.

_____, Chief
Medicaid Fraud Control Unit
Office of the Attorney General

FIGURE 4-2 | Sample Voluntary Disclosure Letter (Continued)

While the goal of the voluntary disclosure is to resolve the overpayment issue without any further investigation or sanction by the OIG or state MFCU, a large overpayment that resulted from conduct occurring over an extended period can cause the Medicare carrier or Medicaid program either to conduct a further review to satisfy the criteria listed above or to make a referral for investigation. Indeed, Medicare carriers routinely notify the OIG of large unexplained refunds not accompanied by detailed explanations as to why the refund was being made. The state Medicaid programs will also make a referral to the MFCU for large unexplained refunds. Because disclosure can trigger an audit or investigation, it is recommended that physicians seek the advice of experienced health care counsel before making such a disclosure.

4.1.7 Timing of the Voluntary Disclosure

A frequently asked question is how much time the physician has to make a disclosure. Although the OIG in different pronouncements has stated that a provider should make a disclosure and refund the overpayment within 30 days of learning of the overpayment, it is not always possible to make disclosure within this time frame. For a physician practice to properly determine the extent of an overpayment situation that may have been going on for a number of years, it is generally necessary to involve the practice's attorney and have the attorney retain an auditor or billing consultant. Therefore, it can take several months before the practice learns the full extent of the problem. As a result, the physician practice may want its attorney to submit an initial disclosure to Medicare or Medicaid addressing the discovery of the problem and explaining that the practice is actively investigating the matter, along with the submission of a detailed follow-up letter once the internal audit has been completed (see Figures 4-3 and 4-4 for sample letters). This practice has the benefit of preventing employees who are aware of the problem, such as billing personnel, from filing a whistleblower action against the practice.

Law Firm No.1

Tom Jones

Direct Dial: (555) 555-8555
Email: xxx@yyy.com

Boston,
MA 01251

March 16, 2007

_____, Manager
Benefit Integrity Unit
National Government Services
P.O. Box 1919
Portland, ME 04104

    Re: Notice of Potential Overpayments for Physical Therapy Services

          Provider: XYZ VNA
            Boston, MA 02114

Dear Ms. _____:

    This office is counsel to the XYZ VNA of Boston, MA. XYZ VNA is a nonprofit agency that provides home health services in over 70 communities throughout eastern Massachusetts. The XYZ VNA is providing this preliminary notice of a potential overpayment situation.

    On or about February 7, 2007, the XYZ VNA discovered that a physical therapist (T.C., RPT) employed to service patients in the Boston, MA area had falsely claimed to have provided physical therapy visits that were never performed. The XYZ VNA terminated Ms. C. and reported her conduct to both the Massachusetts and New Hampshire licensing boards.

    As a result of this physical therapist falsely documenting visits to various patients, the XYZ VNA may have submitted claims to Medicare that included individual therapy visits that were not performed, which could have a monetary impact on the claim. At the present time, the extent of the falsification of records is being investigated. However, many patients cannot remember the exact dates or frequency of Ms. C's visits, which has complicated the process of determining which encounters were performed and which were not. We will provide National Government Services with the results of our investigation once it is completed.

    If you have any questions in the interim, please do not hesitate to contact me.

                     Very truly yours,
                     Law Firm No. 1

                     By: _____
                         Tom Jones

TJ/jag
cc: XYZ VNA

FIGURE 4-3 | Initial Disclosure Letter

Law Firm No.1

Tom Jones

Direct Dial: (555) 555-8555
Email: xxx@yyy.com

Boston,
MA 01251

September 28, 2007

_____, Manager
Benefit Integrity Unit
National Government Services
P.O. Box 1919
Portland, ME 04104

    RE: Notice of Potential Overpayments for Physical Therapy Services

          Provider: XYZ VNA
             Boston, MA 02114

Dear Ms. _____:

    This office is counsel to the XYZ VNA ("XYZVNA") of Boston, MA. I am following up on my letter of March 16, 2007 (copy attached) regarding a potential overpayment situation. XYZ VNA has completed its investigation and reports as follows:

Introduction

    XYZ VNA is a nonprofit agency that provides home health services in over 70 communities throughout eastern Massachusetts. On February 6, 2007, XYZ VNA received a report of a patient complaint that visits by one of its physical therapists, Ms. T. C., RPT, had not been made, while Ms. C. had documented in the patient's medical record as if the visits had been performed. On February 7, 2007, Ms. C. admitted there was one single visit that she falsely documented; she denied any others. Upon discovery of the questionable visit in February 2007, XYZ VNA suspended all claims for visits documented by Ms. C. for the month of January 2007, pending a complete investigation.

    Ms C. was suspended on February 7, 2007 pending further review and her employment was terminated on February 12th due to:

- findings of falsely documented visits, and

- the fact that she was employed by two other VNAs, one of which paid her for full-time employment (and documented patient visits) during the same full-time hours that XYZ VNA employed her.

Case Review Process:

    The following plan was initiated by XYZ VNA to determine the extent to which Ms. C. may have falsely documented visits, as XYZ VNA found that several patients reported a visit history that did not match Ms. C.'s documented visits.

1. Identify and, to the extent possible, call all patients T.C. treated who had a start of care date (or cert period) during the six (6) months prior (August 1, 2006 through January 31, 2007); ask patients to recall the frequency of visits and any details regarding the therapy provided by Ms. C.

2. Based on discussion with patients, identify any discrepancy in documented visits and patient-recalled visits.

FIGURE 4-4   Follow-up Disclosure Letter

_____, Manager
Benefit Integrity Unit
National Government Services
September 28, 2007
Page 2

3. Identify any patterns that emerge in the patient's recollection or in the documented visits that may be used to help determine the extent to which visits may have been falsely documented.

4. Evaluate each case by age and insurer to determine if claims were submitted for falsely documented visits that would need to be refunded to the insurer. (Note, the claims for Ms. C.'s visits in January 2007 had been suspended pending the results of the investigation and that action would be part of the reconciliation process.)

5. Refund insurers for any/all false visits that had been improperly claimed by and paid to XYZ VNA.

Case Review

A full census report was generated for all of Ms. C.'s cases for the prior six months. The list included 9 pediatric patients (four insurers), and 47 adult patients (ten insurers, including Medicare) with a total of fifty-two (52) episodes (admitted for 60-days) of care. Eight pediatric and thirty-eight adult patients/families were reached for discussion.

The table below displays the general findings and assumptions made for the 6-month look-back case review. In order to handle all cases and claims consistently, XYZ VNA arrived at (and applied) some assumptions, which were mostly based on the calls made to patients during the process of discovering the extent to which Ms. C. may have falsified records.

	Case Review/Patient Calls Findings	Recommendations/Assumptions
1	Patients/family members of adult patients (7 of 13) who were called and had only one therapy evaluation visit recorded stated that the visit had been made. Those not reached were ages 36–60.	Based on the findings from seven calls, XYZ VNA considers all one-time therapy visits (that were the patients' first visit for therapy evaluation) to have been performed as documented.
2	Patients who were called consistently stated the "admission visit" or first visit in a series of visits was completed on the day it was recorded as being performed.	Consider all of the first visits documented as an admission or start-of-care episode to have been completed as documented.
3	Ms. C. documented some single therapy visits in a patient's series of visits when she was assigned to "cover" another therapist's visit due to their absence. The primary therapist whose case may be "covered" by a colleague would discuss the "covered" visit with the patient, evaluate for progress, any problems, etc. If the visit did not occur, it would readily be discovered through therapist's discussion or prior to that through a patient report/complaint of a missed scheduled visit.	One-time visits or occasional visits made during an episode of care, when Ms. C. "covered" for another primary therapist's case, were performed as documented.

FIGURE 4-4 | Follow-up Disclosure Letter (Continued)

_____, Manager
Benefit Integrity Unit
National Government Services
September 28, 2007
Page 3

	There were no such instances; thus, it is believed that all Ms. C. "covering" single visits (7) were completed as they were documented.	
4	Generally home health therapy visits would not be required to be performed in consecutive fashion. While it may occur occasionally (more with children), patients requiring physical therapy at home do not usually have a clinical reason to be visited at such a frequency; numerous patients had consecutive-day visits documented and, when asked if Ms. C. visited them two days in a row, responded, "no," "never," "no, I don't believe so," etc.	Except for visits for children (for which the parents confirmed visit frequency) any consecutive-day visits were considered to be false documentation, e.g., consecutive Monday-Tuesday visits, or Thursday-Friday visits. For these visits, XYZ VNA was very conservative and only one of any documented consecutive visits is considered to have been performed.
5	Eleven patients/families reported that Ms. C. visited them "one to two, or two to three times per week" but they could not remember precisely.	A range of 1–3 visits is acceptable in home health. In these cases, XYZ VNA accepted the documentation for 1, 2, or 3 weekly visits to be representative of visits that were actually performed as documented by Ms. C. Without evidence or patient report of any visit discrepancy, the visit is assumed to have been provided.
6	Eight patients stated they could not recall their visit frequency and two patients were not called because they were 86 and 92 years old, with known mental changes. In these cases, unless there were consecutive visits (see #4 above), XYZ VNA could only rely on the medical record to be representative of the actual performed and billable visits.	Without patient recall, XYZVNA accepts visits as having been performed as documented. However in these cases, if there were consecutive-day visits, the VNA only counts and submits claims for nonconsecutive visits.
7	Some patients were clear and specific about the number of visits, time of day, etc.	XYZVNA accepts the patient report as accurate; VNA will count and submit claims for the visits the patient believes and stated they received.

Findings

Regarding the six-month look-back case review process, XYZ VNA found that 26 of 47 (about 55%) of the adults had recollection of their home care and visit frequency. While there was a wide range in the patient's ability to recall dates and times of home therapy visits, the most reliable information clearly came from patients who were still "active" on the VNA caseload. When there was a

FIGURE 4-4 | Follow-up Disclosure Letter (Continued)

_____, Manager
Benefit Integrity Unit
National Government Services
September 28, 2007
Page 4

discrepancy in visits documented and any patient's report, XYZ VNA accepted the patient's report to reflect the accurate record of visits that would be submitted in a claim. In calling patients, XYZVNA found that patient recollection is variable, especially among elderly patients; the six-month look-back clearly reached the limit of most patient's interest or memory.

Patients/Cases Reviewed With Questionable Findings					Discrepant Visit Findings		
Patient/ case type	Case count	Cases discussed w/patient	Cases not discussed	Cases w/ discrepant visits (per patient report & table # 4)	60-day episodes/ visits tagged as discrepant consecutive visits (**)	Additional discrepant visits with documented frequency greater than patient reports	Total discrep- ant visits
Adult	47	38	7 w/one visit only 2 w/ dementia	25	19 episodes/ 47 visits	28	75
(**) To be conservative, one of every two consecutive visits was considered to be false.							

Adult Cases Discrepant Visit Findings

There were 19 adult Medicare episodes of care that had between one and nine visits that were considered to have been falsely documented because they were consecutive with another visit. XYZ VNA considered those consecutive visits to be non-billable visits. Even with those adjustments, none resulted in a change to the 10-therapy visit threshold and the Medicare claim; all cases claimed as having reached the threshold did in fact have at least 10 combined physical, occupational, and/or speech therapy visits. There were 18 additional Medicare questionable visits that could not be substantiated by the patients; XYZ VNA did not bill for those visits.

One or Two Single Therapy Visits

Fifteen of the adult patients were provided only one or two therapy visits by Ms. C. In this 6-month review, there were two types of one-time visits provided by Ms. C.:

Type 1) the single visit that was the first therapy visit for the purpose of evaluating the patient for eligibility for home care services and to set up the therapy plan; when the patient was not admitted for further services, the visits stands as the only visit made and

Type 2) a single visit (or two) in the middle of a series of planned therapy visits where Ms. C. "covered" for one or two visits for another therapist's patient.

FIGURE 4-4   Follow-up Disclosure Letter (Continued)

_____, Manager
Benefit Integrity Unit
National Government Services
September 28, 2007
Page 5

Thirteen patients had Type 1 single visits as her visit was the first therapy evaluation provided by XYZ VNA. When called, seven were reached and all stated that Ms. C. had provided one physical therapy visit. Based on this trend, XYZ VNA believes that all single therapy evaluation visits documented were accurate. Seven Type 2 single therapy visits were performed by Ms. C. and are believed to have been documented accurately. Similarly, XYZ VNA believes all Ms. C. one- or two-visit cases are correctly documented.

Impact on Medicare Billing

Among the Medicare cases with discrepancy in visits documented vs. visits believed to have been performed, the distribution and potential action is as follows:

Claimed & reimbursed	Questionable visits/episodes	Questionable visits affecting reimbursement	Reimbursement required	Action to be taken
44 episodes	75 visits/ 25 episodes	None	None; 100% of 10-visit therapy threshold cases claimed appropriately.	None; no claims affected.

Summary

The physical therapist whose clinical practice was in question delivered care to 56 patients during the six-month evaluation period. With respect to Medicare, while there were 44 episodes of care that were extensively evaluated for evidence of falsely documented visits, there were no episodes with questionable visits that were billed as having reached the MO 825 ten-visit therapy threshold when it was not met; 100% of Medicare claims were correctly submitted. Because there was no financial impact to the Medicare program, I respectfully submit that no additional review or action by Medicare is required.

I trust the foregoing is an adequate explanation for what occurred and the resulting investigation by XYZ VNA. If you have any questions, do not hesitate to call. Thank you for your consideration.

Very truly yours,
Law Firm No. 1

By: _____
Tom Jones

TJ/jag
Enclosure
cc: XYZVNA

FIGURE 4-4   Follow-up Disclosure Letter (Continued)

4.2   Postpayment Audits

4.2.1   Introduction

As health care expenditures have spiraled upward, government and private payers have responded with a variety of cost containment efforts. Increased postpayment reviews and audits to ensure the integrity of the various health insurance programs are one of the myriad of cost containment efforts. While Medicare audits a very small percentage of physician practices annually, it is likely that most physicians during their professional careers will be subject to a postpayment review or audit by Medicaid, Medicare, and/or a private insurer.

4.2.2   Audit Generating Conduct

Civil audits by Medicare, Medicaid, and other third-party payers, as well as criminal investigations by government authorities, are often the result of complaints from beneficiaries, competitors, and current and former employees, as well as computer-generated screenings of the physician's claim submission profile that reveal billing irregularities in comparison with a statistical norm of his or her peer group. Unfortunately, staying within the norms is no guarantee either, as Medicare, Medicaid, and many insurance programs conduct random audits of physicians by computer selection.

While random audits and patient complaints certainly are the source of some investigations (any physician can be subject to a random audit if the computer happens to stop at his or her name), in most cases, a physician is selected for review on the basis of a comparison of his or her utilization rates for particular Current Procedural Terminology (CPT®) codes in relation to those of his or her peers in the same specialty and geographic area. The chances of an audit increase if a physician consistently bills at the upper end of utilization profiles of CPT coding or diagnostic tests.

Common reasons why Medicare and third-party insurers will deny services include lack of documentation, the office visit not being as complex as billed, or the service provided not being medically necessary.

A routine audit can be elevated to a fraud investigation if the audit reveals a pattern of gross upcoding or billing for services that were not performed. Examples of conduct that could result in a referral for criminal investigation include:

- Consistent billing at a higher level of service than what is reflected in the medical record

- Flagrant and persistent overutilization of medical services with little or no regard for results, the patient's ailments, condition, or medical needs

- Duplicate billing that appears to be deliberate, including billing the insurer twice for the same services

- Consistent use of improper or inappropriate billing codes.

Although most physicians do not intentionally engage in any of the above practices, many find themselves subject to recoupment following an audit because their records failed to adequately document the services for which they billed. The outcome of an audit is heavily dependent on the degree to which the records failed to adequately document the services billed.

4.2.3   Laying the Foundation for Accurate Billing

Accurate billing is dependent on compliance with the terms and conditions of the Medicare, Medicaid, and insurance programs, which are most often found in the contract, enrollment material, handbooks, rules, regulations and coding books. This material is updated and periodically changed. Therefore, it is critical that the physician's billing staff be vigilant in complying with any coding and billing amendments. It is recommended that all physicians:

- Obtain yearly, by written request, certified mail with return receipt requested, all updates and amendments applicable to each insurance program in which the physician participates as a provider.

- Either personally attend or have key staff attend any seminars for participating providers sponsored by the Medicare contractor or insurer.

- Document in writing, certified mail with return receipt requested, any confusion over billing codes and the appropriate method for billing; Medicare or the insurer should be asked for appropriate information and instructions (see sample letter in Figure 4-5).

- Document in writing, certified mail with return receipt requested, the oral instructions of the contractor or insurer, or the contractor/insurer's refusal to provide the practice with accurate oral and written instructions.

- Review the office superbill or encounter form periodically for changes and modifications; compare the superbill to the updates received from the insurer.

- Be familiar with the billing codes used by the practice; routinely check the codes used on claim forms against the medical records.

- Ask the insurer for advice if the practice is not sure how to bill a certain procedure. Telephone advice should not be relied on; there is no substitute for a letter, sent certified mail with return receipt requested. The practice should keep all billing correspondence together with any billing information updates sent by Medicare or other insurers in a separate file. These files should be reviewed periodically.

- Make sure the office staff understands the ramifications of their actions or inaction.

4.2.4   Documenting the Physician's Services

There is a common expression used by all auditors: "If it is not documented in the medical record, the service never occurred." All physicians must be knowledgeable of the Evaluation and Management (E/M) Services Guidelines in the CPT codebook. These guidelines are the basis for the different levels of service that can be billed and serve as the criteria by which all medical records are measured by Medicare, Medicaid, and private insurers during overpayment reviews. Too frequently, physicians either are not familiar with the key components required to justify a particular level of service or else fail to adequately document those components. It is also important

JOHN DOE, M.D.
100 Main Street
Boston, MA 02114

July 9, 2009

BY EXPRESS MAIL DELIVERY
Express Mail No. _____

Jane Doe, Provider Relations
Neptune Pluto Insurance Co.
1 Mars Drive
Boston, MA 15183

Re: Documentation of Critical Care Codes

Dear Ms. Doe:

I am writing to confirm the discussion we had today about the documentation necessary to support the use of the critical care codes (CPT Codes 99291, 99292). Specifically, we discussed the necessity for documenting in the medical record the exact amount of time spent providing critical care services to the patient. You informed me that it was sufficient to simply record the total time, and that I am not required to record the actual start and stop times. You further informed me that without the documentation of time spent with the patients, any services provided in the critical care setting should be coded as subsequent hospital care (CPT Codes 99231-99233) rather than critical care.

I trust the foregoing is an accurate recitation of the advice you gave me. If I am incorrect, I would appreciate your letting me know by reply letter. Thank you once again for your time.

Very truly yours,

John Doe, M.D.

FIGURE 4-5   Sample Confirmatory Letter to Medicare Regarding Advice Received on the Telephone

that the documentation support the medical necessity for any diagnostic tests that may have been billed. Every medical record should contain the pertinent facts, findings, and observations about the patient's health history, including past and present illnesses, examinations, tests, treatments, and outcomes.

The best way to maintain patient records that will not cause problems later is to create a system and then use that system consistently. The following are suggestions for maintaining a medical records system that will stand up to scrutiny by Medicare, Medicaid, or a private insurer.

- The physician should dictate or write his or her notes of the patient encounter *during or immediately after* the examination. If the physician writes medical records at the end of the day after seeing a number of patients, there is an increased risk that crucial information will be omitted from the notes.

- If the patient has been treated by other health care providers (such as another physician), the physician should obtain copies of those records and include them as part of the medical record. This includes all related health care reports bearing in any way on the condition being treated.

- All patient questionnaires should contain a request for information about previous health care providers, including names, addresses, and telephone numbers.

- The patient should sign a medical release form to allow the physician to obtain prior medical records.

- If a patient rejects recommended methods of treatment (especially when they are less costly to the insurer), the physician should make a note in the medical record detailing his or her recommendations and the patient's choice.

- If the physician's recommended treatments or procedures are more radical or invasive to the patient, or more costly to the insurer, and the decision to treat in this manner is based on the failure of previous treatments by other health care providers or the patient's expressed desire, this should be noted in the record.

- If the patient was previously treated or seen by other health care providers whose recommendations may have been different from those of the physician, he or she should explain why his or her course of treatment is different.

The conclusion physicians should draw from this is to pay attention to their own records. The physician must view his or her practice as both a profession and a business and must stay on top of the business. The failure to do so can be costly.

4.2.5   Initiation of an Audit

4.2.5.1   *Scope of Initial Audit*

If the review by Medicare, Medicaid, or other insurer was triggered by a beneficiary complaint or for profile irregularities, the initial audit will tend to be very specific and likely will focus on either the subject matter of the complaint or a particular class of records closely related to the irregularity in the physician's billing profile. For example, if the computer screening disclosed an excess number of comprehensive office visits, eg, CPT code 99215, in relation to the number performed during the same period by the physician's peers in the same geographic area, Medicare would request records for a number of patients who were billed for this level of service. At the same time, there may be a legitimate reason for the disparity, such as a primary care physician who specializes in treating complicated patients with human immunodeficiency virus or acquired immunodeficiency syndrome.

Medicare will examine these medical records in detail to determine whether the complaint was valid or whether the reason for the excess profile was the result of a program error or violation. In most cases, the medical records will be examined during this initial audit by a nurse reviewer or physician consultant to determine whether the billing was correct and whether the services were medically necessary. On the basis of the results of this initial review, and which governmental entity conducted the audit, a variety of potential actions can be taken against the physician.

4.2.5.2   Steps to Take on Receipt of a Request for Records

Today's physician is likely to spend a greater percentage of her or his time responding to postpayment inquiries than his or her predecessors of 20 or even 10 years ago. It is essential to have an office procedure in place that can effectively respond to these inquiries and substantially reduce the amount of time required of the physician. The following are some suggestions for responding to initial requests for medical records and documents from Medicare and other health care insurers:

- The physician should establish an office procedure in which all requests for information are placed in a file for regular review by the physician. It is amazing how many times the physician is the last person in the office to know he or she is being subjected to an audit.

- The physician should have the office staff determine what information is being requested, the date of service being questioned, and the procedure being questioned. A simple preprinted form can be developed, filled out by the staff, attached to the file, and provided to the physician for review. If the information sought is billing information, the office staff should be able to handle the inquiry without involvement by the physician. If the information sought is related to medical necessity or the appropriateness of treatment, someone with a medical background should review the request.

- The physician should not let Medicare determine by its request what information is relevant to a claim. Frequently, when Medicare asks for information about a patient's treatment on a specific date, the physician sends only the medical record for that date of service. Some months later, the physician is subjected to a medical review, with Medicare claiming he or she did not adequately document the treatment on that date. To avoid this, the physician should review the patient's entire medical record (including x-rays, laboratory test results, surgery reports, and other dates of service) to determine whether those records contain information pertinent and relevant to the medical care on the specific date requested. If so, those records should be sent to

Medicare as well. Similarly, if the medical record for the particular date of service refers to other records, these records should also be provided.

- The physician should review all the documentation copied by the office staff before it is submitted to Medicare to ensure that it is complete and supports the services provided and the medical necessity of those services. Too often staff may not copy all the relevant notes and may send them to Medicare without the physician having reviewed the submission.

- If the medical records are not entirely legible or are difficult to read, it is perfectly appropriate to attach a handwritten or typed statement that is clearly marked as being a transcription of the original record. However, the original record should not be altered in any manner.

- All information to Medicare or other insurers should be sent with a cover letter by certified mail, return receipt requested. This letter should identify the patient, the information sought, and the information provided. It should be addressed to a particular person at the Medicare carrier (see Figure 4-6). This information should never be sent without being directed to a contact person and never be sent by regular mail. Otherwise, there is the potential that Medicare will claim that it never received the information and may demand an extrapolated overpayment based on the alleged failure to provide the requested information.

- The physician should maintain copies of everything that is sent to Medicare until the audit is resolved.

4.2.5.3   *What Not to Do*

The biggest mistake a physician can make when confronted with a request for records is to either create a "missing" document or alter/amend an existing document. Such conduct will result in a referral for criminal prosecution for obstruction of justice. While medical records should not be changed under any circumstances, it is perfectly appropriate to add an addendum to include any relevant information about the

JOHN DOE, M.D.
100 Main Street
Boston, MA 02114

July 9, 2009

BY EXPRESS MAIL DELIVERY
Express Mail No. _____

_____, Investigator
Medicare Integrity Program
43 Landry Street
Biddeford, ME 04005

    Re: John Doe, M.D.
          CMM #: 12345678

Dear Ms. _____:

    I am responding to your letter of June 10, 2009, in which you requested that I provide your office with the complete patient files for the twenty (20) patients on the attached list. Enclosed you will find the records for each patient in a separate folder. In each, I have placed my entire office medical record, including intake sheet, office notes, consultation reports, test results, records obtained from other medical providers, and all other documentation relating to the patient.

    Please be assured that I will cooperate fully in your review of the services that I provided to these patients. While I believe the records for each patient are complete, do not hesitate to call if you need any additional materials.

    Thank you for your consideration.

                Very truly yours,

                John Doe, M.D.

FIGURE 4-6 | Sample Transmittal to Medicare in Response to Request for Records

patient encounter, such as the patient's condition and treatment, that may not have been in the contemporaneous record. If this is done, however, the addendum must be identified as such and dated as of the date it was created. Similarly, as stated above, if the medical records are not entirely legible, it is permissible to attach a written or typed transcription of the record. However, under no circumstances should the original medical record be altered in any way in an effort to make it legible.

4.2.5.4   *Supplemental Requests for Records and Information*

In some instances, the physician will receive requests for additional information after a response has been made to the first request. This should be considered a warning flag. The physician should establish an office procedure in which these requests for further information are brought to the physician's immediate attention. At this point the physician personally should speak directly with the reviewer from Medicare or the insurer to determine what information is being requested and why the previous response was inadequate. However, the physician must be careful when speaking to representatives of Medicare. All contact with a physician is recorded in the case file and could potentially be used against the physician at a later time.

4.2.6   Notification of the Results of the Postpayment Review

Medicare will provide the physician with the results of the postpayment review. The notice will contain a narrative description of the overpayment situation, including the specific issues involved that created the overpayment. The notice will also include the findings for each claim in the sample, including a specific explanation of why any services were determined to be noncovered or incorrectly coded. It will also contain a list of all individual claims including the actual amounts determined to be noncovered, the specific reason for noncoverage, the amounts denied, and the overpayment determination for each claim. Generally, the notice will also include a demand for repayment of the overpayments (see Figure 4-7 for an example of such a notice).

MEDICARE
NEW ENGLAND BENEFIT INTEGRITY SUPPORT CENTER

CONFIDENTIAL

November 16, 2006

CMM#:

Dear Dr. Doe:

EDS, the New England Benefit Integrity Support Center (NE-BISC) is the Program Safeguard Contractor (PSC) chosen by the Centers for Medicare and Medicaid Services (CMS) to perform specific program safeguard functions for the Medicare program. Included in our responsibilities is reviewing the accuracy and justification of services reimbursed by the Medicare program.

We have completed a review of your claims which were selected using a statistically valid random sample of 20 beneficiaries for the time frame 01/01/05 through 12/31/05. The sample size was chosen to guarantee at least a 90% confidence level and a 8% precision. The calculated overpayment determined from this sample is $3,522.40. Based on the finding(s) of this review, the extrapolated overpayment of $19,296.12 is due the Medicare program. A spreadsheet with a list of the specific claims that have been determined to be fully or partially denied, the specific reasons for the denial and the amount of the overpayment is enclosed.

Briefly, we requested medical records from your office in Boston, MA. Our first request to your office was sent on 04/17/2006.

The medical records received from your office were reviewed by our medical consultant. As a result, the following was determined:

- Exceeded the relatively more-restrictive CMS guidelines for number of NCSs to be performed for a given condition and also exceeded the more liberal AANEM 90th percentile standards. In a majority of instances Dr. Doe could have diagnosed unilateral carpal tunnel with as few as 2 sensory and 2 motor tests; he typically employed 5 sensory for unilateral and as many as 8 for bilateral CTS.

A CMS Medicare Integrity Program, Program Safeguards Contractor

Medicare Integrity Program
43 Landry Street
Biddeford, ME 04005

page 1 of 2

FIGURE 4-7   Notice from Medicare of Audit Result

- Dr. Doe routinely performs motor testing with F wave studies for CTS which is not indicated. He quite frequently test the radial nerve as part of his evaluation for CTS; this is not deemed necessary as part of the routine suite of test needed to deal with a possible CTS diagnosis.

- Question of cervical radiculopathy in a significant proportion of the beneficiaries testing which leads to F wave testing and also to some extent to the use of EMG as well. There is seldom any detail as to the nature of the pain - just "shoulder pain" or something equally vague. This does not justify routine F wave testing. The need for F wave testing depends on the condition being tested for but should not form a routine part of the evaluation for CTS unless there's serious, well-founded concern that there may be a proximal lesion present. If there is reason to suspect a radiculopathy then documentation should offer some detail supporting that suspicion; such documentation was absent across the sample.

- There were a few cases in which all studies were denied—one involving postherpetic tingling and one involving a diabetic where it seemed the diagnosis was obvious and where no documentation of neurological exam appeared at all. The AANEM policy makes it clear that the electrodiagnostic physician should be serving as a consultant in these cases. Therefore, a history, focused exam, and diagnostic hypothesis should form part of the service; such documentation was absent across the sample.

- There was also a pattern noted of the physician billing the various codes with separate -TC and -26 modifiers; sometimes the number of units billed for the -TC and -26 bearing the same CPT code designator differed. These services should have been billed as complete procedures.

The extrapolated overpayment determination of $19,296.12 has been referred to the affiliated contractor for collection. In the near future, you will receive additional correspondence from the affiliated contractor regarding the specifies of the overpayment and repayment process. **Do not forward** payment or appeal this determination until you have been notified by the affiliated contractor.

Please contact me at 207-312-7081 if you have any questions regarding this matter.

―――――――――
Investigator
New England Benefit Integrity Support Center

FIGURE 4-7 | Notice from Medicare of Audit Result (Continued)

HIC Number	Bene Last Name	Bene First Name	HCFA Place of Service Code	ICN	Carrier Claim Paid Date	Claim First Date of Service	HCPCS /CPT CodCe	Modifier Code 1	Modifier Code 2	Units	NEW PROC	ADJUSTED	OVERPAY- MENT AMOUNT	A/D/R	COMMENT
		WILFRED	11		7/25/2005	29-Jun-05	95904	TC	N/A	8			$258.43	D	Deny -TC - should be billing as complete procedure
		WILFRED	11		7/25/2005	29-Jun-05	95904	26	QU	1		4	($177.14)	R	Allow as complete procedure - no 26 or TC modifier
		WILFRED	11		7/25/2005	29-Jun-05	95861	TC	N/A	1			$26.20	D	Deny -TC - should be billing as complete procedure
		WILFRED	11		7/25/2005	29-Jun-05	95861	26	QU	1			($26.20)	A	Allow as complete procedure - no 26 or TC modifier
		WILFRED	11		7/25/2005	29-Jun-05	95903	TC	N/A	3			$95.90	D	Deny -TC - should be billing as complete procedure
		WILFRED	11		7/25/2005	29-Jun-05	95903	26	QU	3			($95.87)	A	Allow as complete procedure - no 26 or TC modifier
		EMMA	11		1/3/2006	08-Dec-05	95904	TC	QU	5			$161.52	D	Deny -TC - should be billing as complete procedure
		EMMA	11		1/3/2006	08-Dec-05	95904	26	QU	5		3	($64.96)	R	Allow as complete procedure - no 26 or TC modifier
		EMMA	11		1/3/2006	08-Dec-05	95860	TC	QU	1			$34.34	D	Deny -TC - should be billing as complete procedure
		EMMA	11		1/3/2006	08-Dec-05	95860	26	QU	1			$44.82	D	Deny - documentation does not support the service billed

page 1 of 2

FIGURE 4-7 | Notice from Medicare of Audit Result

196

HIC Number	Bene Last Name	Bene First Name	HCFA Place of Service Code	ICN	Carrier Claim Paid Date	Claim First Date of Service	HCPCS /CPT CodCe	Modifier Code 1	Modifier Code 2	Units	NEW PROC	ADJUSTED	OVERPAY-MENT AMOUNT	A/D/R	COMMENT
		EMMA	11		1/3/2006	08-Dec-05	95903	TC	QU	2			$63.94	D	Deny-TC - should be billing as complete procedure
		EMMA	11		1/3/2006	08-Dec-05	95903	26	QU	2	95900		($57.15)	R	Need better documentation of necessity for EMG and F wave studies plus radial nerve study
		NORMAN	11		3/30/2005	08-Mar-05	95904	TC	N/A	9			$290.74	D	Deny-TC - should be billing as complete procedure
		NORMAN	11		3/30/2005	08-Mar-05	95904	26	QU	9		4	($49.34)	R	Allow as complete procedure - no 26 or TC modifier
		NORMAN	11		3/30/2005	08-Mar-05	95861	TC	N/A	1			$26.20	D	Deny-TC - should be billing as complete procedure
		NORMAN	11		3/30/2005	08-Mar-05	95861	26	QU	1			($26.20)	A	Allow as complete procedure - no 26 or TC modifier
		NORMAN	11		3/30/2005	08-Mar-05	95930	TC	N/A	4			$127.87	D	Deny-TC - should be billing as complete procedure

FIGURE 4-7 | Notice from Medicare of Audit Result (Continued)

4.2.7   Submitting a Rebuttal Statement

Both Medicare and the state Medicaid programs, as well as private insurers, give the physician the right to submit additional documentation and other information concerning the claims that were subject to review for the purpose of having Medicare redetermine the potential overpayment (see Figure 4-8). At this point, it is critical that the physician review each and every overpayment determination made by Medicare.

First, it is essential that each of the sampled cases be reexamined to determine whether the results reached by the contractor are correct. For example, if it is alleged that the medical records did not disclose the medical necessity of the services rendered, the physician can provide a written justification for the services. If it is alleged that an improper billing code was used, the physician again can justify the use of the billing code on the basis of the overall condition of the patient or inadequate billing instructions from the insurer. In some instances, either the billing instructions or billing codes may have changed during the time period encompassed by the audit.

If the denial was based on an alleged lack of medical necessity for the services, the physician should consider responding with more than medical records. Quite often, Medicare's physician consultants or internal medical review staff substitute their own personal views of the efficacy of a particular procedure as the final word on the professionally recognized standards of the profession. When dealing with an obstinate medical reviewer, the physician should consider submitting the following:

- Texts, articles, and other professional publications supporting the physician's choice of treatment
- Written expert opinions from a medical specialist supporting the choice of treatment. It is important to ensure that the expert has reviewed the same records as the consultant for Medicare or the insurance company.
- Affidavits or letters from the patient(s) confirming that the treatment was performed, the patient's satisfaction with the

(*Continued on page 207*)

CONSOLIDATED REQUEST FOR REDETERMINATION

Re: Worcester Neurology PC
       Worcester, MA
       (John Doe, M.D.)
       (CMM# 12345678)

           Reference No.: _____
           HIC No.: _____
           Internal Control No. _____

Re: John Doe, M.D.
       Boston, MA
       (CMM# 32145678)

           Reference No.: _____
           HIC No.: _____
           Internal Control No. _____

                    Submitted by: John Doe, M.D.
                                        c/o Tom Jones
                                        Law Firm No. 1
                                        Boston, MA 01251
                                        (555) 555-8555

                    Submitted to: NP, Corp.
                                        Redetermination Dept.
                                        P.O. Box 3
                                        Boston, MA 15183

FIGURE 4-8 | Sample Response to Audit

CONSOLIDATED REQUEST FOR REDETERMINATION

INTRODUCTION

This will serve as my Consolidated Request for Redetermination pursuant to 42 C.F.R. §§ 405.940-.944 from the review of samples of my claims by the Medicare Program Safeguard Contractor. This Consolidated Request for Redetermination involves two separate determinations for samples of claims submitted from my offices in Boston and Worcester, Massachusetts between January 1, 2005 and December 31, 2005. Because the issues raised in the initial review of the two offices, and my responses to those issues, are the same, I am filing this Consolidated Request for Redetermination.

PROCEDURAL HISTORY

I maintain offices in both Boston, MA and Worcester, MA (Worcester PC). On November 16, 2006, EDS (as the Medicare Program Safeguard Contractor) issued two separate notices to "John Doe, M.D." (CMM# 12345678) related to a review of claims for 20 beneficiaries from each location for the period of January 1, 2005 through December 31, 2005 (Appendices G and I respectively).

It was not until May 21 and May 22, 2007 that NP Corp issued the overpayment notices to the Worcester office, Worcester Neurology, PC. Thereafter, on July 16 and July 17, 2007, NP Corp. issued overpayment notices for the Boston office. The reference numbers for these overpayment notices are set forth on the cover to this Consolidated Request for Redetermination.

BACKGROUND

Before responding to the comments made by the Medical Consultant who reviewed my charts, I would like to stress that my medical practice is focused on Electrodiagnostic Medicine and Clinical Neurophysiology. I am board certified in neurology, electrodiagnostic medicine, clinical neurophysiology, and disability evaluation. I am an Assistant Professor of Neurology at XYZ University School of Medicine and have published nineteen (19) peer review articles and abstracts relating to electrodiagnostic procedures. (My curriculum vitae is found at Appendix K.)

I perform EMG (Electromyography) testing at two locations: 1) ABC Laboratory, 2 Main St. in Boston, MA, and 2) DEF Laboratory, affiliated with Worcester Neurology, 6 Main St, in Worcester, MA. All patients are referred by other physicians for electrodiagnostic testing only. These include both PCPs and a variety of specialists such as neurologists, neurosurgeons, hand surgeons, orthopedic surgeons, rheumatologists, and endocrinologists. No patient is referred for a neurological consultation. Referring physicians have diagnostic dilemmas and questions and therefore seek electrodiagnostic testing to clarify their differential diagnosis. Because I do not perform consultations or other "Evaluation and Management Services," my charges in this sample of charts are limited to the Nerve Conduction and EMG billing codes only (CPT Codes 95900, 95903, 95904, 95860, 95861, and 95934).

FIGURE 4-8 | Sample Response to Audit (Continued)

Although I obtain a focused history and perform a focused exam on every patient in order to formulate an electrodiagnostic plan of action, I do not charge for those services. I am aware that many electrodiagnostic physicians submit claims not only for the actual testing but also for an Evaluation and Management service for that portion of the evaluation. Thus my approach decreases the total expense for the testing.

I would also like to stress that the primary goal of electrodiagnostic examination is to determine the site of the lesion. Such testing serves a variety of functions:

- to establish the diagnosis
- to evaluate for concomitant conditions
- to argue for or against an alternative diagnosis
- to quantify the severity of the condition

Establishing the correct diagnosis can help select the best therapeutic option. Although clinical evaluation is irreplaceable, electromyography can help in providing in-depth information about the state of the peripheral myelin, axons, or muscles. This position is supported by the comprehensive evaluation by Mary Roe, M.D., the Director of Neurophysiology Laboratory and Vice Chairman of the Department of Neurology at Greater Boston Medical Center, concerning the Medical Consultant's findings (Appendix N).

REPLY TO THE CONCLUSIONS ASSERTED BY THE MEDICAL CONSULTANT

In both letters from the Program Safeguard Contractor, there are four identical assertions made by the Medical Consultant that warrant a specific response before addressing the individual cases that were reviewed.

Bullet No. 1. *Exceeded the relatively more-restrictive CMS guidelines for number of NCSs to be performed for a given condition and also exceeded the more liberal AANEM 90th percentile standards. In a majority of instances Dr. Doe could have diagnosed unilateral carpal tunnel with as few as 2 sensory and 2 motor tests; he typically employed 5 sensory for unilateral and as many as 8 for bilateral CTS.*

Regarding the number of nerve conduction studies (NCSs) that are appropriate for a given condition, the Massachusetts Medicare Carrier has no published policy regarding Electrodiagnostic Medicine or the number of nerve conduction studies per diagnosis.

With regard to the assertion that I exceeded both the CMS Guidelines and American Association of Neuromuscular and Electrodiagnostic Medicine ("AANEM") recommendations, I dispute the Medical Consultant's conclusions. Attached as Appendix A are the AANEM recommendations, which allow for a significantly higher number of nerve conduction studies than the seemingly arbitrary criteria used by the Consultant. In many cases the number of studies that I used was less than recommended. Furthermore, since the diagnostic yield of sensory studies in many cases is higher than that of the motor, I have substituted the motor studies for sensory studies. In that situation not only is the

FIGURE 4-8 | Sample Response to Audit (Continued)

diagnostic yield higher, but also the total amount charged is smaller, as the sensory studies are reimbursed at the lower rate.

Additionally, the Medical Consultant's assertion "puts the cart before the horse" in arguing that a diagnosis of unilateral carpal tunnel syndrome could have been made with fewer tests. The fact of the matter is that a patient is referred because of certain symptoms. Until the actual tests are performed, no definitive diagnosis can be made. This position is fully supported by Dr. Roe's report at Point 1 (Appendix N).

In making the assertion about the appropriate number of tests, the Consultant focused exclusively on one diagnosis (unilateral Carpal Tunnel Syndrome) and neglected the fact that 15 out of 40 patients in the two samples had two or more diagnoses, which were established by the EMGs. Even in patients where only one diagnosis was made with the test, other diagnostic possibilities were excluded by performing a thorough testing; hence other diagnoses were "ruled out." The Consultant is using unpublished, seemingly arbitrary criteria when making a decision about what is "appropriate." The AANEM guidelines specifically state that no rules about the maximum number of nerve conduction studies (which are applicable for a single diagnosis) can be applied in the situation where multiple neurophysiologic diagnoses are established by performing NCS and EMG.

Additionally, the AAEM *"Practice Parameter for Electrodiagnostic Studies of Carpel Tunnel Syndrome"* recites that is appropriate to perform supplementary nerve studies. In all 40 cases the Consultant did not "allow" in any of her comments the use of median and ulnar mixed nerve studies, which have one of the highest diagnostic yields for Carpal Tunnel Syndrome (Appendix C).

Significantly, in a literature review of the usefulness of NCSs and needle electromyography for the evaluation of patients with carpal tunnel syndrome, the AAEM relied on several peer-reviewed studies that I co-authored. Therefore, my scientific work on electrodiagnosis of Carpal Tunnel Syndrome is an integral part of the foundation of the AANEM standards for neurophysiologic testing in CTS (Appendix M: Second AAEM literature review of the usefulness of nerve conduction studies and needle electromyography for the evaluation of patients with Carpal Tunnel Syndrome; pages 926, 936–7, 954, 974).

Bullet No. 2. *Dr. Doe routinely performs motor testing with F wave studies for CTS which is not indicated. He quite frequently test(sic) the radial nerve as part of his evaluation for CTS; this is not deemed necessary as part of the routine suite of test (sic) needed to deal with a possible CTS diagnosis.*

Once again, the Consultant is exclusively focusing on Carpal Tunnel Syndrome, while the fact of the matter is that the F waves were used to evaluate, confirm, or exclude proximal pathology in the affected limbs. In many cases patients had proximal symptoms which warranted evaluation of the F waves and radial nerves in order to evaluate for a cervical radiculopathy and brachial plexopathy. The focus of the EMG test is not only to evaluate for one and only diagnosis, but to establish a correct diagnosis even in situations where the

FIGURE 4-8 | Sample Response to Audit (Continued)

clinical assumption was incorrect. Focusing on only one problem, and stopping the test after only one clinical option was evaluated, would be substandard practice. Even in this sample, 15 out of 40 patients had two or more electrophysiologic diagnoses. By stopping the test prematurely and not evaluating for comorbidity, one would fail to establish the correct diagnosis. In this regard, I would refer to Dr. Doe's report at Points 2 and 3 (Appendix N).

Bullet No. 3. *Question of cervical radiculopathy in a significant proportion of the beneficiaries testing which leads to F wave testing and also to some extent to the use of EMG as well. There is seldom any detail as to the nature of the pain - just "shoulder pain" or something equally vague. This does not justify routine F wave testing. The need for F wave testing depends on the condition being tested for but should not form a routine part of the evaluation for CTS unless there's serious, well-founded concern that there may be a proximal lesion present. If there is reason to suspect a radiculopathy then documentation should offer some detail supporting that suspicion; such documentation was absent across the sample.*

The Consultant is suggesting that proximal arm pain should be neglected if the patient has CTS. As I routinely obtain a focused history and perform a focused exam on every patient in order to formulate an electrodiagnostic plan of action, I do not charge for those services, and I am not obligated to document the details of my clinical conclusions. A focused narrative documentation of the reason for the EMG test is documented for each patient under the heading "History/Comments" on each EMG report. The Consultant is also stating that the role of EMG in evaluation of a cervical radiculopathy is somehow questionable. In some cases in this sample the EMG portion of the test was denied even where the EMG diagnosed cervical radiculopathy. That is incorrect, as the role of EMG in cervical radiculopathy has been clearly established as reported in the AANEM policies (Appendix D: AANEM Practice Parameters for needle EMG in Cervical Radiculopathy). In this regard, I would refer to Dr. Doe's report at Point 4 (Appendix N).

Bullet No. 4. *There were a few cases in which all studies were denied — one involving postherpetic tingling and one involving a diabetic where it seemed the diagnosis was obvious and where no documentation of neurological exam appeared at all. The AANEM policy makes it clear that the electrodiagnostic physician should be serving as a consultant in these cases. Therefore, a history, focused exam, and diagnostic hypothesis should form part of the service; such documentation was absent across the sample.*

The Consultant is incorrect in asserting that the AANEM policy "makes it clear that the electrodiagnostic physician should be serving as a consultant" and therefore a neurological examination, including history, focused exam, and diagnostic hypothesis, should form part of the service. This is true only when the electrodiagnostic physician is asked to perform a consult by the referring physician. There is absolutely no such requirement or policy when only diagnostic testing is performed. Once again, I was never asked to perform a neurological consult on any patient. Additionally, a review of the actual records provided to the Consultant reveals that I did conduct a focused history and exam of each patient. In this regard, I would refer to Dr. Roe's report at Point 6 (Appendix N).

FIGURE 4-8 | Sample Response to Audit (Continued)

With regard to the two cases referenced by the Consultant, she denied the whole study with the explanation that the diagnosis was "obvious." The Consultant never interviewed, saw, or examined the patients. The statement that the diagnosis is "obvious" is unacceptable, as supported by Dr. Doe in her report at Point 5 (Appendix N).

- As more fully detailed in the individual responses to the Consultant's findings, the first patient had neurological symptoms following a herpes zoster infection and the EMG excluded a variety of conditions that can be seen following a herpes zoster infection. Studies have shown that up to 60% of patients have electrophysiologic abnormalities following herpes zoster (Patient #14 Boston List: CCC). Details regarding this issue can be found in Appendix E.

- The second patient is a diabetic with leg pain, low back pain, sensory disturbance in the legs, and balance difficulties. The EMG defined the exact type of neurological problem that the patient has and eliminated a wide spectrum of diagnostic possibilities that can be seen in diabetic patients with neurological complications (Patient #12 Worcester List: PT).

Bullet Specific to Worcester: *There was also a pattern noted of the physician billing the various codes with separate – TC and – 26 modifiers; sometimes the number of units billed for the – TC and – 26 bearing the same CPT code designator differed. These services should have been billed as complete procedures.*

As a general proposition, the Consultant is correct that the various procedures should be billed with a global code. However, this rule does not apply when services are rendered in a medically underserved area such as Worcester. In such cases, Medicare requires the physician to separately bill the professional (26) and technical (TC) components, and to submit the QU modifier with the professional component (26), denoting a medically underserved urban area (HPSA).

All of my charges submitted to Medicare without the QU modifier are automatically denied, and my billing service was instructed by the Medicare Carrier to separate the technical and professional components with the TC and 26, and further that the QU modifier must be used for the year 2005. Appendix L contains a copy of the Medicare Explanation of Benefits (EOB) of a claim that was denied because the TC and 26 modifiers were not used. The same EOB contains specific instructions that TC, 26, and QU must be used. As of January 1, 2006, a new modifier AQ replaced modifiers QU and QB. It appears that the Medical Consultant was unaware of the above requirements.

As a result, all of the denials based on the use of these modifiers for claims involving patients tested at the Worcester location must be overturned.

ADDITIONAL ISSUES INVOLVING THE CONSULTANT'S FINDINGS

- In several cases the MIP consultant denied the EMG portion of the test in patients who had electrophysiologic diagnosis of a cervical radiculopathy. It is not possible

FIGURE 4-8 | Sample Response to Audit (Continued)

to make the electrophysiologic diagnosis of a cervical radiculopathy without the EMG. Details regarding this issue can be found in Appendix D.

- In two cases, the MIP consultant inappropriately replaced the sensory nerve conduction codes (95904) with motor with F wave nerve conduction codes (95903), which is against every rule of proper billing. MIP consultant is changing the billing in a way that is not reflecting the actual tests that were performed, which is prohibited by the proper billing standards (Patient #7 Worcester: GH; and Patient #10 Worcester: ME).

APPEAL OF FINDINGS RELATING TO SERVICES RENDERED AT THE WORCESTER LOCATION
(The patients are listed in alphabetical order)

1) B., Anita

The Consultant had no comments about this patient.

2) B., Carl
   (HIC No. 98765432)

Mr. B. presented with right hand numbness and tingling in the first three fingers, and right hand atrophy. The testing was performed to evaluate for possible median neuropathy vs. proximal cervical or plexus lesion.

Electrodiagnostic testing showed a severe right median nerve lesion distal to the pronator teres, with absent right median motor, sensory, and mixed nerve responses.

The AANEM's *Recommended Policy for Electrodiagnostic Medicine* (Appendix A) recommends performing 3 motor and 4 sensory studies, and 2 H-reflex studies in patients with unilateral pain, numbness, or tingling. Additionally, a one-limb EMG is recommended.

Dr. Doe performed 1 motor study with F waves, 1 motor study without F waves (the right median motor responses were absent), 3 sensory and 2 mixed nerve studies, and a one-limb EMG.

The Consultant decreased the number of sensory units to 2 and downcoded the one motor with F waves study to motor without F waves study (95900).

Testing of the median and ulnar mixed nerves across the palm was necessary to establish the presence of any distal nerve response as the median motor and sensory responses were absent. Radial sensory responses were necessary from two perspectives: 1) to assess a possibility of a plexus lesion, and 2) to assess superficial radial nerve responses in view of absence of median sensory responses. Since the patient had atrophy/weakness of the hand, testing of the F waves was necessary to exclude proximal C8 root lesion.

3) C., Nathalie
   (HIC No. 31456900)

Mrs. C. presented with balance difficulties and distal sensory disturbance. The testing was performed to evaluate for a possible polyneuropathy versus lumbosacral (LS) lesion.

FIGURE 4-8 | Sample Response to Audit (Continued)

Electrodiagnostic testing showed an essentially normal study, with a slightly decreased bilateral peroneal motor amplitude.

The AANEM's *Recommended Policy for Electrodiagnostic Medicine* (Appendix A) recommends performing 4 motor and 6 sensory studies, and 2 H-reflex studies in patients with bilateral pain, numbness, or tingling. A two-limb EMG is also recommended.

Dr. Doe performed 4 motor studies with F waves, 2 sensory studies, 2 H-reflex studies, and a two-limb EMG.

The Consultant downcoded the motor studies with F waves to motor without F waves.

The F waves were medically necessary to evaluate proximal nerve segments and roots. In this patient, NCS did not reveal evidence of a polyneuropathy to explain her sensory disturbance and balance difficulties, hence testing for a LS radiculopathy was necessary. Furthermore, testing showed decreased distal peroneal motor amplitude, which indicated there was a need to assess proximal motor fibers to establish that the amplitude decrease was most likely due to direct trauma to the extensor digitorum brevis (EDB), which may be seen in elderly patients.

FIGURE 4-8 | Sample Response to Audit (Continued)

(*Continued from page 198*)

    treatment, and the fact that no one from Medicare examined the patient

- If the treatment was elective, a statement from the patient detailing the various choices given to him or her by the treating physician and the fact that the patient chose one course of treatment over another.

4.2.8   The Use of Statistical Sampling During Civil Audits

Most postpayment audits involve the use of statistical sampling and extrapolation procedures. Therefore, it is important for health care providers to have an understanding of extrapolation and statistical sampling methods in order to develop effective challenges and defenses to such audits.

4.2.9   How a Statistical Sampling Audit Is Initiated

When an initial audit or investigation discloses billing problems warranting an in-depth review of a physician's billing history, the government has two options: (1) perform a case-by-case review of the physician's patient files or (2) conduct a statistical sampling of the those records. Statistical sampling is by far the more frequently utilized option. Difficulties, such as the time and expense required to perform case-by-case reviews, generally lead third-party payers to apply the more economical, although potentially less reliable, statistical sampling techniques.

Medicare has employed the use of statistical sampling since 1972. Courts have further endorsed the use of these techniques, recognizing that "enormous logistical problems" exist when third-party payers are forced to initiate case-by-case record reviews of providers who have submitted literally hundreds or thousands of claims during a calendar year.

Although efforts to reduce governmental and other third-party payer costs have led to the general acceptance of statistical sampling in medical provider audits, physicians should be cognizant of the fact that such techniques do not always produce accurate or reliable results. In fact, the manner in which statistical sampling is performed may result in significantly exaggerated overpayment amounts that can and should be challenged.

4.2.10 How a Statistical Sampling Study Is Conducted

Medicare's Program Memorandum for Use of Statistical Sampling issued in 2001 contains a detailed technical explanation of the proper methods for establishing and conducting statistical sampling studies. The following is an elementary outline of how such studies are generally performed.

First, the Medicare contractor decides the items of service or types of billings to be reviewed during the sampling study. This entails the determination of whether the audit is to be purely random, or whether the sampling will be focused on particular code groupings. Next, the insurer determines the time period to be reviewed by establishing an explicit beginning and ending date. Finally, the insurer determines the universe of claims so that the results of the study may be extrapolated and a total overpayment estimation can be determined. The universe of claims merely refers to the total number of items of service that were actually paid during the time period selected for the sampling study.

Once these parameters have been set, the insurer selects a sampling unit. Sampling units are obtained by randomly selecting a sample of claims from within the aforementioned parameters established by the insurer. After selection, the insurer will request all documentation relating to the sampling unit. Each of these sample claims is then carefully reviewed for discrepancies and improper billing practices. The third-party payer then calculates an amount of overpayment for each sampling unit reviewed. Overpayment calculations represent the difference between the amount actually paid to the physician and the amount that the insurer contends should have been paid.

Once the overpayment totals are determined for the sample claims, the insurer utilizes extrapolation techniques to set an estimated total overpayment. Specifically, the aggregate amount of overpayments involved in the sampled cases is totaled, and an average overpayment is calculated by determining the percentage of error involved in the aggregate overpayment as compared to the total amount paid for the claims involved in the sampling. This average is then extrapolated across the physician's universe of claims and an estimated total amount of overpayment is determined.

The facts in the 1989 case of *Rockland Medilabs, Inc v Perales* provide a poignant lesson of how the sampling and audit procedure is employed in actual practice. In that case, the state Medicaid carrier performed a random sample audit of a laboratory provider's billings for a 5-month subject period.

> The provider's total Medicaid billings during the subject period amounted to $1,370,099 comprising some 21,912 visits for services rendered to 14,762 patients. A random sample of 100 billings comprising 151 individual visits totaling $9,090 in Medicaid payments was examined. Of that sample, [Medicaid] found 16 improper billings amounting to $3,237 in allegedly fraudulent charges, or some 35% of the random sample. Extrapolating from those figures, [Medicaid] ultimately determined that [the provider] had overcharged Medicaid some $477,933 during the subject period.

Another example of an actual notice of overpayment involved an emergency medicine practice at a suburban hospital. That audit was based on a statistically valid random sampling and extrapolation of a sample of 200 claims for CPT code 99285 submitted to Medicare. After review, Medicare determined that 46% of these Level 5 emergency department claims were inappropriate and thus constituted overpayments. This 46% error rate was applied to the total universe of paid claims for this CPT code for a 2-year period ($456,251) to arrive at a projected overpayment of $209,876.

Large overpayment demands requested by Medicare and other insurers as a result of such audits have led a number of providers to challenge the use of statis tical sampling and extrapolation. Specifically, providers have argued that these procedures are arbitrary, capricious, discriminatory, and/or otherwise in violation of due process. Courts have uniformly rejected these arguments, however, and have approved the use of these statistical techniques. In upholding the use of sampling against challenges that Medicare should have conducted a case-by-case claims review, one federal court stated:

> Absent an explicit provision in the statute that requires individu-
> alized claims adjudication for overpayment assessments against
> providers, the private interest at stake is easily outweighed by the
> government interest in minimizing administrative burdens; in light
> of the fairly low risk of error so long as the extrapolation is made from
> a representative sample and is statistically significant, the government
> interest predominates.

The fact that the use of statistical sampling has been upheld in the health care audit context should not, however, prevent providers from challenging these audits.

4.2.11   Challenging Statistical Sampling

Medicare contractors, such as Recovery Audit Contractors, will generally assert the validity of the statistical sampling utilized during these postpayment audits. However, while courts have consistently upheld the general use of sampling, particular audits have been deemed inappropriate as a result of unacceptable sampling techniques. For example, in an early case, the court took exception to the size of the sample used and found that, in the circumstances of the case, the extrapolation of the sample results to the provider's entire claims universe constituted a violation of due process.

It is prudent, therefore, for physicians and their counsel confronted with the results of audits to closely examine the circumstances of the audit and sampling techniques. In fact, a provider's right to challenge statistical samples has been upheld and recognized by the courts and by Medicare and, in some instances, has been established by state statutes. For example, in a ruling from 1986 regarding the appropriateness of statistical sampling, Medicare stated that:

> Sampling does not deprive a provider of its rights to challenge the sam-
> ple, nor of its rights to procedural due process. Sampling only creates

a presumption of validity as to the amount of an overpayment which may be used as the basis for recoupment. The burden then shifts to the provider to take the next step. The provider could attack the statistical validity of the sample, or it could challenge the correctness of the determination in specific cases identified by the sample . . . . In either case, the provider is given a full opportunity to demonstrate that the overpayment determination is wrong. If certain individual cases within the sample are determined to be decided erroneously, the amount of overpayment projected to the universe of claims can be modified. If the statistical basis upon which the projection was based is successfully challenged, the overpayment determination can be corrected.

Additionally, courts reviewing the use of statistical sampling studies have consistently expressed concern that providers have an adequate opportunity to examine and rebut samplings conducted by insurers.

Providers need to understand the appropriate bases for challenging statistical samples. The following brief list sets out a number of factors on which statistical samples can be challenged:

- *Statistical significance:* Each statistical sample must involve a large enough number of claims to generate statistically valid results. Contrary to what providers may assume, the size of the sample is influenced significantly by the size of the estimated overpayment.

- *Universe stratification:* Stratification involves insurers splitting the universe population into subpopulations for the purposes of conducting a sampling. The use or lack of stratification can lead to improper statistical results. Providers should analyze the appropriateness of the insurer's stratification techniques and challenge these techniques when appropriate.

- *Outliers:* Unrepresentative sample claims, known as outliers, can significantly bias the results of a statistical sample. Providers should review the sampled claims to determine whether any such outliers exist.

- *Extrapolation techniques:* The manner in which insurers extrapolate sampling results may be inappropriate. Extrapolation that fails to take sampling errors and other variables into account may result in overinflated overpayment demands. Providers should request information regarding how an insurer's extrapolation was conducted.

- *Documentation:* Insurers conducting statistical studies must maintain detailed documentation throughout the sampling process so that providers can evaluate and challenge the validity of the sampling techniques. Lack of such documentation can be the basis for invalidation of a sampling.

- *Other nonsampling errors:* Occasionally, the actual process of collecting data and the calculations performed are flawed. Any such flaws can significantly affect the results of a sampling and can be challenged.

4.2.12   Practical Suggestions for Confronting a Statistical Sampling Study

When confronting the results of a statistical sampling, the physician and his or her counsel must evaluate the study to determine whether either the factual findings derived from the sampled cases are in error or the statistical sampling methodology was flawed.

4.2.12.1   *Reexamination of the Audited Cases*

First, as with any type of audit, it is essential that each of the sampled cases be reexamined to determine whether the results reached by the carrier are correct. Pursuant to Medicare's Program Memorandum on the Use of Statistical Sampling, all findings with respect to each case involved in the sample must be documented as to why the original claim was changed and how the overpayment was determined.

4.2.12.2   *Having a Medical Consultant Review the Medical Findings*

Through counsel, the physician should also retain a medical consultant for the purpose of rebutting the findings made by the insurer. Experience with Medicare and other insurers has shown that the insurer will exclude from the sampling well-documented case evaluations that demonstrate the propriety of the services rendered. If the physician can persuade Medicare that a number of the claims involved in the actual sampling were in fact correctly submitted for payment, the resulting percentage of error on which the extrapolation is based will also be reduced, resulting in a much-reduced projected claim for reimbursement from what the insurer initially sought.

4.2.12.3 *Retaining an Expert Statistician*

Additionally, it is vital to retain an experienced statistician to examine the methodology on which the statistical sampling and the resulting projection was conducted. A statistician will understand the process of challenging samplings on the basis of statistical validity, improper stratification, improper presence of outliers, improper extrapolation techniques, insufficient documentation, and other improper nonsampling errors.

4.2.13 Medicare Consent Settlement Procedures

As a result of the administrative problems inherent in constructing and conducting a statistically valid sampling study, Medicare has made a policy decision to obtain consent settlements based on a probable extrapolated overpayment rather than engaging in a full-fledged sampling study. Medicare carriers are authorized to enter into consent settlements in overpayment cases based not on a "statistically valid random sample" of claims but instead on a smaller mini-sample. The stated goal of this program is to successfully recoup an estimated overpayment based on a limited audit in an expeditious manner. It is designed to remove the uncertainty inherent in the fair hearing process involving overpayment claims where both the validity of the sampling study and the correctness of the overpayment determination can be challenged.

The rationale for promulgating this consent procedure is to streamline the recoupment process and to reduce the administrative costs of conducting statistically valid random samplings, while educating the physician as to problems with the billing. The consent settlement process is entirely voluntary on the part of the physician. It affords the physician an opportunity to resolve the disputed issues without further inquiry by the Medicare contractor. However, if the physician does not agree to the consent settlement process, the physician is advised that a full statistical sampling will be conducted.

Medicare requires the contractor to describe the two options available to the physician during this consent settlement procedure. Option 1 is proceeding to a statistically valid random sample for the same universe and time period involved in the audit. By choosing this option, the provider retains all its procedural due process rights to a fair hearing and an appeal to an administrative law judge.

Option 2 allows the physician to agree that there was a problem in the billing and to correct the billing procedure in the future. Under option 2, the physician accepts the capped potential projected overpayment but is allowed to submit additional medical documentation relevant to the individual claims that made up the mini-sample. The Medicare contractor, in turn, will review this material to determine whether an adjustment should be made in the projected sampling results. By agreeing to this option, however, the physician must agree to accept any revised determination made about these claims and to waive any right to appeal. The only concession granted to the physician is that the revised potential overpayment amount will not exceed the initial capped amount. In return, the carrier agrees not to audit the physician's claims for any procedure codes in the future for the period considered in the audit (unless fraud is involved).

4.2.14 Summary

With the increasing emphasis on cost containment for health services, physicians are undergoing audits on a frequent basis. Familiarization with the audit process and the methodologies employed in sampling studies will enable physicians and their attorneys to develop effective strategies for limiting exposure to overpayment demands.

4.3 How to Handle a Health Care Fraud Investigation

4.3.1 Introduction

As a result of the Health Insurance Portability and Accountability Act of 1996 (HIPAA), a number of the administering and investigating agencies are involved in a cooperative effort to identify, determine, and act on fraud and abuse complaints or scenarios warranting a preliminary investigation and those warranting a full investigation. These include the local Medicare carrier and new Medicare Administrative Contractors, the Department of Health and Human Services OIG, the state MFCU, and the single state agencies administering Medicaid.

The principal federal agency charged with investigating health care fraud against the Medicare and Medicaid programs is the OIG. The OIG has broad authority to address health care fraud and abuse enforcement and prevention. The OIG conducts both audits and criminal investigations. Additionally, the Federal Bureau of Investigation (FBI) has responsibility for the investigation of federal health care offenses, as well as other federal crimes. The OIG and FBI work in concert on many cases.

On a local state level, all but 2 states have a MFCU that is generally a part of the state attorney general's office. As the name implies, these units are charged with investigating and prosecuting fraud relating to state Medicaid programs. In addition, the units are also responsible for reviewing complaints of patient abuse and neglect in all residential health care facilities that receive Medicaid funds. It should be noted that federal investigative agencies conduct cooperative investigations with state investigative agencies, such as the MFCU.

4.3.2   How an Investigation Is Initiated

A health care fraud investigation of a physician practice can result from a variety of events. These include the following:

- Tips from informers
- Complaints by patients to the OIG hotline or state Medicaid agency
- Complaints by *qui tam* relators (whistleblowers), including disgruntled employees or competitors
- Referrals from the fraud units of the Medicare contractors or state Medicaid agency
- Statistical analyses of perceived patterns of abusive billing practices, such as coding at unusually higher levels than one's peers.

4.3.3   How a Physician Will Learn of a Fraud Investigation

A physician will learn that he or she is under criminal investigation from one of several sources. Investigators may contact patients and former or current employees and inform them the physician or practice is being investigated for fraud and abuse. In turn, the employees will advise the physician of the contact by the government investigators. Second, an investigator from the OIG, FBI, MFCU, or Medicare contractor will appear at the physician's office. Additionally, the physician may receive a subpoena to either a grand jury or the US attorney's office to produce documents. Finally, a search warrant may be executed at the physician's office.

4.3.4   Informing Employees of the Investigation

If the physician or practice knows that it is under investigation, it is likely that employees will be contacted by investigators at some point during the investigation. In fact, the most commonly used interview technique in health care fraud and abuse investigations is the unannounced after work interview. Investigators employ this tactic of approaching employees at home in the mornings or evenings or on weekends in the hope of catching them off guard and at a location where they will be more likely to talk than at work. Employees confronted at home will usually cooperate with investigators and provide extensive interviews due to nervousness, uncertainty, and the general assumption that they should cooperate with the government. The deliberate or accidental failure to inform employees of an investigation leaves them ill-informed of their rights, responsibilities, and the proper information with which to protect themselves. Therefore, it is usually advisable to inform employees of the existence of the investigation and what their rights are in advance of any such contact. Advance disclosure tends to reduce the shock and surprise when employees are contacted at home and ensures that they have a thorough understanding of their rights and obligations.

In addition, during a health care fraud investigation, speculation and rumor can paralyze a physician's office. By informing employees of the nature of the investigation and the physician's position at the outset of an investigation, counsel can address any concerns the employees may have as well as dispel false rumors that may be circulating in the office. Physicians should be cautioned to not engage in any activity the government might misconstrue as obstructing justice. Because of the potential for misunderstanding, the physician's attorney (rather than the physician himself or herself) should advise employees about not only the existence of an investigation but also what their rights are in the event any employee is contacted by a government investigator. This is generally done by means of a letter or memorandum to eliminate the potential confusion over what was or was not stated to the employee (see Figure 4-9 for an example).

To begin with, each employee has a choice to be interviewed or to decline to be interviewed. Furthermore, absent a grand jury subpoena, the employee cannot be compelled to give any statement. The decision to speak to a government investigator is the employee's decision alone.

If the employee is contacted by an investigator and decides to be interviewed, the employee has a right to consult an attorney before each and

Law Firm No.1

Tom Jones

Direct Dial: (555) 555-8555
Email: xxx@yyy.com

January 8, 2008

RE: Investigation by the federal Office of Inspector General

The federal Office of Inspector General ("OIG") is conducting an investigation into the coding and billing practices of ABC Medical Center. ABC is cooperating fully with the government investigation. The OIG will be requesting to interview certain employees of ABC Medical Center in connection with the investigation. Investigators may also attempt to interview employees at their homes. It is important that you understand your rights and obligations if you are contacted.

1.   You have the right to consent to an interview or to decline to be interviewed. You cannot be compelled to give any statement to an investigator. If you agree to be interviewed, you can decline to answer any question that you do not want to answer and/or even stop the interview at any time for any, or no, reason. *Please be aware that there is no such thing as an "off-the-record" interview with the government.*

2.   However, if you decline to be interviewed, you may be subpoenaed to appear before a federal grand jury to answer questions under oath.

3.   If you are contacted by an investigator and you decide to speak to him or her, or if you agree to be interviewed, you have the right to consult an attorney before, and even during, each and every conversation. You also are entitled to have an attorney with you at all times during any conversations that you might have with investigators.

4.   Massachusetts law allows an employer to pay the legal fees and expenses of its employees for work-related legal representation. ABC Medical Center has made a decision that it is appropriate to do so here. We have conducted a search of Massachusetts lawyers who have experience in the field of federal criminal health care investigations and we find that John Doe of Boston, MA (312-123-4576) comes highly recommended to advise and represent individuals in this matter. If you would like to have counsel for any contacts with government investigators, we recommend that you contact Mr. Johnston, as Mr. Johnston is available to speak to you. He would represent you, and not ABC Medical Center, in this process. At the same time, ABC Medical Center will pay for the costs of your representation, as permitted by Massachusetts law.

5.   Should you decide to be interviewed by a government investigator, you <u>must</u> provide full and truthful information in response to any questions that you choose to answer.

6.   Whether to speak to government investigators is your decision alone. However, I suggest that you consult with attorney Johnston or another attorney about this decision.

7.   Please immediately contact one of us if you are approached by anyone requesting information about ABC Medical Center.

Tom Jones
Law Firm No. 1
(555) 555-8555

FIGURE 4-9 | Sample Notice to Employees Regarding Investigation

every conversation and is also entitled to have an attorney present during any interview with investigators. In the event the employee decides to be interviewed by a government investigator, the employee must provide full and truthful information in response to any questions that are asked. It is a crime to knowingly make a false or misleading statement to a government agent during an investigation.

Under no circumstances should the physician or practice administrator tell an employee not to speak to an investigator. In fact, the safest course of action is to advise the employee to speak to an attorney regarding his or her rights. It is recommended that employees be advised of the name of the attorney hired to represent the physician/practice during the investigation and also be further informed that the attorney is available to answer any questions any employee may have. The physician's attorney may be able to help and provide some clarification to the employees. Finally, employees should be requested to immediately contact the physician's attorney if the employee is approached by anyone requesting information about the physician and/or the practice.

4.3.5   Hiring an Attorney for Employees

While the attorney for the physician can appropriately inform a physician's employees about the nature of the investigation, as well as answer certain questions raised by the employees, the attorney hired by the physician cannot ethically represent the physician's employees. While it may initially be less expensive to have one attorney represent both the physician or practice and its employees, there is an overwhelming risk that the attorney will have to withdraw from the case at a later time if a conflict of interest arises. Therefore, it is recommended that separate attorneys be hired for the employees at the outset of the investigation.

In regard to hiring local counsel, the following information provides several practical tips. As stated above, neither the physician nor the attorney can advise employees not to talk to investigators. The physician can, however, advise employees that he or she will pay for an attorney to represent the employee's interests. The attorney can then make an independent decision as to whether the employee should speak to an investigator. If an interview is conducted, the attorney will be present with the employee. This serves to protect not only the employee but the physician as well, as the attorney will prevent the employee from being intimidated or unduly influenced by government investigators.

4.3.6   Receipt of a Subpoena or Investigative Demand

In the vast majority of cases, health care fraud investigations involve a variety of requests for documents and investigatory subpoenas. It is not unusual for the receipt of a request for records, or *subpoena duces tecum*, to be the first notice a physician or practice receives that it is the subject of an investigation. The following includes an outline of the various tools used by law enforcement agencies to obtain documentary material during the course of a health care fraud investigation, as both federal and state agencies have authority to summons records in certain circumstances.

4.3.6.1   *HIPAA Investigative Demands*

The most important enforcement tool provided to the Department of Justice is the HIPAA *investigative demand*. In connection with *federal* health care investigations, grand jury subpoenas are less common than in other types of investigations because the Justice Department is authorized to issue investigative demands. Under HIPAA, the local US attorney can issue an investigative demand to obtain records in connection with a criminal health care fraud investigation. These investigative demands are the principal tool used by federal prosecutors during joint civil and criminal investigations of health care fraud (see the sample investigative demand in Figure 4-10).

The US attorney can require the production of not only documents but also other tangible things (ie, date stamps, signature stamps, computers, floppy disks). While the government cannot use these investigative demands to compel witnesses to give testimony, the government can require a custodian of records to testify about the production and authentication of such records. The authority granted by the enabling statute is very broad and has been upheld against arguments

(Continued on page 227)

UNITED STATES OF AMERICA

DEPARTMENT OF JUSTICE

SUBPOENA DUCES TECUM

TO:

YOU ARE HEREBY COMMANDED TO APPEAR BEFORE _____

<u>*Assistant United States Attorney*</u> *an official of the U.S Department of Justice, and you are hereby required to bring with you and produce the following: See attached*

which are necessary in the performance of the responsibility of the U.S. Department of Justice to investigate Federal health care offenses, defined in 18 U.S.C. § 24(a) to mean violations of, or conspiracies to violate: 18 U.S.C §§669,1035,1347, or 1518; and 18 U.S.C §§ 287, 371, 664, 666, 1001, 1027, 1341, 1343, or 1954 if the violation or conspiracy relates to a health care benefit program (defined in 18 U.S.C § 24(b)).

PLACE AND TIME FOR APPEARANCE:

United States Attorney's Office, One Courthouse Way, Suite 9200, Boston, MA 02210, on September 15, 2006 at 10 o'clock A.M, or at your option, the documents may be mailed to the Assistant U.S. Attorney listed at:

> U.S. Attorney's Office, 5th Floor
> 408 Atlantic Avenue (John Williams Coastguard Building)
> Boston, MA 02110

if received prior to the date and time for appearance.

Failure to comply with the requirements of this subpoena will render you liable to proceedings in the district court of the United States to enforce obedience to the requirements of this subpoena, and to punish default or disobedience.

Issued under authority of Sec. 248 of the Health Insurance Portability and Accountability Act of 1996, Public Law No. 104-51 (18 U.S.C. 9 3486;

IN TESTIMONY WHEREOF

Health CareZ Fraud Chief, USAO Massachusetts the undersigned official of the U.S. DEPARTMENT OF JUSTICE, has hereunto set her hand this 4th day of August, 2006.

_____

(SIGNATURE)

FORM CRM l8o
MAR. 97

FIGURE 4-10 | HIPAA Investigative Demand

SCHEDULE A TO SUBPOENA DUCES TECUM

I.   DEFINITIONS

A.   "Document(s)" means, without limitation, any written, printed, typed, photo graphed, recorded, transcribed, taped, filmed, or otherwise reproduced or stored communication or representation, whether comprised of letters, words, numbers, pictures, sounds or symbols, or any combination thereof. This definition includes copies or duplicates of documents contemporaneously or subsequently created which have any non-conforming notes or other markings, including any additions, deletions, alterations, or notations, as well as the backsides of any communication or representation which contain any of the above. "Document" also includes all attachments, enclosures, or other matter affixed to or incorporated by reference within documents responsive to this Attachment, including, but not limited to, any pages that show who reviewed, approved or rejected a particular document.

By way of example, "document(s)" includes, but is not limited to: writings; correspondence; memoranda; notes; drafts; records; files; letters; envelopes; messages; electronic mail; electronic messages; analyses; agreements; accounts; working papers; reports and summaries of investigations; trade letters; press releases; comparisons; books; ledgers; journals; bills; vouchers; checks; statements; worksheets; summaries; notices; drawings; diagrams; graphic presentations; instructions; manuals; calendars; diaries; telephone message records or logs; routing slips; activity reports; articles; magazines; newspapers; brochures; guidelines; notes or minutes of meetings or of other communications of any type, including inter- and intra-office or Company communications; reports; plans; questionnaires; forecasts; briefing materials; surveys; charts; graphs; diagrams; compilations; computations; photographs; films or videos; tapes; discs; data cells; databases; spreadsheets; software; bulletins; voice mails; information stored or maintained by electronic data processing or word processing equipment; electronic claims filings; invoices; computer and network activity logs; all other data compilations from which information can be obtained including electromagnetically sensitive stored media such as floppy disks, hard disks, hard drives and magnetic tapes; Web pages; any preliminary versions, drafts or revisions of any of the foregoing; and all attachments to any of the items set forth in this paragraph.

B.   "You," "_____" or the "Company" means any and all of the following:

1.   the entity on which this subpoena was served, irrespective of the name under which it has operated;

page 1 of 5

FIGURE 4-10 | HIPAA Investigative Demand (Continued)

2. _____and any of its predecessors, parents, subsidiaries, affiliates, segments, departments, branches, groups, operations, units, plants, and divisions, both presently existing and those which previously existed, as well as any joint ventures of which it is a part;

3. each of their present or former officers, directors, representatives, employees, attorneys, consultants, contractors, or agents acting or pur-porting to act or appearing to act on behalf of the Company, whether or not their actions were authorized by the Company or were within the proper scope of their authority.

C. "Employee" means any person, including but not limited to any independent contractor or agent, all past and present directors, officers, agents, representatives, attor-neys, accountants, advisors, and consultants who acted or purported to act on behalf of the Company or who have performed any service for the Company or under its name (whether on a full-time, part-time, piece-work, commission, or other basis, and whether paid or unpaid).

D. "Person" includes within its meaning natural persons and corporations, com-panies, partnerships, unincorporated business associations, and any other entity com-posed of natural persons.

E. "Concerning" means referring to, evidencing, describing, or constituting.

F. "Communication" means any transmission or exchange of information between two or more persons orally or in writing and includes, without limitation, any conversation or discussion, whether face-to-face or by means of telephone or other media, whether by chance or by design.

G. "Contact" means any communication, whether written or oral, including telephone conversations or any personal encounter, whether by chance or by design, in a meeting or otherwise.

H. The term "_____" means any of the following:

_____

_____ as well as any entity in which _____ has a controlling interest, directly or indirectly.

INSTRUCTIONS

A. In lieu of appearing at the date and time specified, you may, at your option, produce the records sought to Assistant United States Attorney Susan Winkler, United States Attorney's Office, 5th Floor, 408 Atlantic Avenue, Boston, MA 02110.

FIGURE 4-10 | HIPAA Investigative Demand (Continued)

B.   The recipient of this subpoena shall identify a qualified custodian of records who will be available to testify at the place and time indicated, concerning the production and authentication of documents and records required to be produced by this subpoena.

C.   If a claim of privilege is asserted in response to any document requested by this subpoena, and such document, or any part thereof, is not produced on the basis of such claim, for each such document or part thereof that is not produced, you are directed to provide a privilege log wherein you identify the type of document being withheld (e.g, letter, memorandum, handwritten notes, marginalia, etc.), all actual and intended recipients of the document, its date, and the specific privilege being asserted, all with sufficient particularity so as to allow the U.S. Attorney's Office, and potentially the Court, to assess the validity of the claim of privilege. In addition, where a document is pulled for privilege, please insert a colored piece of paper containing the same bates-number as the document pulled so that it is clear from whose files the privileged documents were pulled.

D.   All documents provided in response to this subpoena are to be the original documents and are to include all copies that differ in any respect (such as marginalia and/or notations), and are to include all markings and post-it notes and other similar documents attached thereto, as well as all attachments referred to or incorporated by the documents. In addition, to the extent records are kept electronically in the normal course of business, they are required to be produced in that format, with sufficient identification of software and provision of any proprietary software as required to access and manipulate the documents to the same extent accessed and manipulated by the Company,

E.   The words "and" and "or" in this subpoena shall be read in both the conjunctive and the disjunctive (i.e., "and/or"), so as to give the document request its broadest meaning.

F.   The term "any" shall be construed to include the word "all" and the term "all" shall be construed to include the word "any."'

G.   Scope of search required: This subpoena calls for all documents in your possession, custody or control, including, but not limited to, your officers, directors, employees, agents, consultants and contractors. You are required to search all files, including electronic sources, reasonably likely to contain responsive documents, including files left behind by former officers, directors, agents and employees.

H.   Manner of production: All documents produced in response to this subpoena shall comply with the following instructions:

  i. You shall conduct a search for responsive documents in a manner sufficient to identify the source and location where each responsive document is found.

page 3 of 5

FIGURE 4-10 | HIPAA Investigative Demand (Continued)

ii. All documents produced in response to this subpoena shall be segregated and labeled to show the document request to which the documents are responsive and the source and location where the document was found.

iii. To the extent that documents are found in file folders, computer disks, hard drives and/or other storage media which have labels or other identifying information, the documents shall be produced with such file folder and label information intact.

iv. To the extent that documents are found attached to other documents, by means of paper clips, staples or other means of attachment, such documents shall be produced together in their condition when found.

I. In the event there are no documents responsive to a particular subpoena request, please specify that you have no responsive documents.

J. If you know of documents you once possessed or controlled, but no longer possess or control, which would have been responsive to this subpoena, state what disposition was made of such documents, including identification of the persons who are or are believed to be in possession or control of such documents currently.

K. To facilitate the handling and return of the submitted documents, please mark each page with an identifying logo or the first three letters of your company's name and number each page sequentially beginning with "000001." The marks should be placed in the lower right hand corner of each page but should not obscure any information on the document. All documents should be produced in enclosures bearing the name of your company, the date of the subpoena and the paragraphs of the subpoena to which the documents pertain.

L. The time period of this subpoena is January 1, 1999 to the present, unless otherwise specified.

III. SPECIFICATIONS

1. "All contracts between _____

2. All documents concerning contracts to which any of the _____ Companies is a party.

3. All documents concerning payments to any of the _____

4. All documents concerning communications with any of the _____ Companies since August 2003.

page 4 of 5

FIGURE 4-10 | HIPAA Investigative Demand (Continued)

5. All documents concerning communications with _____ since August 2003.

6. All documents concerning communications with _____ since August 2003.

7. All documents concerning communications with _____ since August 2003.

8. All documents concerning contracts or agreements with _____.

9. All documents concerning communications with _____ since August 2003.

10. All documents concerning contracts or agreements with _____.

11. All documents concerning communications with _____ since August 2003.

12. All documents concerning communications with _____ since August 2003.

13. All documents concerning contracts or agreements with any entity owned, controlled, or operated by _____.

14. All documents concerning communications since August 2003 with any entity owned, controlled, or operated by _____.

15. All documents concerning communications with _____ since August 2003.

16. All hard drives used by _____.

17. All documents concerning communications to or from_____to or from _____.

18. All documents concerning communications to or from _____ to or from Any _____regional _____director, or to any _____.

19. All reports and other documents concerning the performance of _____.

20. All reports and other documents concerning the performance of _____.

21. All reports concerning grants and other support provided to_____ by any pharmaceutical manufacturer or distributor.

22. All e-mails to which the following persons were a sender or recipient:

23. All documents concerning complaints or concerns about _____.

page 5 of 5

FIGURE 4-10 | HIPAA Investigative Demand (Continued)

(Continued from page 220)

that it constitutes an unreasonable search and seizure under the Fourth Amendment, which requires a showing of probable cause.

Although HIPAA investigative demands may be issued only in connection with criminal health care fraud investigations by the US attorney's office, the information obtained may be shared with civil and administrative enforcement agencies, such as the OIG. As a result, these administrative demands facilitate the conduct of joint criminal and civil investigations because the documents produced are not subject to the secrecy requirements governing a grand jury subpoena. In fact, these investigative demands are used at the same time as an ongoing grand jury or other criminal investigation to enable the sharing of information with any civil component of the joint investigation.

A physician subject to an investigative subpoena should be aware that HIPAA affords protection to providers who comply with an investigative demand. The statute explicitly provides immunity from civil liability to a physician or other entity that complies in good faith with a demand and produces the requested materials. This is an absolute grant of immunity that overrides any federal or state laws governing the confidentiality of medical records.

4.3.6.2   *OIG Requests for Assistance and Administrative Subpoenas*

By statute, the OIG has broad authority to request access to examine a health care provider's books and records. As a result, the OIG is not required to issue a summons in order to gain access to records or information, but may simply submit a request in writing to the provider (see Figure 4-11). In general, denial of the request can result in eventual suspension or exclusion from the federal health programs. The OIG's authority with regard to access requests is limited to obtaining documentary materials related to the Medicare and Medicaid programs. As a rule of thumb, recipients of such a request should ensure that only the materials the OIG is authorized to examine and has requested are provided. While there

(Continued on page 230)

DEPARTMENT OF HEALTH & HUMAN SERVICES   OFFICE OF INSPECTOR GENERAL

Washington, D.C. 20201

July 07 1999   REQUEST FOR INFORMATION
                                                     OR ASSISTANCE

Our Reference: 01 File No. 1-99-,
Your Reference:

To: Tom Jones, Esquire
      Law Firm No. 1
      Boston, Massachusetts 01251

The Inspector General of the Department of Health and Human Services, pursuant to the authority contained in 5 USC Appendix 3 et seq., requests that you furnish information or assistance as follows:

　　All patient records identified in the _____ investigation be made
　　available to agents for their review at

Pertinent sections of the United States Code are set forth on the reverse hereof. The request is made for law enforcement purposes and in connection with an official investigation being conducted by the Department.

CAUTION: Representatives of the Office of Inspector General are required to show their
                official identification when personally requesting information or assistance.

Requested by: _____   Special Agent
                                    Name and Title

                         DHHS/OIG/OI
                         P.O. Box 8767
                         Boston. MA 02114 _____
                         Office

page 1 of 2

FIGURE 4-11 │ OIG Request for Records

Pursuant to the authority contained in 5 USC Appendix 3 et seq., the Inspector General (or his delegate) is authorized to:

(1)   have access to all records, reports, audits, reviews, documents, papers, recommendations, or other material available to the applicable Department which relate to programs and operations with respect to which the Inspector General has responsibilities under this Act (section 6(a)(1));

(2)   request such information or assistance as may be necessary for carrying out the duties and responsibilities provided by this Act from any Federal, State, or local government agency or unit thereof (section 6(a)(3));

(3)   require by subpoena the production of all information documents, reports, answers, records, accounts, papers, and other data and documentary evidence necessary in the performance of the functions assigned by this Act, which subpoena, in the case of contumacy or refusal to obey, shall be enforceable by order of any appropriate United States District Court (section 6(a)(4)).

Other provisions state:

(1)   Upon request of the Inspector General for information or assistance under section 6(a)(3), the head of any Federal agency involved shall, insofar as is practicable and not in contravention of any existing statutory restriction, or regulation of the Federal agency from which the information is requested, furnish to the Inspector General, or to an authorized designee, such information or assistance.

(2)   Whenever information or assistance requested under subsection 6 (a)(1) or 6 (a)(3) is, in the judgement of the Inspector General unreasonably refused or not provided, the Inspector General shall report the circumstances to the head of the establishment involved without delay.

FIGURE 4-11 | OIG Request for Records (Continued)

(*Continued from page 227*)

may be many other considerations bearing on the issue of whether or not additional documents should be provided, this decision is best made after careful consideration of a number of issues, including patient confidentiality, privacy, and privilege, agency jurisdiction, a thorough grasp of the focus of the investigation, and the related factual issues.

The OIG also has broad administrative authority to subpoena information, documents, records, reports, and other data during a Medicare/Medicaid-related investigation (see the sample subpoena in Figure 4-12). OIG subpoenas for documents can be used in support of any OIG investigation. While the power to compel the production of documentary material is very broad, the OIG does not have the authority to depose witnesses. However, when an OIG investigation becomes the subject of a federal grand jury proceeding, it is OIG policy that relevant documents should be obtained by grand jury subpoena or a HIPAA investigative demand issued by the US attorney. As a result, the OIG will rarely issue a subpoena in furtherance of a criminal investigation that has been referred to the local US attorney.

4.3.6.3 Grand Jury Subpoenas

The federal US attorney and the state MFCU can issue a subpoena for both testimony and records to a grand jury during the course of a criminal investigation (see Figure 4-13). If the physician receives a grand jury subpoena, this signifies that a criminal investigation is ongoing. At the same time, the issuance of grand jury subpoena, rather than a search warrant, is generally an indication that the prosecutor does not believe the physician or his or her staff are likely to destroy documents. Unlike a HIPAA investigative demand or OIG subpoena, a grand jury subpoena can be issued to compel the testimony of witnesses as well as for the production of documentary material.

Documents produced and testimony given in response to a federal or state grand jury subpoena are subject to the requirements of grand jury secrecy. As a result, such information cannot be shared with civil or administrative agencies without a court order. As stated above, given the powers of the US attorney and OIG to issue administrative subpoenas during a health care fraud investigation, grand jury subpoenas are less

DEPARTMENT OF HEALTH & HUMAN SERVICES

OFFICE OF THE INSPECTOR GENERAL

OFFICE OF INVESTIGATIONS

233 N. Michigan Ave

Chicago. IL 60601

Accompanying this letter is a subpoena addressed to you returnable at the Office of Inspector General, Office of Investigations, Detroit Sub-Office, before my designee, Special Agent _____. The subpoena has been issued pursuant to the authority of the Inspector General by Section 6 (a) (4) of Public Law 95-452 [5 U.S.C. Appendix 3 Section 6 (a) (4)), as amended by Public Law 100-504.

All documents provided in response to the attached subpoena are to be originals (including any copies maintained in your files), or legible certified copies, unless otherwise noted. If any copies are provided in response to the subpoena, the original records must be maintained and made available to employees of my office, upon request, during normal business hours.

Failure to appear at the time and place specified in the subpoena may be taken as a failure to comply with the subpoena. However, as a convenience, you may assemble the documents requested and return them via certified mail on or before May 1, 2001 to:

Special Agent _____

Department of Health and Human Services

Office of Inspector General

Office of Investigation

477 Michigan Avenue, Suite 40

Detroit, MI 48226

If you have any questions, please contact Special Agent _____ at (313) 555-555.

Sincerely,

_____

Regional Inspector General

for Investigations

page 1 of 5

FIGURE 4-12 | OIG Subpoena

UNITED STATES OF AMERICA

DEPARTMENT OF HEALTH AND HUMAN SERVICES

OFFICE OF INSPECTOR GENERAL

SUBPOENA DUCES TECUM

To:

YOU ARE HEREBY COMMANDED TO APPEAR BEFORE Special Agent _____,
an official of the Office of Inspector General, at 477 *Michigan Avenue Suite*
1140, *in the City of Detroit and State of Michigan, on the 1st day of May,* 2001,
at 9:00 *o'clock, am of that day, in connection with* an investigation relating
to possible violations of Titles 18, 31 and 42 of the U.S. Code with respect to
Medicare, Medicaid and other Federal Health Care Programs; *and you are hereby required to bring with you and produce at said time and place the following*:
See Attachment A (Definitions)

And

Attachment B (Instructions)

*which are necessary in the performance of the responsibility of the Inspector
General under Public Law* 45-452 *[5 USC App. 3 Section 6(a)(4)], as amended by
Public Law* 100-504f, *to conduct and supervise audits and investigations and
to promote economy, efficiency and effectiveness in the administration of and
to prevent and detect fraud and abuse in the programs and operations of the
Department of Health and Human Services.*

IN TESTIMONY WHEREOF

*the undersigned official of the Office of
Inspector General of said DEPARTMENT OF
HEALTH AND HUMAN SERVICES, has hereunto
set his hand this 3rd day of April 2001*

page 2 of 5

FIGURE 4-12 | OIG Subpoena (Continued)

ATTACHMENT A

DEFINITIONS

A.   "Document(s)" means, without limitation, any written, printed, typed, photographed, recorded or otherwise reproduced or stored communication or representation. This definition includes copies or duplicates of documents contemporaneously or subsequently created that have any non-conforming notes or other markings and the backsides of any communication or representation that all contain any of the above.

By way of example, documents include, but arc not limited to: correspondence; memoranda; notes; drafts; records; letters; envelopes; telegrams; messages; electronic mail; analyses; agreements; accounts; working papers; reports and summaries of investigations; trade letters; press releases; comparisons, books; notices; drawings; diagrams; instructions; manuals; calendars; diaries; articles; magazines; newspapers; brochures; guidelines; notes or minutes of meetings or of other communications of any type, including inter- and intra-office or company communications; questionnaires; surveys; charts; graphs; photographs; films or videos; tapes; discs; data cells; bulletins; printouts of information stored or maintained by electronic data processing or word processing equipment; electronic claims filing, invokes, all other data compilations from which information can be obtained including electromagnetically sensitive stored media such as floppy discs, hard discs, hard drives and magnetic tapes; and any preliminary versions, drafts or revisions of any of the foregoing.

B.   The "Hospital" means any and all of the following: _____,

_____, its parents, successors, subsidiaries, and affiliates, departments and subunits, both presently existing and those in existence at any time between January 1, 1992, and the present.

C.   The term "relationship" means any and all of the following: an association or affiliation of the identified institution and the Hospital or common ownership or control between the identified institution and the Hospital as further set forth in 42 C.F.R. §413.17; an understanding, contract, agreement or arrangement between the identified institution, including its officers, agents, consultants, contractors or employees, and the hospital, including its officers, agents, consultants, contractors or employees.

INSTRUCTIONS

A.   If a claim of privilege is asserted in response to any document requested herein, and such document, or any part thereof, is not produced on the basis of such claim, for each such document or part thereof that is not produced, you arc directed to provide a privilege log identifying the type of document being withheld (e.g. letter, memorandum, handwritten notes, marginalia, etc.), all actual and intended recipients of the document, its date, and the specific privilege being asserted, all with sufficient particularity so as to allow the Office of the Inspector General, and potentially the Court, to assess the validity of the claim of privilege.

page 3 of 5

FIGURE 4-12 | OIG Subpoena (Continued)

B.   All documents provided in response hereto are to be the original documents and are to include all marginalia and post it notes and other similar documents attached thereto, as well as all attachments resorted to or incorporated by the documents.

C.   The words "and" and "or" as used herein shall be read in both the conjunctive and the disjunctive (i.e., and/or), so as to give the document request its broadest meaning.

D.   Relevant time period: Unless otherwise indicated, the relevant time period for each document request herein shall be January 1, 1992 to the present, and shall include all documents created or prepared during that period, or referring or relating to that period, regardless of when the document was created or prepared.

E.   If any document, information or data called for herein exists as, or can be retrieved from, information stored in computerized form then you are directed to produce the information in computerized form, including sufficient identification of the applicable software program to permit access to and use of the document.

F.   Scope of search required: This request calls for all documents in the possession, custody or control of the Hospital, as defined above, including but not limited to its officers, directors, employees, agents, consultants and contractors. The Hospital is required to search all files reasonably likely to contain responsive documents, including files left behind by former officers, directors, agents and employees.

G.   Manner of production: All documents produced in response hereto shall comply with the following instructions:

(a)   The Hospital shall conduct a search for responsive documents in a manner sufficient to identify the source and location where each responsive document is found.

(b)   All documents produced in response hereto shall be segregated and labeled to show the document request to which the documents are responsive and the source and location where the document was found.

(c)   To the extent that documents are found in file folders and other similar containers which have labels or other identifying information, the documents shall be produced with such file folder and label information intact.

(d)   To the extent that documents are found attached to other documents, by means of paper clips, staples or other means of attachment, such documents shall be produced together in their condition when found.

H.   In the event there are no documents responsive to a particular request, state for each Hospital that the Hospital has no responsive documents.

I.   If requested documents are no longer in the possession or control of the Hospital, this request requires that the Hospital state what disposition was made of such documents, including identification of the person(s) who are or are believed to be in possession or control of such documents.

page 4 of 5

FIGURE 4-12 | OIG Subpoena (Continued)

ATTACHMENT B

SPECIFICATIONS

B-1   For each hospitalization identified in Attachment C: all documents from the patient's medical record or file that discuss, refer, or relate to the patient's discharge or transfer to another facility, including but not limited to discharge summaries, nurses' notes, physicians' notes and orders, discharge planning documents, social workers' notes, ambulance records, and requests for information or medical records from subsequent providers.

B-2   For each hospitalization identified by date of discharge on Attachment C, all documents relating to the coding and billing of any claims submitted to the Medicare program.

B-3   For the period January 1, 1992, to the present, all documents relating or referring to the manner in which discharges or transfers of Medicare beneficiaries were billed to Medicare, including, but not limited to: reports; manuals; guidelines; notes; training materials; alerts; publications; Health and Human Services Inspector General reports; minutes of meetings; analyses; audits; overpayment notices; policies; complaints; reviews; claim denials; communications or correspondence with local, state or national trade and/or professional associations; inquiries; appeals of payment denials and decisions related thereto. This specification does not include individual patient files or billing records for individual patients except where payments were denied because transfers were incorrectly coded as discharges.

B-4   All documents relating or referring to any relationship regarding the transfer of patients between _____ and each of the following entities:

B-5   Documents sufficient to identify (a) the Hospital's Board of Directors or equivalent governing board; (b) the Hospital's executive officers; and (c) the Hospital's supervisors and employees with job duties that include coding inpatient hospitalizations or billing Medicare and Medicaid for those services.

FIGURE 4-12 | OIG Subpoena (Continued)

UNITED STATES DISTRICT COURT

EASTERN DISTRICT OF MICHIGAN

TO: Keeper of Records
John Doe, M.D., P.C.

Grand Jury No.
**SUBPOENA TO TESTIFY
BEFORE GRAND JURY**

SUBPOENA FOR:
☐PERSON   ☑DOCUMENT(S) OR OBJECT(S)

YOU ARE HEREBY COMMANDED to appear and testify before the Grand Jury of the United States District Court at the place, date, and time specified below.

PLACE	COURTROOM
	Room 1056, 10th Floor
Grand Jury	
Theodore Levin U.S. Courthouse	DATE AND TIME
231 W. Lafayette	July 16, 2008 at
Detroit, MI 48226	9:00 A.M.

YOU ARE ALSO COMMANDED to bring with you the following document(s) or objects(s):*

Items on attached Schedule A.

☐ *Please see addition information on reverse.*

This subpoena shall remain in effect until you are granted leave to depart by the court or by an officer acting on behalf of the court.

Clerk of Court	DATE
David J. Weaver	July 16, 2008

This subpoena is issued on application of the United States of America	NAME, ADDRESS AND PHONE NUMBER OF ASSISTANT U.S. ATTORNEY
	U.S. Attorney's Office
	211 W. Fort Street, Suite 2001
	Detroit, Michigan 48226 (313) 226-9168

*If not applicable, enter "none".

page 1 of 2

FIGURE 4-13 | Grand Jury Subpoena

SCHEDULE A

1. Complete patient files for the following individuals identified by name and UPIN, including not only the medical record, but also all billing records, correspondence, referrals, consultations, test results, and all other documentation or information relating to the patient without limitation.

    A.

    B.

    C.

    D.

    E.

    F.

    G.

    H.

    I.

    J.

    K.

    L.

    M.

    N.

    O.

    P.

2. A mirror image of the hard drive of the office computer.

3. All original calendars, datebooks, and/or scheduling books that contain any information regarding scheduling of patient appointments.

4. The original of all documents (a) constituting or regarding referrals for consultations on every patient, without limitation; (b) constituting or regarding reports provided to referring physicians, without limitation.

5. A copy of all CPT books, coding references, and training material regarding billing, without limitation.

6. A copy of all documents constituting or regarding communications with all representatives of the Medicare carrier or intermediary, the Department of Health and Human Services, the administrative hearing officer, and/or the Centers for Medicare and Medicaid Services.

7. The original of all materials provided to the administrative hearing officer, including without limitation all calendars, notebooks, and patient files.

page 2 of 2

FIGURE 4-13   Grand Jury Subpoena (Continued)

(Continued from page 230)
frequently used during such an investigation involving parallel criminal and civil investigations (where the potential exists for a civil enforcement action as well as criminal prosecution). Generally, a grand jury subpoena will be issued after criminal prosecutors have clearly identified the targets of the investigation, and the government wants to secure the testimony of witnesses under oath prior to actually returning criminal indictments.

4.3.7   Responding to a Subpoena or Investigative Demand

A physician who receives either a subpoena or an investigative demand for records should immediately notify experienced counsel. A physician should not attempt to handle the matter by himself or herself. The receipt of a subpoena or investigative demand for records is a critical development: the handling and outcome of this situation could determine the path, pace, and result of future events (ie, disposition of the case, continued investigation, filing of civil suit, or criminal indictment). Some of the most serious errors a physician can make often occur at this stage of an investigation.

4.3.7.1   Initial Assessment of the Subpoena and Contacting the Government

An initial review of the subpoena or investigative demand issued to the physician will often apprise counsel of the scope of the investigation. For example, a subpoena directed at billing records regarding patients who have received evaluation and management services is a strong indication that the investigation is focused on the appropriateness of the code levels submitted for those services. On the other hand, a subpoena for business records related to the leasing of rental space to health care providers and/or suppliers indicates that the investigation is centered on whether or not the rental charge was in fact an inducement for the referral of services prohibited by the anti-kickback statute (AKS).

Identifying which governmental agencies are involved in the investigation can also provide an understanding of the nature of the investigation, which is an important step in determining and anticipating how the investigation will develop. For example, a document request or subpoena issued by the OIG will, in many circumstances, be a clear indication that the investigation is still in the early stage. Alternatively, the receipt of a HIPAA investigative demand is a definite confirmation that the US attorney is conducting the investigation, which indicates a more serious scenario. Regardless of such initial assessment of the nature of the document request or subpoena, counsel should contact the government agent named in the request or subpoena as soon as possible. If there is an attorney involved (such as an assistant US attorney or a Department of Justice or MFCU attorney), counsel should arrange a conference as soon as possible in an effort to determine the nature and scope of the investigation.

One of the first tasks during the initial meeting or conversation with the government representatives will be to determine whether the investigation is criminal and/or civil in nature, the specific issues under investigation, and, if possible, the client's status and that of the employees (ie, target, subject, or witness). However, if a *qui tam* false claims action by a whistleblower has been filed under seal, the government is prohibited from disclosing this fact to counsel absent court approval. Where the initial contact from the government is a HIPAA investigative demand issued by the US attorney, this is a good indication that a *qui tam* action was filed against the physician or medical practice. Therefore, some thought should be given to which particular individual(s) or employee(s) may have filed the action, when the action was filed, what position they occupied, and what information may have been accessed.

4.3.7.2 *Review and Analysis of the Subpoena/Investigative Demand*

Subpoenas and/or investigative demands will generally seek production of a series of generic categories of documents. For example, a subpoena may seek lists of employees, various specified patient records, billing records, remittance advices for a particular procedure or code, provider manuals, and bulletins issued by the Medicare carrier. The OIG or US Attorney will often use a stock list of documents it seeks during the course of a health care fraud investigation. For some medical practices, some of those categories may not exist and the government should immediately be informed of this fact.

If a subpoena is facially overbroad in terms of both the categories of documents requested and the time period involved, a reasonable attempt should be made to narrow the scope of the subpoena, including consideration of a motion to quash for overbreadth. Where compliance with the subpoena is either unreasonable or impossible, counsel should notify the government as soon as possible, carefully documenting the unreasonableness or impossibility of compliance.

Generally, subpoenas call for the production of the documents within a short period of time, such as 14 to 30 days from issuance. Typically, the government will be flexible on extending the date of production, particularly with voluminous documents involving a significant time period. Another solution would be to ask that the production of records be staggered over a reasonable period of time. Where voluminous records are requested for an extended time period, the government may be receptive to initially selecting and reviewing a sample of the requested records, and then deferring inspection of the remainder for some agreed-upon time. This allows the physician to postpone the assembly and delivery of the remaining requested records until after the initial grouping has been evaluated, with the hope that no further records will be sought.

4.3.7.3   *Ensuring the Integrity of the Subpoenaed Documents*

Nothing is more critical to the successful outcome of an investigation than ensuring that the documents, items, and other materials summonsed are not altered or destroyed. If the physician receives a subpoena for the production of medical records, billing records, financial information, or other materials, subject to any applicable privilege, the records specified in the subpoena must be produced. Too often, a physician or other health care client will panic on receipt of a subpoena and either make additions to a clinical record or otherwise withhold or destroy potentially incriminating material. In other cases, physicians may falsely represent that the documents requested could not be found. Under no circumstances should the physician or an employee create a missing document or alter an existing one. Altering or otherwise enhancing the records will necessarily give rise to charges of obstruction of justice. The gathering, reviewing, and production of requested documents in response to a subpoena or other investigative demand must be handled carefully to avoid obstruction of justice allegations. Obstruction of a health care investigation is itself a federal crime punishable by imprisonment and fines.

While complicated billing patterns based on technical requirements of the Medicare laws may not rise to the level of a criminal charge, nothing will result in a criminal prosecution faster than the destruction, alteration, or enhancement of documents. Indeed, in more than a few cases, the US attorney has concluded that, even though the underlying facts do not support either a criminal or civil prosecution for health care fraud, an obstruction of justice charge for interference with the investigation was warranted. Consequently, it is imperative that a physician faced with a subpoena or investigative demand circulate a written memorandum to employees that emphasizes the importance of fully complying with the subpoena (see Figure 4-14 for a sample letter). One additional benefit of a written memorandum is documentary proof of the employer's good-faith intentions should an employee alter, enhance, or destroy records on his or her own.

4.3.7.4   *Providing Written Instructions That Relevant Documents Are Not to Be Destroyed*

Additionally, even without the service of an investigative demand or subpoena for records, once the physician becomes aware of an investigation, he or she should take steps to preserve all tangible evidence that may related to the investigation. This includes both hard-copy documents and electronic documents. Therefore, it is advisable that a medical practice that is under either subpoena or investigation suspend any general document destruction policies until counsel can determine whether those documents scheduled for destruction are responsive to

ABC MEDICAL GROUP

October 30, 2008

ABC Medical Group has received a subpoena for a number of records regarding its billing practices to Medicare and Medicaid. ABC Medical Group believes that it has billed in compliance with all regulatory requirements, and will fully cooperate with the government in its investigation. Over the next several weeks, we will be meeting with various employees to determine what responsive documents each may have. It is imperative that every employee fully cooperate in this task.

As a result of the receipt of this subpoena, all ABC Medical Group employees have a duty to preserve any documents and data, including electronic documents, which could be relevant to billing to the Medicare and Medicaid programs. We therefore request that you immediately preserve all existing documents and data concerning billing of any nature, and not delete or destroy any potentially relevant documents, including, without limitation, any electronic documents such as emails. Failure to take appropriate steps to preserve and protect potential evidence can result in very severe penalties and have adverse consequences, including monetary and other sanctions.

With respect to electronic data, the preservation obligation is not limited simply to avoiding affirmative acts of destruction. We are required to suspend any routine document retention/destruction policy, including any automatic deletion features that periodically purge electronic documents, such as e-mail. We are essentially putting a "litigation hold" on the destruction of any documents or data to ensure the preservation of relevant documents.

If you have any questions regarding this directive, please contact General Counsel John Doe at 617-856-0000.

| FIGURE 4-14 | Letter to Employees Regarding Compliance with Subpoena |

the subpoena (see letter to personnel in Figure 4-15). This also applies to e-mail messages, if covered by the subpoena.

4.3.7.5 *Responding to the Subpoena/Investigative Demand*

Subpoenas are often drafted by persons with limited knowledge about the operation of a medical practice and the specific types of records maintained by the practice. In most instances, therefore, it is beneficial for counsel to meet with the government agent or attorney who issued the subpoena in an attempt to clarify any ambiguities and, if appropriate, discuss narrowing the subpoena's scope. The government may limit the scope of a subpoena if the physician or medical practice can demonstrate valid reasons regarding why compliance with the literal terms of the subpoena is overburdensome. In other cases, as stated above, the government will generally allow the physician or medical practice to stagger production over time, a process commonly referred to as *rolling production.*

In all cases, the physician's attorney will confirm, by means of a letter, any agreements reached with the government regarding the scope and manner of production. Documenting the efforts to negotiate a reasonable scope for the discovery demand will only improve the physician's position if the government seeks court enforcement (see Figure 4-16).

4.3.7.6 *Appointing an Independent Custodian*

In any case involving a large medical practice where the government has requested a large number of documents, a key employee, such as the office manager, should be appointed as custodian for the purpose of gathering the requested documents. This person should be uninvolved in the underlying allegations. The custodian should be informed that he or she may be questioned under oath by the government about the search for records and the response made to the subpoena. The appointment and duties should be in writing in order to eliminate any question about the custodian's responsibilities (see Figure 4-17).

It is vital that the medical practice carefully select not only an appropriate custodian, but also any additional employees who will be involved in the document gathering and review process, as any employee with

(*Continued on page 247*)

Law Firm No.1

Tom Jones

Direct Dial: (555) 555-8555
Email: xxx@yyy.com

Boston,
MA 01251

September 22, 2008

Distribution List of Physician Members
Greater Boston General Surgery, P.C.

This office is counsel to Greater Boston General Surgery, P.C. ("GBGS"). GBGS has received an inquiry from the Massachusetts United States Attorney's Office regarding its affiliation with ABC Medical Center's surgical residency training program. The U.S. Attorney has requested information concerning the following from GBGS:

- whether residents or students in ABC's surgical residency program were performing procedures under the direction and/or supervision of any GBGS physician, and, if so,
- how those procedures were billed to Medicare and Medicaid.

Federal law requires us to put a "hold" on any documents and data, including electronic documents, that could be relevant to the inquiry. We therefore request that you immediately preserve all existing documents and data concerning the affiliation of either GBGS or yourself with the surgical residency training program at ABC Medical Center as well as any data/documents relating to the billing for procedures performed under your direction and/or supervision by residents or students in the training program. You should not delete or destroy any documents, including, without limitation, any electronic documents such as emails, concerning these matters. Failure to take appropriate steps to preserve and protect potential evidence can result in very severe penalties and have adverse consequences, including monetary and other sanctions.

The inquiry by the U.S. Attorney is not a public matter. As a result, you should keep the fact that there is such an inquiry confidential.

If you have any questions regarding this directive, please contact counsel at Law Firm No. 1:

Tom Jones (555-555-8555) or xxx@yyy.com

FIGURE 4-15 | Letter to Key Personnel Regarding Document Preservation

aw Firm No.1

INITIAL LETTER TO U.S. ATTORNEY

Tom Jones

Direct Dial: (555) 555-8555
Email: xxx@yyy.com

Boston,
MA 01251

August 25, 2008

_____, Assistant U.S. Attorney
Health Care Fraud Chief
U.S. Attorney's Office
408 Atlantic Ave, 5th Floor
Boston, MA 02210

       Re: Subpoena duces tecum issued to the Custodian of Records of the XYZ
              Healthcare Corporation pursuant to 18 U.S.C. §3486

Dear _____:

       This will confirm that the law firm of Law Firm No. 1 represents the XYZ
Healthcare Corporation in connection with the subpoena duces tecum issued on August 19,
2008. During our telephone conference, I stated that it was unlikely that XYZ could comply
with the subpoena by Thursday, September 9, 2008. Based on this representation, you
agreed to extend the compliance date. With regard to Paragraph 5 of the subpoena, you
also agreed that XYZ does not have to produce regular payroll checks issued to persons
who fell within the definition of "Sales Representative" but only commission and bonus
checks for the period of 2005 to date.

       I will be in contact with you once I meet with XYZ's management and support staff
to determine when these records can be produced. If you have any questions in the interim,
please do not hesitate to contact me.

                               Very truly yours,
                               Law Firm No. 1

                               By: _____
                                      Tom Jones

TJ/jak

cc: General Counsel
       XYZ Healthcare Corporation

FIGURE 4-16 | Initial Letter to US Attorney Regarding Scope of Subpoena

MEMORANDUM TO CUSTODIAN OF RECORDS

TO: Robert So-and-So
             ABC Medical Center

FROM: _____
             General Counsel/Senior Officer

RE: Document Review Responsibilities

DATE: September 1, 1999

You have agreed to act as corporate document custodian for the limited purpose of ABC Medical Center's response to requests for information from the United States Attorney. A description of those requests, as well as a memorandum I have sent to relevant department heads, are attached.

Your responsibilities are as follows:

1.   Work with each department head who received the attached memorandum to ensure that copies of the memo are distributed to employees within his/her department who may have documents responsive to the U.S. Attorney's requests.

2.   Compile a list of employees to whom my memo is circulated.

3.   Follow up with those employees believed to have responsive documents to assure compliance.

4.   Obtain certifications from such employees of their search and forwarding of responsive documents.

5.   Forward all responsive documents to the company's attorneys for their review and submission to the U.S. Attorney.

If you have any questions regarding these matters, please contact me or our outside counsel, Tom Jones (555) 555-8555, representing us in this matter.

_____

*   This form is reprinted with permission from the AHLA "Best Practices Handbook in Advising Clients on Fraud & Abuse Issues" (1999).

FIGURE 4-17 | Memorandum to Custodian of Records

(Continued from page 243)

access to crucial documents has the potential to file a *qui tam* lawsuit. As a general rule, most medical practices should rely on the smallest control group possible.

4.3.7.7   *Providing Written Instructions to the Custodian and Document Searchers*

As every unrecorded conversation is subject to each participant's interpretation, physicians and medical practices should avoid supplying the custodian with undocumented oral instructions regarding the particular records to be gathered. The custodian and any other individual responsible for locating relevant documents should receive written instructions that are clear and easy to follow and that incorporate any arrangements the attorney for the physician or medical practice has reached with the government (see Figure 4-18 for an example). All such requests should contain the following:

- A detailed description of the various types of documents subject to the subpoena
- The time period covered by the subpoena
- The potential location of the documents.

Any requests to employees regarding file searches should also be in writing, and the custodian should receive written confirmation from each person or department queried that such responsive documents have been produced or exhaustively searched for. In addition, negative results should be documented. Instructional memoranda should also address the often overlooked adhesive notes that, depending on the language of the subpoena, may have to be produced. All instructional memoranda should be drafted with the clear expectation that they will ultimately be provided to the grand jury or investigating agency.

4.3.7.8   *Review of the Gathered Documents by Counsel*

After the custodian has assembled all potentially responsive documents, they should be reexamined by counsel to determine whether they are in fact responsive to the subpoena. This crucial step ensures that no document

(Continued on page 251)

INSTRUCTIONS TO DOCUMENT SEARCHERS

Confidential

TO: Distribution List

FROM: _____
           General Counsel/Senior Officer

RE: Request for Information from the United States Attorney's Office

DATE: September 1, 1999

Enclosed as Attachment A is a description of categories of documents and records requested by the United States Attorney's Office (the "Requester"). Please read the description carefully and forward copies of this memo, with its attachments, to those employees in your department who may have documents that fall within one of the categories of documents sought by the Requester.

Your employees (and you, if you have responsive documents) should deliver the originals and existing copies of all documents sought by the Requester to Robert Recordkeeper, the person acting as custodian of records, at [location of custodian's office] as they are located. If there is any doubt about whether any item or object or document is sought by the Requester, it should be provided as part of the collection process. E-mail and computer files should also be searched for responsive data. You and your employees should be careful not to destroy or discard any documents sought by the Requester. All responsive documents should be delivered no later than September 15, 1999. If, for any reason, you or your employees cannot respond by or before that time, you should notify Robert Recordkeeper.

In order to demonstrate full compliance with the Requester's request, it is important that we be able to document fully the collection process. You and your employees should keep a written record of the search technique utilized. After the searches have been completed, the Certification included as Attachment B should be signed and sent to Robert Recordkeeper.

The documents forwarded to Robert Recordkeeper will be returned to you and your employees. However, if you anticipate that you or your employees may need the document or information from the document, in the near future, a copy of the document should be made for you to retain before the original is submitted.

Please note that negative responses are required on the attached certification form if no documents are located.

If you have any questions regarding the scope of the Requester's request or the instructions in this memorandum, please contact me as soon as possible.

cc: Robert Recordkeeper, Custodian of Records

_____
*   This form is reprinted from the AHLA "Best Practices Handbook in Advising Clients on Fraud & Abuse Issues" (1999).

page 1 of 3

FIGURE 4-18 | Instructions on Conducting Search for Responsive Documents

ATTACHMENT A

CATEGORIES OF DOCUMENTS SOUGHT BY
THE UNITED STATES ATTORNEY

Request 1.

Request 2.

Request 3.

Request 4.

Request 5.

Request 6.

Request 7.

Request 8.

page 2 of 3

FIGURE 4-18   Instructions on Conducting Search for Responsive Documents (Continued)

ATTACHMENT B

CERTIFICATION

I have received the memorandum from _____ [general counsel], dated September 15, 1999, which seeks documents requested by the United States Attorney's Office. I have reviewed all files within my possession, custody or control, and hereby state that:

_____ I have found no responsive documents.

_____ I am forwarding all responsive documents with this certification.

_____ I have previously forwarded all responsive documents.

_____ I have previously forwarded some responsive documents and am attaching additional documents.

I UNDERSTAND THAT THE DOCUMENTS IN QUESTION ARE BEING SOUGHT BY THE GOVERNMENT PURSUANT TO SUBPOENA, AND THAT THERE MAY BE SERIOUS CONSEQUENCES TO THE COMPANY AND TO ME, INDIVIDUALLY, IN FAILING TO PRODUCE RESPONSIVE DOCUMENTS.

_____
Date

_____
(Signature)

_____
(Print Name)

_____
(Location)

_____
(Telephone No.)

Return to: Robert Recordkeeper

page 3 of 3

FIGURE 4-18 | Instructions on Conducting Search for Responsive Documents (Continued)

(Continued from page 247)

protected by the attorney-client privilege or attorney–work product doctrine is inadvertently produced and no unnecessary documents are disclosed.

At this stage, a privilege log will be created, listing any documents withheld under a claim of privilege. A privilege log will identify:

- The person who wrote the document
- The named recipient
- The date
- A brief description of the subject matter of the document
- The privilege or doctrine relied on.

4.3.7.9   Keeping a Record of the Documents and Materials Produced to the Government

All documents produced, including originals, should be Bates-stamped and copied, potentially eliminating any dispute as to what was or was not produced to the government. A cover letter and detailed memorandum specifying the documents being produced should be addressed to the government by counsel and, where applicable, should reference Bates-stamped numbers (see Figures 4-19 and 4-20 for a sample cover letter and memorandum). A signed receipt for the delivery of the records should be obtained in every case.

4.3.8   What to Do If an Auditor or Investigator Appears at the Office

Most postpayment audits involve a review of documents and other records submitted by the physician after a written request by Medicare or Medicaid. It is extremely rare that an auditor will physically come to the physician's office. In the event that an auditor or investigator does actually appear at the physician's office, it is critical for the physician or office manager to initially determine which agency the auditor or investigator is from.

(Continued on page 255)

Law Firm No.1
Boston,
MA 01251

Tom Jones

Direct Dial: (555) 555-8555
Email: xxx@yyy.com

November 6, 2008

VIA MESSENGER

_____, Assistant United States Attorney
United States Attorney's Office
United States Courthouse – Suite 9200
1 Courthouse Way
Boston, MA 02210

Re: Subpoenas to ABC Medical Center and XYZ University Surgery, Inc.
relating to the Graduate Training Program in Surgery

Dear Ms. Rollins:

In connection with the above-referenced subpoenas, enclosed please find a document entitled *Initial Response by ABC Medical Center and XYZ University Surgery, Inc. to the Various Requests Contained in Attachment "C" to the Subpoenas Issued to ABC and XYZ*. Copies of the responsive documents referenced in the *Initial Response* are also enclosed.

We are in the process of having these documents scanned to a disk. Once that process is completed, I will forward a copy of the disk to your attention.

If you have any questions, do not hesitate to call.

Law Firm No. 1

By: _____
Tom Jones

TJ/jak
Enclosures

cc: OIG S/A Ben Celso
_____, Trial Attorney
_____, Assistant General Counsel, ABC Medical Center
_____, Assistant General Counsel, XYZ University
(w/ Initial Response)

FIGURE 4-19 | Cover Letter to US Attorney Regarding Document Production

w Firm No.1

Tom Jones

Boston,
MA 01251

Direct Dial: (555) 555-8555
Email: xxx@yyy.com

November 6, 2008

INITIAL RESPONSE BY ABC MEDICAL CENTER ("ABC") AND XYZ UNIVERSITY SURGERY ("XYZ") TO THE VARIOUS REQUESTS CONTAINED IN "ATTACHMENT C" TO THE SUBPOENAS ISSUED TO ABC AND XYZ

1. Organizational chart(s) showing key ABC and XYZ organizations and contacts.

    Responsive documents are appended as Bates Nos. "ABC/XYZ 000001-15."

2. Documents identifying all current and former personnel at ABC's Surgery Department and XYZ. Such documents shall include, but, are not limited to, personnel listings or other documents identifying the name, title and job description, last known address and telephone number, Social Security Number, and dates of employment of each current and former physician, resident, nurse, administrative personnel, and any independent contractor(s).

    ABC and XYZ have compiled listings containing responsive information which are appended as Bates Nos. "ABC/XYZ 000016-31."

3. Documents or a list reflecting the Medicare provider and subprovider identification number(s), as well as the tax identification numbers, for ABC, and for ABC's Surgery Department, any and all providers (including medical residents, fellows and students in the Graduate Training Program) in the Surgery Department.

4. The Medicare provider and subprovider identification number(s), as well as the tax identification number(s), for ABC and XYZ, and for any and all providers affiliated or employed by ABC and XYZ.

5. For each provider number produced in response to specifications 3 and 4 above, please provide documents identifying the corresponding tax identification number, the mailing address used for the billings, and a name and telephone number of a contact.

    ABC and XYZ have compiled listings containing the responsive information to Requests Nos. 3-5 which are is appended as Bates Nos. "ABC/XYZ 000032-34."

6. A copy of the current by-laws and charter for ABC and XYZ.

    Responsive documents are appended as Bates Nos. "ABC/XYZ 000035-120."

7. All contracts or other agreements made or entered into between ABC and XYZ.

    Responsive documents are appended as Bates Nos. "ABC/XYZ 000121-159."

8. Any ABC and/or XYZ training materials, guidance, policies, instructions or manuals which address how medical records are to be prepared and/or reviewed.

9. Any ABC and/or XYZ training materials, guidance, policies, instructions or manuals that refer, reflect, or relate to billing Medicare, Medicaid, or any other third-party payer for services performed by teaching physicians, and by participants in any graduate medical training program.

page 1 of 2

FIGURE 4-20   Memorandum Listing Documents Being Produced in Response to Subpoena

> Responsive documents to Requests Nos. 8 and 9 are appended as Bates Nos. "ABC/XYZ 000160-278."

10. A complete copy of ABC and/or XYZ's policy manual(s) and the State of Massachusetts' Medical Board Regulations.

> As agreed on October 21, 2008, ABC is providing an index to ABC's policies as well as providing the available policies of the Faculty Practice Plan and XYZ. Responsive documents are appended as Bates Nos. "ABC/XYZ 000279-299."

11. Any and all internal or external reviews that refer, reflect, or relate to the evaluation of ABC and/or XYZ's billing practices and/or monitoring compliance with Medicare regulations concerning billing for services provided by (or procedures performed by) teaching physicians.

> As we agreed on October 21, 2008, ABC is providing the compliance reviews of XYZ. Responsive documents are appended as Bates Nos. "ABC/XYZ 000300-425."

12. Documents reflecting the number and amount of Medicare Part B services and reimbursements for ABC's Department of Surgery by place of service, e.g., inpatient Medical Center, clinic, emergency room, etc.

> As agreed on October 21, 2008, XYZ providing from its billing agent a "Medicare Analysis by Group by CPT for FY09" as a sample of the information that it has access to with regard to Medicare billings. Responsive documents are appended as Bates Nos. "ABC/XYZ 000426-431."

13. All contracts or agreements between ABC and/or ABC's Department of Surgery and the DEF Institute.

> All responsive documents have been produced in response to Request No. 7.

14. All documents referring, relating, or discussing to any current and/or former ownership interest in the DEF Institute.

> ABC and XYZ are not in possession of any responsive documents.

15. All documents which identify the current and/or former officers and/or directors of the DEF Institute.

> ABC and XYZ are not in possession of any responsive documents.

16. All space and equipment rental or lease agreements by and between ABC and/or XYZ and the DEF Institute, and any appendices or amendments to any such agreements.

> All responsive documents have been produced in response to Requests Nos. 7 and 24.

17. All documents that disclose or discuss the number of anticipated referrals to ABC from the DEF Institute and/or Dr. John Doe.

> ABC is not in possession of any responsive documents.

18. All documents that disclose or discuss the number of actual patient referrals to ABC from the DEF Institute and/or Dr. John Doe.

> ABC is not in possession of any responsive documents.

page 2 of 2

FIGURE 4-20 | Memorandum Listing Documents Being Produced in Response to Subpoena (Continued)

(Continued from page 251)

If the investigator is from a criminal agency, such as the state MFCU, FBI, or OIG, counsel should immediately be called for advice. The physician/practice has certain rights in a criminal investigation. Physicians should not assume that they have nothing to hide and give away the keys to the office. In any event, the physician and staff are under no obligation to answer any questions. The practice's attorney will want to speak directly to the investigator and inform the investigator that no interview will be conducted without the presence of the attorney.

If the investigator is not from a criminal agency but is from the Medicare carrier, the state Medicaid agency, or a private insurance company, he or she has a right to examine specific patient files relating to the particular program he or she is from. For example, an auditor from the state Medicaid agency has the ability to review only medical records for Medicaid members, and not records from Medicare members or a private insurer.

4.3.8.1   *Right to Immediate Access to Records*

Both the federal OIG and the state MFCU have authority to gain immediate access to a physician or other health care provider's office upon reasonable request in writing to examine records, documents, and other data relating to the Medicare and Medicaid programs. Private insurance companies, such as Blue Cross, do not have this power.

Immediate access is defined as being within 24 hours of the request unless the investigator believes the records will be altered or destroyed. Failure to comply with an OIG subpoena or request for access to records can result in exclusion from the Medicare and Medicaid programs. Similarly, failure to grant immediate access to the state MFCU can result in exclusion from the Medicare and Medicaid programs for a minimum of 90 days.

In the event the OIG or MFCU investigator provides an appropriate notice of the request for immediate access to records, the practice should not give the investigator free run of the office, as the investigator could use his or her observations to gather additional evidence to obtain a search warrant. The written request will provide a description of the documents or types of documents to be examined. The physician or a staff member should take the time to select the specific records the investigator wants to examine and turn over only those records.

4.3.8.2 Guidelines for Interacting with an Auditor/Investigator

In the event an auditor or investigator does appear in the office, the following guidelines should be considered:

- The physician and the employees should not discuss the case with the investigator/auditor. This is a task best suited for the practice's attorney. It is important to understand that there is no such thing as an off-the-record discussion with government auditors or agents.

- Any substantive questions should be presented in writing and reviewed with the attorney.

- The investigator/auditor should always be asked for his or her card, or name, unit or department, address, and telephone number.

- The investigator/auditor should be allowed access to patient medical records only for the particular program with which he or she is affiliated. If the investigator is from Medicaid, he or she has a right to review only records of Medicaid patients, etc.

4.3.9 Search Warrants

A search warrant authorizes designated law enforcement personnel to enter onto private property and search for evidence specified in the warrant (see sample search warrant in Figure 4-21). If a search warrant is executed at the physician's office or home, or the home of an employee, it is a very serious matter as it indicates that the government has probable cause to believe that a crime was committed and that evidence will be found during the search. To obtain a search warrant, the government must submit an application and an affidavit to a court setting forth the facts of the investigation and the reasons why it is believed that evidence or the proceeds of a crime are located at the place sought to be searched.

(Continued on page 260)

UNITED STATES DISTRICT COURT

EASTERN DISTRICT OF MICHIGAN, SOUTHERN DIVISION

In the Matter of the Search of
(Name, address or brief description of person or property to be searched)

SEARCH WARRANT

CASE NUMBER:

TO: [Name of agent], FBI, and any Authorized Officer of the United States

Affidavit(s) having been made before me by _____, who has reason
to believe that ❑ on the person of or ❑ on the property or premises known as (name,
description and/or location):

SEE ATTACHMENT "A"

in the Eastern District of Michigan, Southern Division, there is now concealed a certain
person or property, namely (describe the person or property)

SEE ATTACHMENT "B"

I am satisfied that the affidavit(s) and any recorded testimony establish probable cause
to believe that the person or property so described is now concealed on the person or
premises above-described and establish grounds for the issuance of this warrant.

YOU ARE HEREBY COMMANDED to search on or before **April 26, 2006** (not to exceed 10
days) the person or place named above for the person or property specified, serving this
warrant and making the search (in the daytime - 6:00 A.M. to 10:00 P.M.) and if the person or property be found there to seize same, leaving a copy of this warrant and receipt
for the person or property taken, and prepare a written inventory of the person or property
seized and promptly return this warrant to the Honorable Charles E. Binder, United States
Magistrate Judge, as required by law.

_____   at   <u>Bay City, Michigan</u>

Date Time Issued

Honorable Charles E. Binder   _____
United States Magistrate Judge   Signature of Judicial Officer

page 1 of 3

FIGURE 4-21   Sample Search Warrant

ATTACHMENT A

___, including a pole barn located on the property, said premises being described as a single-story commercial building with green wood siding, brown shingle roof, and three red entrance doors. The driveway to the building is asphalt and has a parking area located on the south side of the building. The building is located on the south side of north _____

Michigan. The address numbers. _____

re affixed to the sign located in front of the building on the south side of _____
1. The pole barn sits to the south of the premises, adjacent to the parking lot, and has green metal siding with white doors.

FIGURE 4-21   Sample Search Warrant (Continued)

ATTACHMENT B

1. Medical records for patients listed in Attachment C, including but not limited to:

   (a) Patients' treatment plans for services,

   (b) Documents reflecting diagnoses,

   (c) Doctors' orders and progress notes,

   (d) Nurses' notes and activity flow sheets,

   (e) Therapists' notes,

   (f) Equipment supply/order sheets,

   (g) Test results,

   (h) Hospital records,

   (i) Billing records (to include: patient ledgers, ledger cards, claims for payment, accounts receivable and payable),

   (j) Appointment books and calendars,

   (k) Patient sign-in, and

   (l) Any and all correspondence relating to patients listed in Attachment C.

2. Claims submission and provider guidance issued by [Name of insurance provider] of Michigan:

   (a) All Provider/Claims related manuals

   (b) All [Name of insurance provider] provider bulletins (also known as The Record)

page 3 of 3

FIGURE 4-21 | Sample Search Warrant (Continued)

(Continued from page 256)

Fortunately, search warrants are not the typical investigative tool used during health care fraud investigations. Government investigators will generally apply for a search warrant in situations where there is evidence that the physician subject to the investigation is likely to alter, destroy, or conceal documents if served with an investigative demand or subpoena to produce materials to the US attorney or grand jury.

While search warrants are rarely used, health care providers should be prepared in the event government investigators appear with one. At the time a search warrant is executed, the agents must provide the owner or controller of the place to be searched with a copy of the warrant. At the conclusion of the search, the agent in charge must provide a receipt for any property taken. Government agents are also required to file a fully detailed inventory of the property seized with the court promptly after the search, as well as provide, on request, a copy of this inventory to the person from whom or from whose premises the property was taken.

If at all possible, counsel should be present during the execution of a search warrant to witness and monitor the process. Government agents frequently attempt to interview employees during the course of a search, but the search warrant itself provides no authority to detain an employee during a search for the purpose of questioning. Investigative techniques of this sort are employed to extract as much information as possible. In most instances, they work quite well. The risks to a provider posed by these tactics make it advisable for provider's counsel to brief key employees about the potential for a search and their respective rights in the event a search is conducted or if they are contacted by the government.

In the event a search warrant is executed at the office, there are several items to remember (see Figure 4-22). First, the physician or employees must *not* refuse entrance to the investigators. This can result in arrest for obstruction of justice. The physician or employee should ask to see the warrant and then allow the investigators access to his or her office or home. Second, the physician's attorney should be contacted immediately. Additionally, a copy of the actual search warrant itself as well

MEMORANDUM

TO: Medical Director
             ABC Medical Center

FROM: Tom Jones, Esq. Law Firm No. 1

DATE: November 27, 2008

RE: What to Do in Case of a Search Warrant

The following is an overview of the issues that can arise during the execution of a search warrant. In the event government agents appear with a search warrant, we suggest you immediately call me and do the following:

1.   Ask to see the government investigators' identification and/or business cards. You should write down the name and positions of the government investigators participating in the search.

2.   The agents are required to provide you with a copy of the search warrant.

3.   You should provide the agents with my name and contact information as the attorney for the practice: Tom Jones (555-555-8555).

4.   The warrant will authorize the agents to search specific premises and seize specific property. The warrant will identify the locations the agents are permitted to search. If the agents attempt to search in an area not designated by the warrant, ask them to wait so that counsel can be consulted. If they refuse to wait, do not interfere with their efforts.

5.   The warrant will also include an attachment listing all of the items (or categories of items) to be seized. If the agents attempt to seize items not designated by the warrant, ask them to wait so that counsel can be consulted. If they refuse to wait, do not interfere with their efforts.

6.   Do not "agree" that the search can be expanded beyond the specific limits or objects described in the search warrant.

7.   The agents are entitled to take the original documents and items described in the warrant. While you can ask for copies of the documents before they are taken by the agents, the agents are not required to give you copies of the documents. As a

page 1 of 2

FIGURE 4-22 | Memorandum on Potential Search Warrant

result, consider asking only for copies of specific documents that are essential to your conducting business. If the agents refuse to give you copies, do not be concerned, as copies can be obtained later.

8. Do not attempt to impede, physically or otherwise, the person(s) serving and executing the warrant. You should instruct all personnel not to impede or obstruct the agents' efforts to execute the warrant in any way. Obstruction of the execution of a search warrant is a felony under federal law.

9. **It is advised that all nonessential employees be sent home on paid leave.**

10. The search warrant authorizes the agents to search and to seize property only. **It does not give the agents the authority to interview employees or ask questions.** Neither you nor any employees are required to answer any questions of a substantive nature, such as "tell us about your activities," "what operations are carried on at this site," etc. You may politely decline to answer these questions.

11 If the agents do interview any employees, make a note of who was interviewed and the questions that were asked by the agents.

12. The agents may serve grand jury subpoenas on employees. The grand jury subpoenas require attendance before the grand jury on a specified date for the purpose of giving testimony. ***The subpoena does not require the employees to speak with the agents during the search.*** If any subpoenas are served on employees, make a list of all employees who are subpoenaed. In addition, ask the employee for a copy of the subpoena, because it is likely to reflect the names of the government attorneys involved in the investigation and their phone numbers.

13. Observe the search and take notes regarding where the agents searched and what documents or items were taken from particular locations. Also record any comments or statements made by the government agents.

14. The agents may seize legal files or other attorney-client privileged materials as part of the search. If the agents attempt to seize any attorney-client privileged materials, ask to speak with the agent in charge of the search. If the agent will not cooperate on this issue, counsel should be notified so they can attempt to contact the Assistant United States Attorney. Ultimately, if the agents decide to take privileged materials, you cannot stop them and you should not try.

15. The agents are required to give you an inventory of all property taken pursuant to the warrant.

page 2 of 2

FIGURE 4-22 | Memorandum on Potential Search Warrant (Continued)

as any attachments that specify both the areas to be searched and the items to be seized should be requested. The physician should also obtain the name and business card of the investigator in charge of the search and if possible, of all personnel who assist in the search. The physician should also record what areas the investigators search and the records/documents seized.

The warrant authorizes agents to search and seize property only. It does not give investigators any right to interview the physician or the employees. The physician and employees should not answer any substantive questions posed by any investigator; instead, the attorney should be called, and he or she will have all contact with the investigators. Just as no substantive questions should be answered, no information should be volunteered. Once again, it is important to remember that there is no such thing as an off-the-record conversation with a government agent, no matter what the investigator says.

The physician can appropriately tell the employees that they cannot be compelled to speak to a government investigator. At the same time, an employee can agree to be interviewed during the search. For this reason, it is generally advisable to tell your employees to simply leave the office for the day. Under no circumstances should the physician instruct an employee not to be interviewed. Instead, the physician should keep track of who was interviewed and, if possible, what was said.

The warrant will authorize the agents to search specific premises and seize specific property. Under no circumstances should a physician conceal, destroy, or remove from the premises any documents or property of any nature during the course of the search. The physician should keep track of the areas searched and the items seized. If the agents appear to go beyond the scope of the warrant either in the areas being searched or the items being seized, this should be brought to their attention. However, the physician must not interfere with the search even if he or she believes it goes beyond the scope of the warrant. Finally, the agents are required to provide a receipt for all property taken pursuant to the warrant.

4.3.10   Preliminary Actions the Physician's Attorney Will Take When Faced with an Investigation

Once the physician believes he or she is the subject of an investigation, his or her attorney will generally contact the government agent in charge of the investigation. It is critical to the physician's defense to learn as much as possible about the nature and scope of the investigation. The attorney will want to know whether the case is criminal, civil, and/or administrative in nature. If it is a criminal investigation, the attorney will also want to learn whether key personnel are targets or subjects of the investigation or if they are simply witnesses.

If the attorney is successful in finding out the nature and scope of the investigation, the attorney will interview key employees about the issues involved in the investigation as soon as possible. In essence, the attorney will often talk to the practice's employees first and possibly obtain a written statement. Too often government investigators can scare employees into making inaccurate statements. By having an attorney speak to the employee, the attorney can convey accurate information about the investigation and obtain useful information.

4.4   Conclusion

This chapter highlighted some of the issues involved in a health care investigation. It is strongly recommended that a physician confronted with a postpayment audit or criminal investigation retain an attorney experienced in this very specialized field as soon as possible, as it is critical to mount an affirmative defense while the investigation is being conducted.

APPENDIX*

The Litigation Center[1] of the American Medical Association (AMA) and State Medical Societies is the voice of America's medical profession in legal proceedings across the country. Established in 1995, the Litigation Center provides physicians with legal expertise assistance and has participated in more than 200 cases, many with precedent setting results.

The center's legal staff works tirelessly to ensure physicians' rights are upheld in the most important challenges facing today's working physician. Whether it is protecting the integrity of hospital medical staffs or challenging abusive litigation against physicians, many cases have set important legal precedents and have broad, practical applications for the medical profession and patients. The Litigation Center's docket of cases covers a wide range of topics across the medical-legal landscape, including: physician payment, medical staff privileges, medical liability, peer review, scope-of-practice and many other topics.

The Litigation Center's recent activity includes successful efforts to preserve the rights of medical staffs and ensure fair compensation for physician services—a few of the many ongoing AMA efforts to protect physicians' rights. See the following case samples.

---

*The content in this appendix is not the work of the authors, but was prepared by and is reproduced with the permission of the AMA Litigation Center.

Fraud and Abuse

United States ex rel. Mikes v. Straus, 274 F.3d 687 (2d Cir. 2001)[2]

Issue

The issue in this case was whether physicians can be held liable for a violation of the False Claims Act (FCA) under a theory of false implied certification.

AMA Interest

The AMA has consistently maintained that FCA liability should require a violation of definite and understandable laws.

Case Summary

Patricia S. Mikes, MD, sued Mark J. Straus, MD, and two other physicians under the FCA qui tam (whistleblower) provisions. The defendants were partners in a medical group specializing in problems of oncology and hematology. Mikes was a former employee of the defendants, and she had been involuntarily terminated. The defendants had submitted Medicare claims for spirometry tests, which measure breathing capacity. According to Mikes, these tests were performed improperly, because the measuring equipment was calibrated incorrectly, and the technicians who performed the tests were insufficiently trained to do so. Mikes contended that the defendants' protocol for calibrating the measuring equipment fell beneath the standards recommended by the American Thoracic Society (ATS).

The trial court held for the defendants. It found that, when they submitted their payment claims, the defendants had neither explicitly nor implicitly promised that the tests met any specific standard of care. The defendants had complied with the standards set forth by the equipment manufacturer, which were less rigorous than the ATS recommendations, and this was sufficient. The court rejected Mikes's theory that, by submitting the claims, the defendants implied that they satisfied the customary standard of care. The court also noted that, although the case had proceeded for several years, Mikes was unable to identify any specific test results that were incorrect. Mikes appealed. The United States Department of Justice, the American Association for Respiratory Care, and Taxpayers Against Fraud filed amicus curiae briefs on her behalf.

Litigation Center Involvement

The Litigation Center, along with the Medical Society of the State of New York and several specialty medical societies, filed an amicus brief on behalf of the defendants. Amici's counsel participated in oral argument.

United States ex rel. Swafford v. Borgess Medical Center, 2001 U.S. App. LEXIS 26669 (unpublished opinion) (6th Cir. 2001)[3]

Issue

The issue in this case was whether physicians can be held liable for a violation of the False Claims Act (FCA) under a theory of false implied certification.

AMA Interest

The AMA supports physicians' right to exercise professional judgment in choosing the most appropriate billing code to use in identifying medical services they have rendered (or have caused to be rendered) and billed to Medicare.

Case Summary

Plaintiff Swafford was a registered vascular technologist employed by defendant Borgess Medical Center's vascular ultrasound department. Swafford analyzed the results, through videotape, of venous ultrasound studies ordered by defendant physicians for patients with suspected deep vein thrombosis. Swafford performed the ultrasound tests, examined the data for five risk factors identified by the physicians, and indicated on a worksheet the presence or absence of the risk factors. The physicians reviewed the worksheets and prepared a final report, setting forth findings and conclusions.

Swafford filed a qui tam (whistleblower) lawsuit, which the government declined to join. Swafford alleged that the defendant physicians billed Medicare for conducting venous ultrasound tests although, in fact, they did not provide those services. Swafford insisted that the doctors did not really interpret the test results, as the physicians represented to Medicare, but rather plagiarized the worksheets prepared by Swafford and other technicians and submitted them as interpretations. Swafford further alleged that Borgess Medical Center was aware of these practices and conspired with the physicians.

The district court granted defendants summary judgment. It ruled that Swafford failed to demonstrate that the claims submitted were, in fact, false. The Health Care Financing Administration (HCFA) Provider Guidelines do not include a billing code for venous ultrasound studies, so the physicians had to exercise their professional judgment in choosing the most appropriate billing code. The defendants had sufficient information to form a professional opinion regarding the test results. The court also found that the defendants' readings of the test results were within the standard of care and therefore constituted a proper submission. Further, insufficient evidence existed to suggest that defendants possessed the requisite scienter (ie, a mental state embracing intent to deceive or defraud) to render them liable under the FCA. Swafford appealed to the Sixth Circuit.

The Sixth Circuit affirmed. Swafford petitioned the Supreme Court for certiorari, but the Court denied that request.

AMA Involvement

The Michigan State Medical Society and the AMA filed an amicus brief in the Sixth Circuit to support the defendants.

United States ex rel. Walker v. R & F Properties, 433 F.3d 1349 (11th Cir. 2005)[4]

Issue

The issue in this case was whether the federal False Claims Act (FCA) was violated by physicians submitting claims to Medicare for services rendered by nonphysicians when physicians were not on the premises.

AMA Interest

Because the AMA has consistently maintained that FCA liability should require a violation of definite and understandable laws, the Litigation Center filed an amicus curiae brief to support the physicians in their defense of this appeal.

Case Summary

In this qui tam (whistleblower) action under the FCA, Karyn Walker contended that the defendant physicians should be bound by the Medicare Carrier's Manual (MCM) rules for the billing of incidental services, even though those rules were not set forth in the Medicare Act or the Code of Federal Regulations.

R & F Properties of Lake County, Inc. is a medical corporation in Lake County, Florida, which provides family care. Most of its patients are covered by Medicare. R & F formerly employed Karyn Walker as a nurse practitioner. From time to time, R & F used its physician assistants/nurse practitioners, including Walker, to service its Medicare patients without a physician being physically present on the premises. The physicians were, however, always available by telephone or pager. R & F's billings to Medicare included charges for the services rendered by the physician assistants/nurse practitioners.

At the time covered by the lawsuit (prior to 2002), the relevant federal regulation stated:

"Medicare Part B pays for services and supplies incident to a physician's professional services... if the services or supplies are of the type that are commonly furnished in a physician's office or clinic, and are commonly...included in the physician's bill."

The Medicare regulations did not explicitly say whether a physician had to be physically present on the premises in order to qualify incidental services for payment. However, the MCM stated that services rendered by nonphysicians could be deemed "incident to a physician's professional service" only if the physician were "present in the office suite and immediately available to provide assistance and direction throughout the time that the aide is performing services."

Walker filed a qui tam action, alleging that R & F had violated the FCA by billing for services of nonphysicians while physicians had not been physically present. She claimed that R & F was bound by the MCM requirement that a physician be physically present on the premises when the services were rendered. The United States Department of Justice, although notified of the suit, declined to intervene.

The trial court entered summary judgment for R & F. It held that, during the relevant time period, "neither the Medicare statutes nor the regulations provided much guidance on the level of supervision required in order to bill...services...as 'incident to.'" R & F had complied with the federal law and regulations in existence at the time of the billings, and the MCM requirements did not carry the force of law. The court noted that its holding was consistent with Florida law, which encouraged physicians to delegate health care tasks to qualified assistants.

Walker appealed to the Eleventh Circuit, which reversed the trial court's opinion. While the appellate court acknowledged that the Medicare regulations did not fully define the term *incident to* during at least the majority of the time at issue, it held that Walker should be allowed to introduce evidence as to how the industry and CMS defined that term.

Litigation Center Involvement

The Litigation Center filed a brief amicus curiae in the Eleventh Circuit to support R & F.

Physician Self-Referral

Garcia v. Health Net of New Jersey (N.J. Super. Ct. App. Div.)[5]

Issues

The issues in this case are whether physician-owners of a surgical center properly referred patients to that center and whether those physicians committed fraud both by submitting insurance claims to Health Net of New Jersey and by not undertaking more vigorous collection efforts against their patients for their co-insurance obligations.

AMA Interest

The AMA believes that: (1) physician ownership interests in health facilities, products or equipment can benefit patient care; (2) physicians should be able to refer patients to a facility in which they have an investment interest when they are directly providing the care or services; (3) fraud and abuse in medical practice should be limited to intentional acts of misconduct and activities inconsistent with accepted medical practice; and (4) physicians should be able to use discretion in sending patient accounts to collection.

Case Summary

The plaintiff physicians (and a podiatrist) sued Health Net of New Jersey for an injunction to prevent termination of their network participation contracts. Health Net countersued, alleging that the plaintiffs sought payment for care of patients referred in violation of the Codey Act, a state law prohibiting the referral of patients to a facility in which a physician has an ownership interest. Health Net also challenged the surgery center's out-of-network billing practices.

The trial judge found that the physicians had violated the Codey Act, notwithstanding an opinion of the New Jersey Board of Medical

Examiners that doctors may personally treat their patients in facilities that they own, as well as bill for those services. However, the court found that private parties are not authorized to enforce the Codey Act. The judge also found that there was no evidence supporting the scienter element of Health Net's fraud claim, since Wayne Surgical Center and many other similar facilities had been allowed to operate under a largely unenforced law. Additionally, the judge found no wrongdoing in the doctors' not collecting co-insurance payments from patients for out-of-network surgeries.

Health Net appealed to the Appellate Division of the Superior Court.

Litigation Center Involvement

The Litigation Center, along with the Medical Society of New Jersey filed an amicus curiae brief in support of the physician-owners and the surgery center.

Abusive Litigation Against Physicians

United States v. Vargo (D. Mont.)[6]

Issue

The issue in this case was whether a physician had knowingly overbilled for medical services.

AMA Interest

The AMA strives to avoid the expansion of liability theories against physicians, which can lead to overzealous and abusive litigation.

Case Summary

This civil False Claims Act case contended that Dr Patsy Vargo knowingly overbilled the United States Air Force for medical services performed on an independent contractor basis for four years.

The United States previously had brought a criminal suit against Vargo for the same activities, but voluntarily dropped the criminal charges after it hired an independent medical expert, Dr Glenn D. Littenberg, to review Vargo's records. Dr Littenberg, a longtime member of the AMA's Current Procedural Technology panel, determined that Vargo had complied with the regulations in effect and billed properly for her services.

In the civil suit, Vargo retained Dr Littenberg as her expert, but the prosecution hired its own experts to oppose him. Vargo also obtained a number of written testimonials from physicians who worked with her and, in some cases, in more senior positions, while she rendered her services.

The case ultimately settled, pursuant to a confidential settlement agreement and an undisclosed payment from Vargo.

Litigation Center Involvement

The Litigation Center paid a small portion of Vargo's defense costs. Although the monetary contribution was modest, the Litigation Center wanted Vargo and others to know that her fellow physicians supported her.

References

1. www.ama-assn.org/ama/pub/physician-resources/legal-topics/litigation-center/about-us.shtml.

2. www.ama-assn.org/ama/no-index/physician-resources/18583.shtml.

3. www.ama-assn.org/ama/no-index/physician-resources/18583.shtml.

4. www.ama-assn.org/ama/no-index/physician-resources/18583.shtml.

5. www.ama-assn.org/ama/no-index/physician-resources/18829.shtml.

6. www.ama-assn.org/ama/no-index/physician-resources/16176.shtml.

INDEX

A

Abuse, definition of, 23

Abusive litigation against physicians, 272–273

Addendum to medical record for audit, 191, 193

Ambulance companies, inducements resulting from competition among, 73

Ambulatory surgery centers (ASC), physician-owned, 76–80, 271–272

American Health Lawyers Association (AHLA), partnership with AMA in developing guide of, xx

American Medical Association (AMA) levels of office visit set by, 54–55

Litigation Center of, 265, 267, 270, 272, 273

partnership with AHLA in developing guide of, xx

Anti-kickback statute (AKS), 7

aim of, of preventing inappropriate referrals, 8–9, 18

ASC violations of, 77–78

civil prosecutions under, 59

criminal fines and prison sentences for violating, 16, 59, 101

exceptions to, 13–14

intent in determining violations of, 60

joint ventures involving referral sources violating, 73–81

knowledge requirement of, 9

OIG advisory opinions declining protection from, 80

professional services among physicians violating, 68, 69, 71–73

remuneration in violation of, 27, 62

safe harbor for prosecutions under, 60–61

settlement of violations of, incidence of, 60, 62

voluntary self-disclosure of violation of, 15

waiver of Medicare co-pays and deductibles as implicating, 66–67

Attorney. *See* Counsel, health care

Attorney–client privilege, 251

Attorney–work product doctrine, 251

Auditing and monitoring program, 124–125

Audits of physician files, 43

Audits, postpayment, 184–215

changing or creating documents for, 191, 193

elevated to fraud investigation, 185

frequency of, 214

initiation of, 189–193

interaction with auditor or investigator in, 256

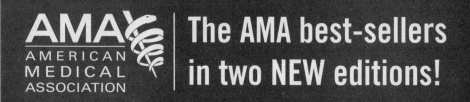
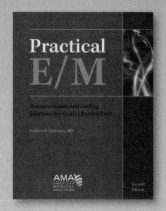